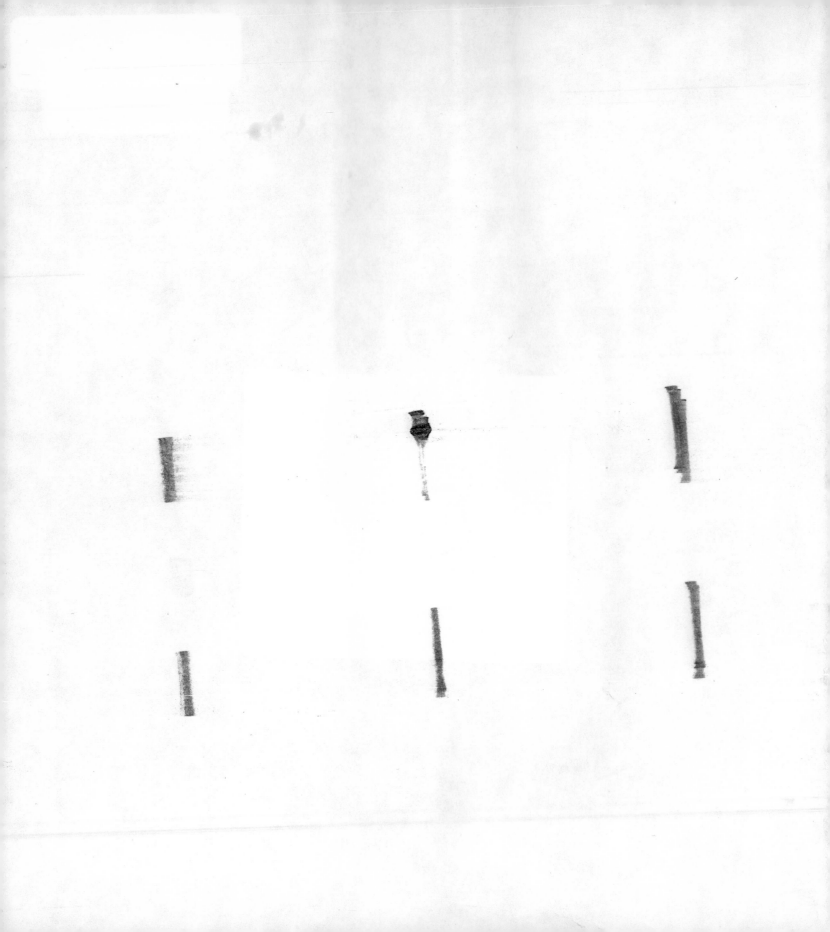

Better Homes and Gardens®

BLUE RIBBON
BAZAAR
CRAFTS

© Copyright 1987 by Meredith Corporation, Des Moines, Iowa.
All Rights Reserved. Printed in the United States of America.
First Edition. First Printing.
Library of Congress Catalog Card Number: 86-61616
ISBN: 0-696-01495-5

BETTER HOMES AND GARDENS® BOOKS

Editor: Gerald M. Knox
Art Director: Ernest Shelton
Managing Editor: David A. Kirchner
Editorial Project Managers: James D. Blume, Marsha Jahns,
   Rosanne Mattson, Mary Helen Schiltz

Department Head, Crafts Books: Joan Cravens
Senior Crafts Editors: Beverly Rivers, Sara Jane Treinen
Associate Crafts Editor: Elizabeth Porter

Associate Art Directors: Linda Ford Vermie, Neoma Alt West
   Randall Yontz
Assistant Art Directors: Lynda Haupert, Harijs Priekulis, Tom Wegner
Senior Graphic Designers: Jack Murphy, Stan Sams, Darla Whipple-Frain
Graphic Designers: Mike Burns, Blake Welch, Brian Wignall
Art Production: Director, John Berg; Associate, Joe Heuer;
   Office Manager, Emma Rediger

President, Book Group: Fred Stines
Vice President, Retail Marketing: Jamie Martin
Vice President, Direct Marketing: Arthur Heydendael

BETTER HOMES AND GARDENS® MAGAZINE
Vice President, Editorial Director: Doris Eby
Executive Director, Editorial Services: Duane L. Gregg

Blue Ribbon Bazaar Crafts
Editor: Joan Cravens
Contributing Editors: Gary Boling, Judith Veeder
Editorial Project Manager: Marsha Jahns
Graphic Designer: Kimberly Zarley, Linda Ford Vermie
Electronic Text Processor: Mary Louise Mathews

W hether you are staging a holiday sale, a bazaar for a community service group, or any crafts fund-raising event, you'll find designs, ideas, and suggestions by the score in **Blue Ribbon Bazaar Crafts.** We've filled our pages with practical information to make every bazaar run smoothly and profitably. Best of all, we've filled them with delightful and inexpensive projects in a variety of styles and techniques. You and your fellow crafters are sure to enjoy making them, and bazaar shoppers will find them irresistible.

CONTENTS

COUNTRY PRIDE

Country crafts combine our folk art heritage with the charm of a one-of-a-kind item, so they're natural best-sellers at bazaars.

Hand-carved of sugar pine and highlighted with handsome colors, this house-blessing plaque, *left*, offers a cheery greeting at a front door or in an entryway.

To begin, cut out the shape with a jigsaw, and enhance the design with wood-carving tools. Dip the plaque in brown dye to highlight the wood's grain, and add touches of color with acrylic paints.

Instructions for projects in this chapter begin on page 16.

7

Wooden trivets, plates, and bowls are easily transformed into delightful accessories with clever painting techniques. Apply an undercoat to the objects and then add a contrasting color of paint in one of four ways.

For example, to add a geometric pattern to the heart trivet, *left,* or the picture frame, *right,* dip a sponge into contrasting-color paint, and press it gently on the painted surface.

Or, create lively waves of pattern such as those on the bowl and heart by comb painting. Notch one edge of a strip of cardboard, then pull the "comb" across the paint while it's still wet.

Marbleized finishes, used on the medium-size bowl and platter, *left,* and smaller picture frame, *right,* are easy to create by dabbing on paint randomly and making swirl designs with a dry paper towel.

Dripping paint into a bowl and tipping it to one side creates a striking effect on the small bowl, *left, center.*

You'll be pleased with the merchandise your group can assemble for pennies. Scour secondhand shops, garage sales, and flea markets for wooden items to become these quick-to-sell accessories.

The paper cutout wall decorations, *left* and *opposite,* were inspired by delicate European cut-paper artwork. Craft these updated heart motifs from parchment or bond paper to provide a textured surface.

To begin, fold the paper and cut out the basic heart shapes. Then add pierced designs and two schoolgirls cut in paper-doll fashion. Use scraps of gift wrap to cover the background, which can be framed as shown or trimmed with ribbon.

The checkerboard, *opposite,* is a simplification of another traditional craft—wood-block printing. To prepare the board, cut a heart-shape opening at each end. Then, cut another heart to use as a printer, coating it with acrylic paint "ink" to print the heart motifs at the ends. Using additional wood blocks, print the checkerboard squares and geometric border in the same manner.

If desired, make checkers to sell with the checkerboard by cutting ⅝-inch-diameter wood dowels into ¼-inch-thick slices and painting them to match.

When planning projects for group members to work on, be sure to consider techniques that don't require a lot of previous experience. Here are two techniques that won't overwhelm a novice crafter.

Few knit-by-the-batch projects can be worked as quickly and easily as the sleeveless pullover and child's crewneck, *opposite.* The pattern used for the adult's pullover is an easy way to work with many colors at once without complicated color changes. The child's pullover is decorated with a heart-and-hand motif knitted into the front.

More hearts show up on the patchwork projects, *right.* The skirt has the look of an antique quilt, with patched triangles of calico, check, and striped fabrics, but look closely for the heart square tucked in near the hem. Repeat the heart motif in the child's clothes hanger crafted of pine.

The berry-color lap throw, *right,* is a woolen square that was machine-washed and dried to give it the heft and warmth of traditional European boiled wool—without the cost. Finish the edges of this easy-to-make afghan with purchased braid. Stitch the accompanying tote bag from canvas, adapting the pattern used for the house-blessing plaque, pages 6 and 7, for the appliqué motif.

These knitted and patchwork projects are excellent money-makers for your bazaar because they make efficient use of scrap yarn and fabrics.

Whether you market them as children's toys or as knickknacks for the young at heart, these three little kittens, *left*, are bound to bring smiles to your bazaar shoppers. Their 6-inch-tall bodies are stitched from felt, and an attached muzzle and button-on arms are unusual construction features. Tiny black beads form the eyes, and snippets of carpet thread make perfect whiskers. Scrap-bag fabrics, laces, and ribbons are good choices for the kittens' wardrobes.

Dressed for afternoon tea in the garden, the aristocratic bunny couple, *opposite*, is sure to be a country favorite. They're stitched from scraps of wool, with natty costumes created from bits of wool, cotton print, and muslin. For charming details, work a small knitted strip to make a tie, and add tiny buttons to the dress and jacket.

The furniture shown with all the dolls is made from pine scraps, with simple shapings cut with a jigsaw. After completion, the furniture is tinted with fabric dye and decorated with stencils.

Country critters as cute as these will be successful at any bazaar. Construction is simple, and the everyday fabrics and notions used are available everywhere.

HOUSE BLESSING

Shown on pages 6–7.
Finished size is 9x16 inches.

MATERIALS

10x17-inch piece of ¾-inch
  sugar pine
Wood-carving tools; jigsaw
Brown fabric dye
Red, yellow, and green acrylic
  paints; exterior-grade
  varnish; picture hangers
Tissue and carbon paper

INSTRUCTIONS

Note: Use care when carving; keep free hand tucked behind carving hand.
Trace pattern, *opposite,* onto tissue. Flop to trace remainder of design. Transfer outline to pine and cut out with jigsaw; sand edges.
Trace remaining details on board surface. With a narrow tip, carve lines. Using a wider blade, cut away wood around all shapes (gray areas on pattern) to ⅛-inch depth.
Apply dye to board. Paint the design using acrylics. Varnish; add picture hangers.

COUNTRY FINISHES

Shown on pages 8–9.

MATERIALS

Purchased wooden bowls,
  trivets, or frames
Latex paints in rust, green,
  and yellow; varnish
Brushes; fine sponges
Cardboard; paper towels

INSTRUCTIONS

Paint woodenware with desired undercoat color. Allow to dry thoroughly. Add finish according to instructions below; varnish when dry, if desired.

TO SPONGE: Spoon contrasting paint onto cardboard. Cut a small square from sponge and dab one end into paint. Press check design on wood.

TO COMB: Cut "comb" for painting from a piece of cardboard. Paint a contrasting color over undercoat on bowl, trivet, or frame. Comb the design into the wet paint; wipe excess paint from cardboard before combing next row.

TO MARBLEIZE: Place a brush or sponge in contrasting paint and dab randomly onto bowl or plate. Rub paint with dry toweling in swirling motions, picking up excess paint and rubbing wet paint into texture of undercoat.

TO DRIP: Spoon a small amount of paint onto bowl, plate, or trivet. Tip to allow paint drip to run.

CHECKERBOARD

Shown on page 11.
Finished size is 8¼x13½ inches.

MATERIALS

8¼x13½-inch piece of ½-
  inch clear pine
Wood scraps; fine sandpaper
Acrylic paint in rust and gray
Jigsaw; clear varnish
Small brush; heavy paper

INSTRUCTIONS

For heart cutouts, refer to photograph. Trace the full-size heart pattern, *below,* onto tissue, then center it on the short ends of the board, ¼ inch from the edges. Using carbon paper, trace the heart outline onto wood. Drill holes in the center of the heart to provide an opening for the saw blade; cut out the heart. Sand all surfaces.
Next, cut a 6½-inch square from heavy paper. Center the paper widthwise on the board (see the photograph) and draw around it to establish placement of the checked area. Mark a small line every ¾ inch (spacing for checks) all around.
To print the checks, cut a ¾x¾x3-inch wood scrap. For the borders, cut a ¼x1x3-inch scrap; for ends, cut a heart (see pattern).
To print the checkerboard, paint the end of ¾-inch wood scrap with rust paint; press the end onto the corner of the cen-

ter square. Skip a ¾-inch space; print the next check. Repeat until the checkerboard is filled, using previous line of checks as a guide.
Decorate the borders around the checks with gray-painted ¼-inch scrap; print ends with rust hearts printed over gray hearts. (Refer to photograph for placement.) Varnish.

PAPER CUTOUTS

Shown on pages 10–11.

MATERIALS

Good-quality bond or
  parchment paper
T-pin or other large pin
Stapler or cellophane tape
Rubber cement or white glue
Cuticle or surgical scissors
Artist's knife; mat board;
  pencil
Cardboard or wood (for
  cutting surface)
Scraps of wallpaper or gift
  wrap
Picture frame

INSTRUCTIONS

Carefully fold paper in half. Using a pencil, lightly trace patterns (page 18) onto paper, placing fold of paper on broken lines of pattern.
Staple around the outer edge of the design, or tape the edges of the paper together to prevent paper from shifting while cutting the design.
For the Little Girl design, place paper on the cutting surface; prick through all dots with a pin.
For both designs, begin cutting at center of the design (using artist's knife); work toward the edges. Using scissors, cut the outside edge. Use artist's knife to cut inside small hearts.
Open the design; press flat, and place paper under a heavy book overnight.
If desired, glue gift wrap or wallpaper to surface of mat board. Then, with pencil-traced side down, mount design on mat board, using tiny dots of rubber cement or white glue. Frame as desired.

Center

Fold

Fold

CHILD'S SWEATER

Shown on page 12.
Directions are for child's Size 8.
Changes for sizes 10, 12, and 14 follow in parentheses. The finished chest size is 26½ (28¾, 30½, 32) inches.

MATERIALS

Schaffhauser Salvatore (50-gram balls): 5 (6, 7, 8) balls of No. 35 rose (MC) and 1 ball *each* of No. 81 brown (A), No. 33 jade (B), and No. 97 light green (C)
Sizes 4 and 6 standard knitting needles, or size to obtain gauge below
Size 4 circular knitting needle (16-inch length) or 1 set of double-pointed needles
Tapestry needle
11 yarn bobbins

Abbreviations: See *opposite.*
Gauge: With larger needles over st st, 5 sts = 1 inch; 7 rows = 1 inch.

INSTRUCTIONS

Note: When changing yarn colors, always twist the new color around color in use to prevent holes. Do not carry the unused color across back; use separate bobbins for each color used on row.

FRONT: With smaller needles and MC, cast on 66 (72, 76, 80) sts. Work in k 1, p 1 ribbing until length measures 1½ (1½, 1½, 2) inches. Change to larger needles and st st (knit 1 row; purl 1 row) and work even for 6 (10, 14, 16) rows, ending with wrong-side row. Wind 11 bobbins as follows: 1A, 5B, 1C, 4MC.

Continuing in st st, work color pat as follows: *Row 1* (right side): With MC work first 16 (19, 21, 23) sts; continuing with MC, work Row 1 of chart, *opposite,* joining A bobbin and second ball of MC as indicated on chart. Complete row with MC. Continue working from chart, working MC at each edge from separate balls and using bobbins for remaining colors as indicated.

At the same time, keeping to chart as established, work even until total length measures 10 (11, 12, 13) inches; end with a wrong-side row.

FRONT ARMHOLE SHAPING: Keeping to chart, bind off 4 (4, 5, 5) sts at beg of next 2 rows. *Dec row:* K 1, k 2 tog, k to last 3 sts, k 1, sl 1, psso, k 1. *Next row:* Purl. Rep last 2 rows until 50 (56, 58, 58) sts rem. Work even in st st until length from beg of armhole shaping measures 4 (4¼, 4½, 4¾) inches; end with a wrong-side row.

NECK SHAPING: K 19 (22, 23, 23), sl center 12 (12, 12, 12) sts to holder for front of neck, join second ball of yarn and k to end of row. Working both sides at the same time, dec 1 st at each neck edge every row 3 times. Work even 1 row; dec 1 st at each neck edge once more—15 (18, 19, 19) sts each side. Work even until length from beg of armhole shaping measures 6 (6¼, 6½, 6¾) inches; end at armhole edge.

SHOULDER SHAPING: At armhole edge bind off 4 (6, 6, 6) sts 3 (3, 2, 2) times, then bind off rem 3 (0, 7, 7) sts.

BACK: Cast on and work ribbing as for Front. Change to larger needles and st st, working even until the total length measures same as Front to beg of armhole shaping; end with wrong-side row.

BACK ARMHOLE SHAPING: Work as for Front. Work even on rem 50 (56, 58, 58) sts until the length past the beg of the armhole shaping measures the same as the Front to the beg of the shoulder shaping.

SHOULDER SHAPING: Bind off 4 (6, 6, 6) sts at beg of next 6 (6, 4, 4) rows; bind off 3 (0, 7, 7) sts at beg of following 2 rows. Sl rem 20 (20, 20, 20) sts to a holder for back of neck.

SLEEVES: Using the smaller standard needles and MC, cast on 33 (35, 37, 39) sts. Work in k 1, p 1 ribbing until length measures 2 inches, inc 13 (13, 13, 15) sts on last row—46 (48, 50, 54) sts.

Change to larger standard needles and st st, inc 1 st at each side every 1½ inches 5 times—56 (58, 60, 64) sts. Work even until total length is 11½ (12½, 13½, 14½) inches or desired length to underarm; end with a wrong-side row.

TOP SHAPING: Bind off 4 (4, 5, 5) sts at beg of next 2 rows. Dec at each end of next row and every other row as for armhole shaping until length from beg of top shaping measures 4 (4¼, 4½, 4¾) inches. Bind off 2 sts at beg of next 4 rows. Bind off rem sts.

NECKBAND: Sew shoulder seams. With double-pointed or circular needle, right side facing, MC and beg at right shoulder, k 20 (20, 20, 20) sts from back neck holder, pick up 18 (18, 20, 22) sts along left neck edge, k 12 (12, 12, 12) sts from front neck holder, pick up 18 (18, 20, 22) sts along right neck edge—68 (68, 72, 76) sts. Join; work k 1, p 1 rib in rnds until band measures 1 (1¼, 1¼, 1½) inches; bind off with larger needle, working very loosely. Sew in sleeves; sew side and sleeve seams.

Row 1

1 Square = 1 Stitch

COLOR KEY

☐ Rose   ⊡ Jade
☒ Lt. Green   ■ Brown

KNITTED VEST

Shown on page 12.
Directions are for sizes 12–14. Changes for sizes 16 and 18 follow in parentheses. Finished bust size is 38 (40, 41¾) inches.

MATERIALS

Lane Borgesia Hilton (50-gram balls): 6 (7, 7) balls of No. 3365 burgundy (MC) and 3 (4, 4) balls *each* of No. 3821 turquoise (A), No. 3355 brown (B), No. 3687 peach (C), and No. 1938 camel (D)
Sizes 4 and 8 standard knitting needles, or size to obtain gauge given below
Size 4 circular knitting needle (16-inch length)

Abbreviations: See page 19.
Gauge: With larger needles over st st, 9 sts = 2 inches; 11 rows = 2 inches.

INSTRUCTIONS

Note: The yarn is doubled throughout. When changing colors of yarn, always twist new color around color in use to prevent holes. Carry the unused color loosely across back.

BACK: With smaller standard needles and 2 strands of MC held tog, cast on 70 (74, 78) sts. *Row 1* (right side): K 2 through back lps (tbl), * p 2, k 2 tbl. Rep from * across.
Row 2: P 2, * k 2 tbl, p 2. Rep from * across. Rep these 2 rows for ribbing until length measures 2¾ inches; end with a wrong-side row and inc 16 sts evenly spaced on last row—86 (90, 94) sts.
Change to larger standard needles and st st (knit 1 row,

purl 1 row) and work in color pat as follows, remembering to use 2 strands of each color held tog: *Rows 1–2:* MC.
Row 3: Join A; 2 MC, * 2 A, 2 MC. Rep from * across.
Rows 4–5: Work in colors as established. Break off MC.
Rows 6–7: A.
Row 8: Join B; 2 A, * 2 B, 2 A. Rep from * across.
Rows 9–10: Work in colors as established. Break off A.
Rows 11–12: B.
Row 13: Join C; 2 B, * 2 C, 2 B. Rep from * across.
Rows 14–15: Work in colors as established. Break off B.
Rows 16–17: C.
Row 18: Join D; 2 C, * 2 D, 2 C. Rep from * across.
Rows 19–20: Work in colors as established. Break off C.
Rows 21–22: D.
Row 23: Join MC; 2 D, * 2 MC, 2 D. Rep from * across.
Rows 24–25: Work in colors as established. Break off D. Rep these 25 rows for pat.
At the same time, work even until total length measures 13 (13½, 14) inches.

ARMHOLE SHAPING: Bind off 4 sts at beg of next 2 rows. Dec 1 st each end of next row and every other row 4 times—70 (74, 78) sts. Work even until length from beg of armhole shaping measures 8 (8½, 9) inches. Bind off loosely, marking off center 34 (38, 42) sts for back of neck.

FRONT: Work same as for Back until length from beg of armhole shaping measures 5 (5½, 6) inches; end with a wrong-side row.

NECK SHAPING: Keeping to color pat, k 25, join doubled

strand of yarn and bind off center 20 (24, 28) sts for front neck; complete row.
Working each side separately, dec 1 st at neck edge every other row 7 times—18 sts each side. Work even until length from beg of armhole shaping measures 8 (8½, 9) inches. Bind off loosely.

NECKBAND: Sew shoulder seams. With right side facing and using circular needle with 2 strands of MC held tog, beg at right shoulder and pick up 32 (34, 34) sts along back of neck; pick up 15 (13, 13) sts along left neck edge; pick up 18 (20, 20) sts along front neck; pick up 15 (13, 13) sts along right neck edge—80 (80, 80) sts. Join; * k 2 tbl, p 2. Rep from * around. Continue in twisted rib as established until neckband measures 1 inch deep. Bind off loosely in rib.

ARMBANDS: With the right side facing and using smaller standard needles with 2 strands of MC held tog, beg at underarm and pick up 86 (90, 94) sts along the entire armhole edge. Work in twisted rib same as for lower edge of Front and Back until length of armband is 1 inch. Bind off loosely in rib. Sew side seams.

PATCHWORK SKIRT

Shown on page 13.

MATERIALS

Calico scraps in desired colors
Purchased pattern; thread
Cardboard or lightweight plastic for templates

INSTRUCTIONS

Following directions below, make a sufficient number of patch work blocks to accomodate the length and width of your skirt pattern.
From template material cut one 5-inch square and one 3½x3½x5-inch triangle. Trace heart appliqué, *right*, onto cardboard or plastic and cut out.
On the wrong side of fabric scraps, draw around templates. Add ¼-inch seam allowances and cut out. Cut enough triangles and squares to make desired yardage. Cut out heart appliqués for square blocks.
Using ¼-inch seams, join two triangles; repeat for two more triangles. Join the two pieced triangles into a square (seams will run diagonally across center of block). Press seams.
Appliqué hearts atop calico squares by hand, turning under raw edges ¼ inch.
Sew the pieced and heart-motif blocks into strips for the width of the skirt. Make enough strips to establish its length. Then join the strips together. Press seams. Cut out pattern pieces and assemble skirt, following pattern instructions.

LAP ROBE

Shown on page 13.

MATERIALS

60 inches of 60-inch-wide, finely woven wool fabric; thread
Fold-over braid (approximately 6⅔ yards)

INSTRUCTIONS

Wash wool in hot water; tumble dry in hot dryer; the fabric will shrink to resemble boiled wool. Bind edges with fold-over braid, using thread to match fabric.

HANGERS

Shown on page 13.

MATERIALS

½-inch scraps of pine
Colored cord
Paint or stain; brushes
Fine sandpaper; jigsaw
Drill with ¼-inch bit

INSTRUCTIONS

Trace pattern, *left*, onto paper; transfer to wood scraps. Cut out; drill holes (indicated by heavy line on pattern) through hangers. Sand; finish as desired. Tie 15-inch cords through holes, knotting ends on hanger undersides.

HEART-MOTIF TOTE BAG

Shown on page 13.
Finished size is 5x14x16 inches.

MATERIALS

⅔ yard *each* of canvas and lining fabric
Fabric scraps in dark red, rose, blue-greens (solid and print); thread to match fabrics
Scrap of tan bias tape
4 yards of 1-inch-wide tan webbing
Stiff cardboard
Fusible webbing; tracing paper

Fold

Doll's · — · — · —
Child's ————

Fold

INSTRUCTIONS

Use ½-inch seams throughout. Cut canvas as follows: two 15x17-inch rectangles for front and back, two 6x17-inch rectangles for sides, and one 6x15-inch rectangle for bottom. Cut lining fabric to correspond.

Referring to the diagram, *below*, select and trace motifs from the house blessing (page 17). Cut shapes from fabrics and fusible webbing. (*Note:* Cut the large leaves in one piece; bias-tape stems will be placed atop the leaves.)

Referring to diagram, center and pin heart and fusible webbing atop canvas front, 1 inch from bottom edge. Pin large leaves then remaining appliqués, and fusible webbing in place. Using a warm iron, fuse all appliqués, then satin-stitch the edges with coordinating thread. *continued*

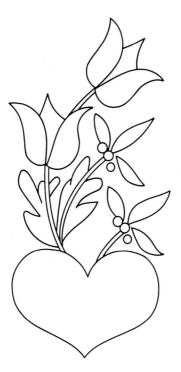

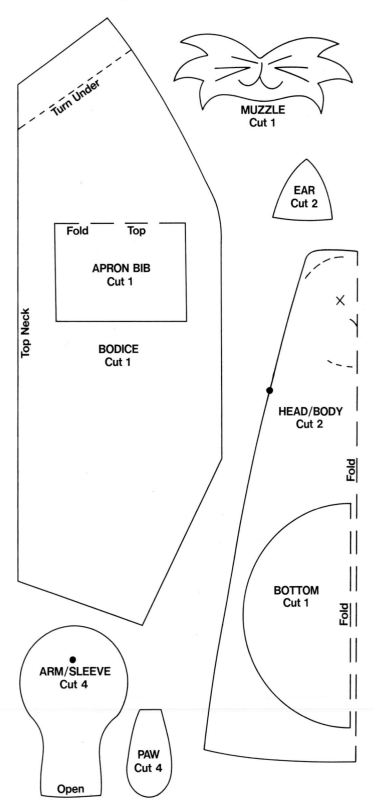

Turn Under

MUZZLE
Cut 1

EAR
Cut 2

Fold | Top

APRON BIB
Cut 1

Top Neck

BODICE
Cut 1

HEAD/BODY
Cut 2

×

Fold

BOTTOM
Cut 1

Fold

ARM/SLEEVE
Cut 4

PAW
Cut 4

Open

Sew bottom canvas bag piece to bottom of front and back, making a long rectangle. Lightly pencil a line 2½ inches from each long edge for placement (outside edge) of straps. Starting at bottom of bag, sew the webbing strap in place (refer to photograph), ending the stitches ⅝ inch from top of bag.

Sew sides to bag, breaking stitches at corners.

Cut a 5x14-inch cardboard rectangle; place in the bottom of the bag.

Sew lining as for bag; leave opening at bottom. Insert canvas bag inside lining, right sides facing; move straps out of way of top. Stitch tops together. Turn; close opening. Tack the straps at top to canvas.

❖

MINIATURE FELT KITTENS

Shown on page 14.
Finished cats are 6 inches tall.

MATERIALS
Felt scraps
Polyester fiberfill
5-mm black beads for eyes
5-mm black pom-pom for nose
Carpet thread in black and white
4 inches of 18-gauge wire for *each* cat; fabric glue
Fabric scraps for clothes; lace and ribbon trims
Tiny beads for buttons
Two ¼-inch flat buttons for *each* cat

INSTRUCTIONS
BODY: *Note:* For ease in sewing, do not cut out the body shapes from felt until matching pieces are sewn together.

Trace around the head/body pattern, *opposite,* onto double thickness of felt. Leaving bottom open, stitch atop the traced line; cut out close to stitching; turn. Using fiberfill, stuff to within ¼ inch from bottom edge. Cut out bottom circle and pin it to bottom edge of body; sew together using a buttonhole stitch.

Draw around muzzle pattern on double thickness of felt and stitch along outside edges. Cut out close to stitching. Position on face as indicated by broken lines and place a small amount of stuffing behind center of muzzle. Hand-stitch muzzle to face along chin and nose curves.

With doubled black thread, outline-stitch mouth. Sew two beads in place for eyes and glue a pom-pom in place for nose. Thread three strands of black carpet thread through muzzle for whiskers.

Cut out ears, place in position and stitch bottom edge of ears to head (on broken lines).

Stitch clothing, following directions below, then make arms as follows: Cut two 2-inch-long wires and four felt paws. Glue one wire between two paws. Repeat for second wire and paws. Allow to dry.

On double thickness of fabric, trace around arm/sleeve pattern. Stitch, leaving bottom open; trim and turn.

Stuff upper part of sleeve, insert wire with paws into the narrow part of sleeve. Add more stuffing around wire and hand-sew bottom edge of sleeve to top edge of paw. Glue lace trim over raw edges. Use a needle-nose pliers to bend half of the paw downward.

To attach arms, use doubled white carpet thread and push needle in one side of the body and out the other side at points indicated by dots on the pattern. Thread needle through arm at dot, then through one of the holes in the tiny button. Pass needle back through second hole in button, through arm and body to opposite side. Pull thread tightly to pull arm snugly against body.

Attach remaining arm and button in the same manner, returning thread to opposite side of body. Repeat process one more time; secure thread.

CLOTHING: Cut out the bodice and turn under the top raw edge ¼ inch; glue. Wrap the bodice around the body of the cat, overlapping the ends in front. Turn under one raw edge of front; glue overlap together.

Cut a 3¾x12-inch rectangle for the skirt. Sew the short ends together using a ¼-inch seam. Turn under a ¼-inch hem. Gather the top edge. Slip the skirt onto the cat; gather to fit. Secure the gathering thread, adjust the gathers, and stitch the skirt to both the bodice and the body.

If you are not planning to add an apron, cover the raw edges of the skirt with lace or ribbon trim.

For the bibbed apron, cut the bib out on folded fabric. With right sides facing, sew short sides together; turn. Center the bottom edge of the bib over the top edge of the apron; topstitch in place. Sew a ribbon tie across the top edge, hiding raw edges.

For the skirt apron, cut a 6-inch square and fold in half, right sides facing (3x6 inches). Stitch the two sides together and turn. Gather top raw edge to 3 inches. Center apron onto a 15-inch length of ribbon and sew in place.

COUNTRY BUNNIES

Shown on page 15. Finished size of Papa Bunny is 15 inches; Mama Bunny is 14 inches tall.

MATERIALS

⅛ yard of wool camel fabric (head, ears, feet, and paws)
⅛ yard of gray herringbone wool (jacket)
⅛ yard of gray lining fabric (jacket)
⅛ yard of gray wool fabric (pants)
¼ yard purple calico (dress)
¼ yard *each* of muslin (body, arms, and legs), and white cotton or muslin (petticoat, bonnet)
Scrap of camel satin lining (ears)
½x10-inch piece of wool or hand-knit strip (tie)
Scraps of gray felt (hat)
Scraps of black felt (eyes)
20 inches of ½-inch-wide lace (petticoat trim)
¾ yard of ¼-inch-wide lace (bonnet)
3 small buttons (coat)
4 small buttons (dress)
16 inches narrow ribbon (tie for girl bunny neckline)
Black carpet thread or fish line; sewing thread
Needles (1 long)
Polyester fiberfill

INSTRUCTIONS

Note: The body pieces for the bunnies indicate cutting directions for one body only. To make the pair you must cut twice the number of pieces.

Trace the full-size patterns (see pages 25–27) onto tissue paper; add ¼-inch seam allowances to all edges. Cut pieces from appropriate fabrics.

In addition to pattern pieces on the charts, cut the following: *For girl bunny:* Cut one 7½ × 20-inch piece *each* of purple calico (dress skirt) and white cotton (petticoat). For sleeves, enlarge arm pattern ⅛ inch all around. Cut four sleeve pieces from purple calico.

For boy bunny: Cut sleeves for jacket from gray herringbone as for girl bunny sleeves. For pant legs and pants (lower side body), enlarge patterns ⅛ inch all around. Cut four pieces of each pattern from gray fabric.

Note: When sewing, join pieces with right sides facing unless otherwise indicated.

For the bunny bodies

HEAD: Sew long edges of face piece to lower edges of each head side, beginning at nose (dots).

Sew head center to head side beginning at nose dot and stitching to back of neck. The front section of face (nose), which overlaps onto the face, remains unstitched at this time. Turn head right side out. Stuff firmly with fiberfill. Turn raw edges of nose under ¼ inch; blind-stitch closed. Hand-sew the mouth with black carpet thread as shown on pattern.

EARS (make two): Sew inner ear linings to outer ear pieces; sew dart on inner ears only. Turn ears right side out. Attach ears to head as indicated on pattern (between the Xs), opening seams only enough to insert ears ¼ inch. Stitch opening closed.

EYES: Insert threaded needle into position for one eye and draw through head to other eye. Pull thread slightly to shape head; knot. Punch eyes from black felt with hole punch. Glue or sew eyes to head.

ARMS AND PAWS: Stitch two arm pieces together, leaving lower edges open. Clip seams, turn arm right side out, and stuff firmly. Turn raw edge of opening under ¼ inch. Repeat for other arm.

Sew two paw pieces together, leaving top ends open. Turn paws right side out and stuff firmly. Slip paw into one arm opening and hand-sew in place. Repeat for other paw. Set aside.

LEGS AND FEET: Sew two leg pieces together, leaving bottom open. Turn leg right side out, and stuff. Turn raw edge of opening under ¼ inch. Repeat for other leg.

Stitch two side foot sections together from top edge to toe (dot). Clip seams and press. Sew foot bottom to lower edges of side foot, beginning at back edge and matching dots. Turn and stuff. Insert foot ¼ inch into leg bottom opening and hand-sew in place. Repeat for other foot. Set aside.

BODY: Sew one body side to one side of center body gusset, leaving opening at neck. Repeat for other side. Clip seams, turn, and stuff. Turn raw edges of neck opening under ¼ inch and insert head into body ¼ inch and hand-sew in place.

Note: Arms and legs are attached to bodies after the clothing is made.

For the girl bunny's clothing

DRESS: Open one section of dress bodice; cut on fold line to make back opening. Turn back opening edges under ¼ inch; stitch down. Sew back bodice to front bodice at the sides. Overlap the back opening edges ¼ inch at the bottom; stay-stitch along the waistline edge.

continued

Join the short sides of the dress skirt. Gather the top of the skirt; sew the gathered edge to the bodice waistline, placing skirt seam under the bodice back opening.

Sew the petticoat as for the dress skirt; place the petticoat inside the dress and sew to the bodice. Hem dress and petticoat with a ½-inch rolled hem. Trim the petticoat hem with lace. Turn under the raw edges of the neck edge ¼ inch. Put dress and petticoat on bunny; sew bodice in place at center back and blindstitch neck edge to bunny. Tie ribbon around neck.

SLEEVES: Sew two sleeve pieces together, leaving a 2-inch opening in the upper back of each sleeve. Clip, turn, insert one stuffed arm, and hand-sew closed. Turn under cuffs. Repeat for other sleeve.

BONNET: Sew around bonnet circles, leaving an opening for turning. Turn right side out; sew closed. Run a gathering thread around the bonnet ⅝ inch from the edge. Topstitch ¼-inch lace around bonnet edge. Cut slits for ears. Place on head, pushing the ears through the slits; pull gathering thread to fit head; tie off thread.

For the boy bunny's clothing
COAT: Sew center seams of coat back from dot to neck. Sew coat fronts to coat back, matching dots. Sew coat front facings to the coat front, matching the dots. Press seams open.

Sew the center seam of the coat back lining as for the coat back. Sew coat front linings to back lining. Sew lining to front coat facing. Sew hem of coat to hem of lining and along slit edges at center back. At neck

edges, sew only the wool facings together. Trim all corners; turn the coat right side out. Press.

Sew collars between the dots, leaving neck edge open. Trim; turn. Sew bottom edge of collar to coat neck, right sides facing (do not sew collar to lining). Turn collar up; turn neck lining under ¼ inch and hand-sew atop collar seam. Press collar and front of coat open to form lapels. Add buttons. Sew sleeves same as for dress sleeve (see dress *above*).

SHIRT: *Note:* Shirt is only a front piece that is tacked to the body front. Hand-sew shirt front to bunny body, folding all raw edges under ¼ inch.

Fold collar in half, *widthwise*, raw edges even; sew around all raw edges, leaving an opening for turning. Turn and press; sew opening closed. Hand-sew collar over shirt at neckline.

PANTS: Sew pant (lower side body) pieces to center pant gusset as for the bunny body; turn. Put on bunny bottom; baste in place. Turn edges of waistband under ¼ inch. Hand-sew on bunny over raw edges of pant waistline.

Sew pant legs as for body legs, leaving 2-inch openings at the tops for inserting legs. Insert legs and hand-sew open seams closed.

HAT: Sew top of hat sections. Cut slits for ears. Glue bottom edge under ¼ inch with white glue. Glue front and back brim in place. Slip over bunny's ears.

TO ASSEMBLE: Tack coat to body leaving front slightly open. Attach arms and legs to bunny bodies with a large needle threaded with carpet

thread. With large knot at one end, push a double thread through left arm, body, and out right arm; pull thread securely and knot. Repeat for legs. Sew gray buttons to boy bunny's coat and white buttons to girl bunny's dress. Fold tie in half and tack in place under collar.

❖

MINIATURE FURNITURE

Shown on page 15.
Finished size of chair and settee is 11 inches tall; stool is 3 inches tall.

MATERIALS
Hammer; dovetail saw
Crafts knife
Drill with ⅛-inch bit
Wood glue; sandpaper
Wood block; 1-inch brads
Acrylic paints in desired colors; varnish
For the stool: ½x½x12-inch, ½x4x4-inch, and ¼x¼x18-inch pieces of pine
For the chair: ½x½x32-inch, ½x4x6-inch, ¼x¼x18-inch, and ⅛x3x6-inch pieces of pine
For the settee: ½x½x32-inch, ¼x¼x40-inch, ½x7x10-inch, and ⅛x6x8-inch pieces of pine

INSTRUCTIONS
For the stool
For patterns, see pages 28 and 29. Cut top to size; cut ½-inch-square notches in each corner. Cut legs to length and bevel each edge of both ends with medium-fine sandpaper on a block, making bevel a little less than ⅛ inch.

Cut rungs 3¼ inches long; use crafts knife to trim a ⅛-inch-diameter by ¼-inch tenon on the end of each rung.

Mark hole positions on legs according to dimensions; bore ⅛-inch-diameter holes in stool legs ⅜ inch deep for mortises.

Test-fit rungs in legs; then, test-fit this assembly with the top. If rungs fit snugly and assembly is square, pull apart and reassemble using wood glue. Coat tenons lightly to prevent glue from squeezing out.

Dab a bit of glue into the top notches and position top so the legs extend beyond the top by the height of the bevel. When the assembly is square, secure the legs with one brad driven through the leg side into the top; let glue dry for four hours.

Set brads, sand lightly, paint, and decorate with diluted acrylic paint as desired. Stencil heart onto stool or chair. Varnish project when dry.

For the chair
Cut the legs, rungs, and chair seat to length. Bevel tops and bottoms of legs, but give the tops of the back legs a wider, rounded bevel.

Transfer back pattern to ⅛-inch pine; cut out. Cut a groove ⅛ inch wide by ¼ inch deep in *each* back rail before shaping and cutting pieces.

Transfer pattern for top rail; cut out. Cut bottom rail to length. Trim tenons on ends of rungs; test-fit parts that form the back. Glue all back parts together and secure rails with 1-inch brads through legs. Test-fit this assembly with the front legs, rungs, and chair seat; glue. Finish as for stool.

For the settee
Assemble same as for chair, measuring carefully. Space the back pieces properly before gluing, making sure back is square. Let the glue dry thoroughly before attaching seat, front legs, and rungs.

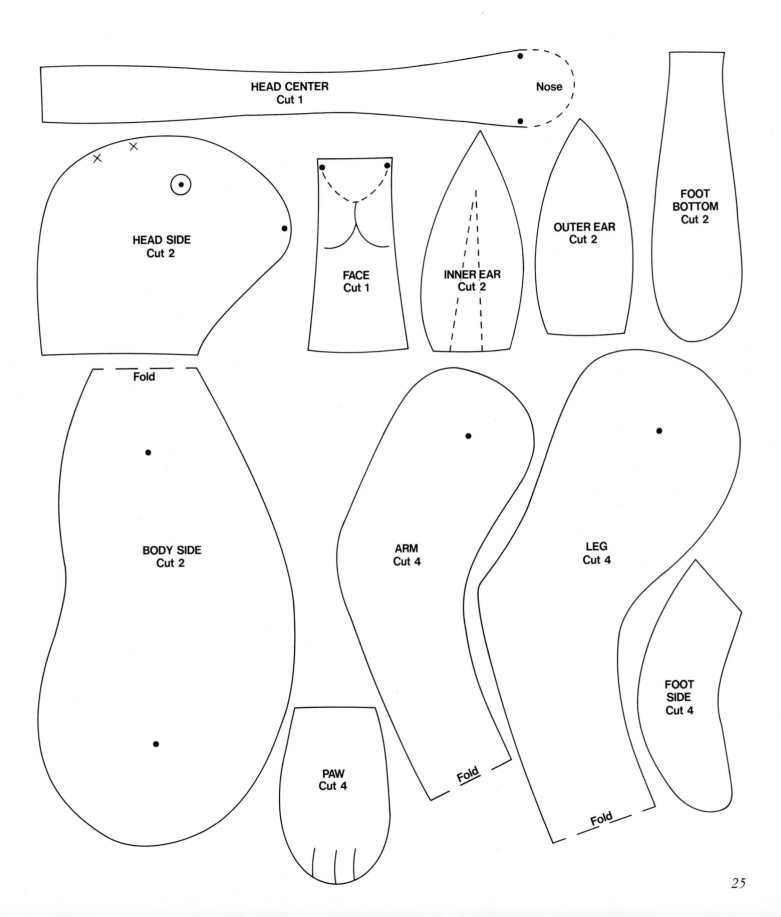

25

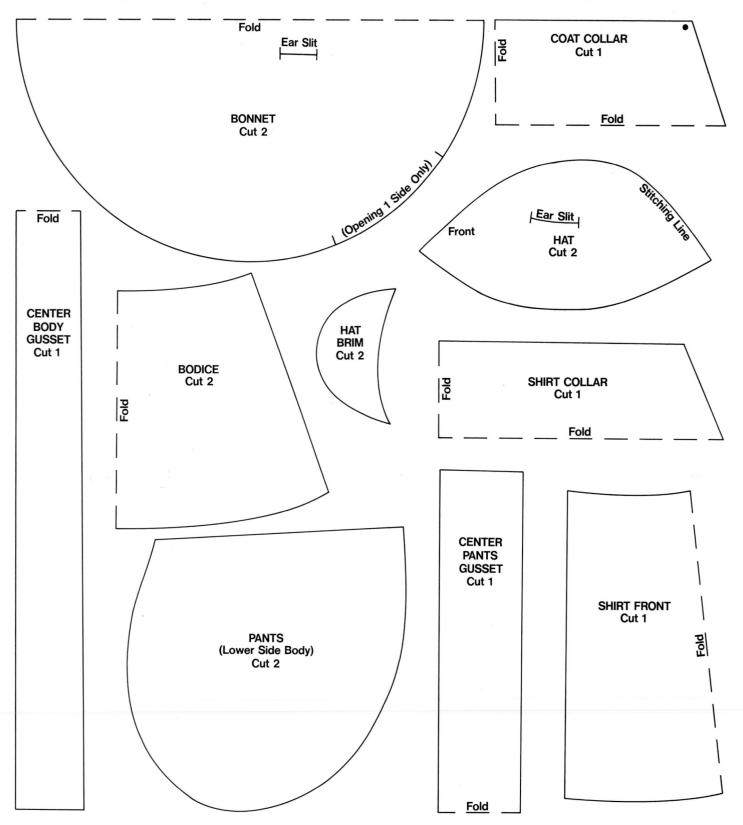

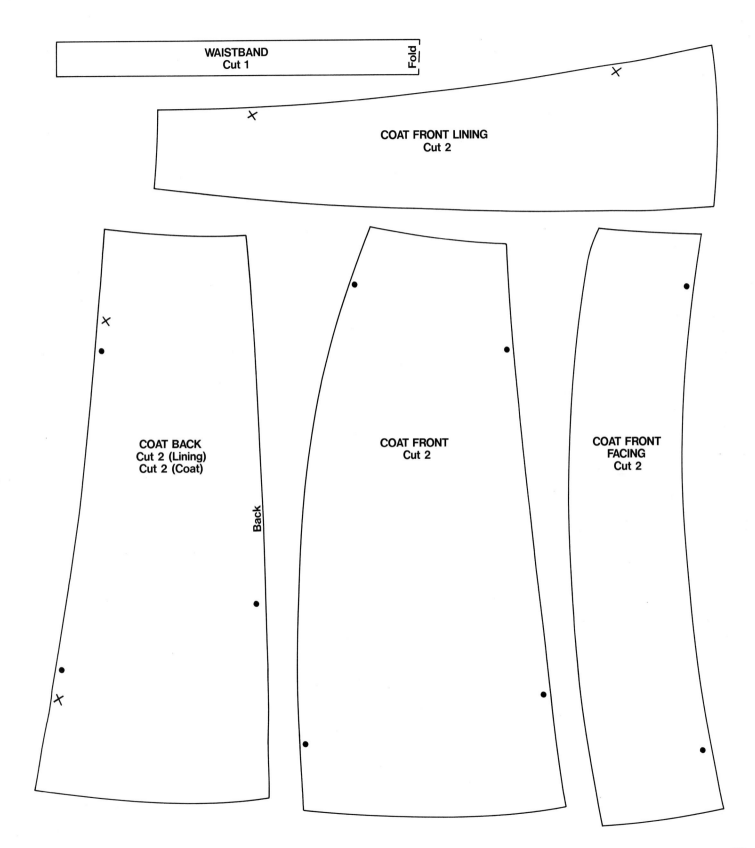

WAISTBAND
Cut 1

Fold

COAT FRONT LINING
Cut 2

COAT BACK
Cut 2 (Lining)
Cut 2 (Coat)

Back

COAT FRONT
Cut 2

COAT FRONT
FACING
Cut 2

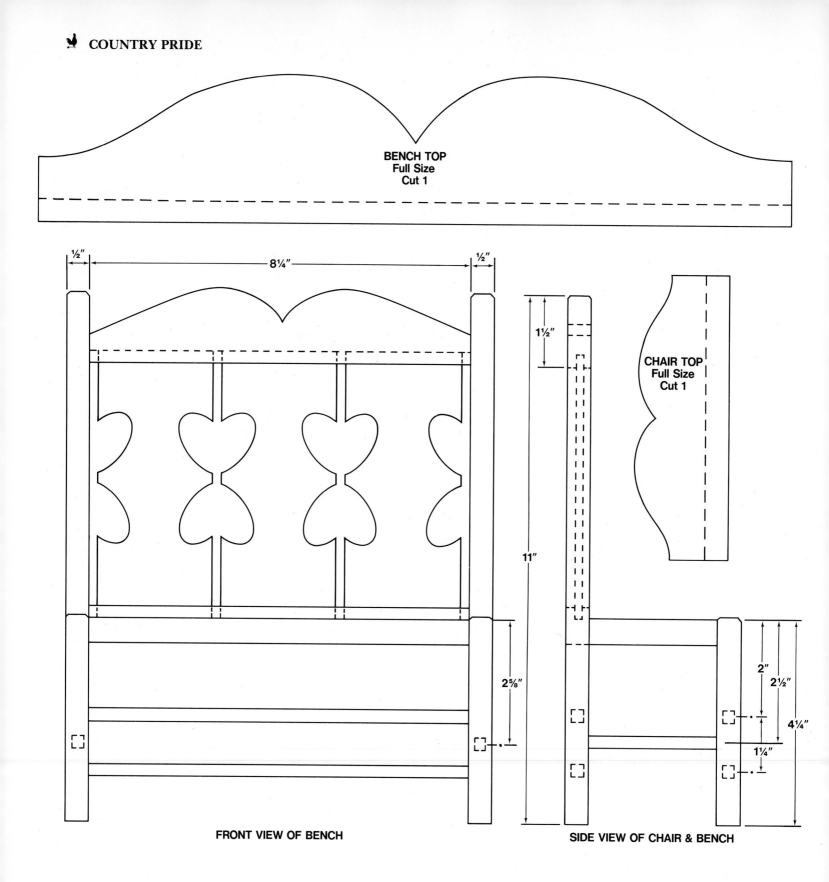

BENCH TOP
Full Size
Cut 1

½" 8¼" ½"

CHAIR TOP
Full Size
Cut 1

1½"

11"

2⅝"

2"
2½"
4¼"
1¼"

FRONT VIEW OF BENCH

SIDE VIEW OF CHAIR & BENCH

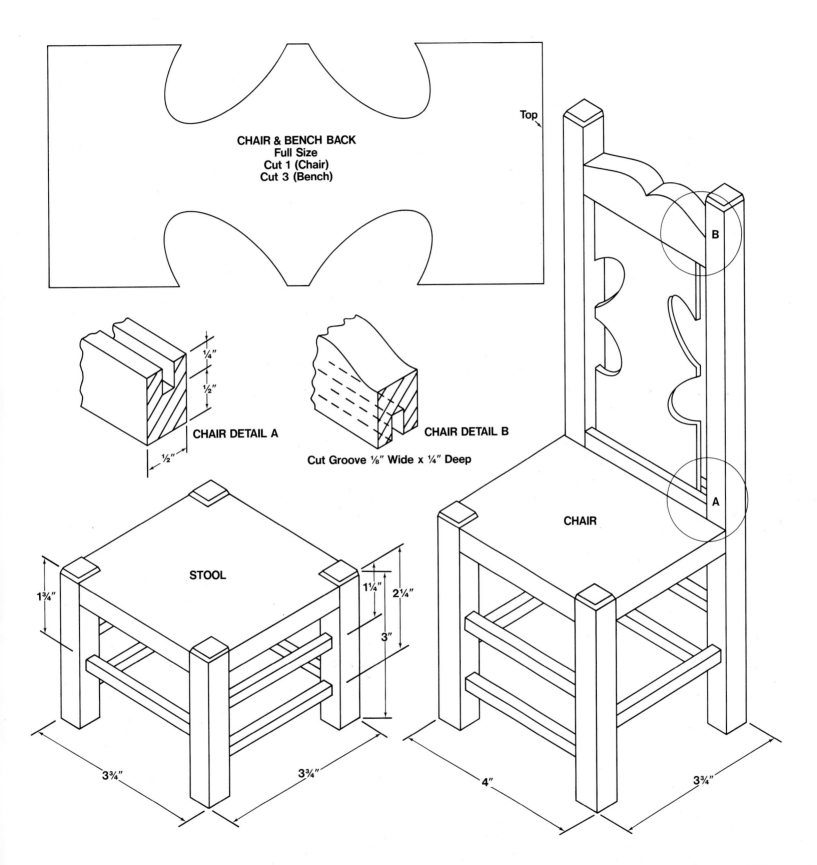

CHAIR & BENCH BACK
Full Size
Cut 1 (Chair)
Cut 3 (Bench)

Top

B

CHAIR DETAIL A

¼″

½″

½″

CHAIR DETAIL B

Cut Groove ⅛″ Wide x ¼″ Deep

A

CHAIR

STOOL

1¾″

3¾″

3¾″

1¼″

2¼″

3″

4″

3¾″

PUBLICITY

A large turnout for your bazaar or sale depends upon a carefully planned and well-organized publicity campaign.

The best planned bazaars, and the ones that are best attended, are those that are so well publicized that people in the community know about them long before opening day.

The key to successful attendance is a well-executed publicity campaign that answers some of the questions potential shoppers have. Where will the bazaar be held? (Are there directions, perhaps even a map, to an out-of-the-way location?) What dates, and during what hours, will booths be open? Who is sponsoring the event? What organization or group will be the recipient of the bazaar's profits?

You also will encourage attendance by including information in your publicity that tells potential shoppers whether parking, child care, food and beverages, and even entertainment will be available to make shoppers' visits to your bazaar easy and enjoyable.

Weighing the options

Publicity strategies should accompany the planning of the bazaar, and should begin well before the bazaar's opening day. Once the location, dates, theme, and organizing personnel are selected, publicity efforts can begin.

For best results, plan several different types of publicity—word-of-mouth, posters, and advertising in local media. Map

out a timetable of various publicity events so these efforts are spread evenly over the month preceding the bazaar, with more concentrated efforts as the bazaar draws near.

Deciding on a theme

A bazaar theme is important to publicity because it provides a focus for slogans, advertising illustrations, decorations, and entertainment ideas. Many bazaars are scheduled so that the

time of year suggests a theme, such as a harvesttime festival or a sale designed to relieve the winter doldrums. The seasonality of the bazaar dictates the theme, and all that is needed is a catchy, inviting name for the event.

Or, the bazaar is given for a particular reason, to raise funds for a community service organization, for example, or as part of a larger community event or celebration—perhaps a Fourth

of July or a Founder's Day celebration. These bazaars call for themes that fit the situation. For example, a sale to raise money for a local recreation center building fund should have a theme and title that tie the purpose of the sale to the goals of the community effort.

Creating and using handbills

For many local events, you can use handbills (printed on standard- or legal-size paper) to spread the word about your bazaar efficiently and inexpensively. Not only are handbills this size easy to reproduce, but shopkeepers are more willing to display small handbills than large posters.

In addition to posting handbills in stores, tack them up in libraries, schools, and municipal and office buildings. (Before posting handbills, obtain permission from the proper authorities. You might also offer to send volunteers to remove them after the sale date.)

Some merchants—operators of crafts stores who have provided materials for items sold at bazaars, for example—may be willing to tuck handbills inside paper bags, or to have bazaar representatives distribute handbills during peak hours.

To create a handbill, make arrangements through a local printer—quick-service print shops are commonplace—or through a school or church.

Learn what's needed for reproduction before designing the handbill. For example, ask if you can duplicate photographs or illustrations and use more than one color of ink. (Multi-colored printing can be expensive; you may want to request a cost estimate.)

Most print shop owners can help you plan and design a handbill. They will at least have samples of similar work they've produced to provide you with ideas.

Ask one or more artistic and imaginative members of the group sponsoring the bazaar to design the handbill. Have them include some visual representation of the event—a drawing that fits the theme or an illustration of the types of merchandise for sale. Accent the basic design with a few simple motifs or borders.

When designing the handbill, make sure that the important information is clear and prominent—the date, time, and place. Also include other pertinent information, such as special entertainment, and provisions for children.

If the site of the bazaar is obscure or difficult to find, include a map or directions, and give some indication of available parking. In large metropolitan areas, instructions for access via public transportation might be helpful. If possible, provide a telephone number prospective visitors may call to learn more about the bazaar.

Designing posters

Posters are effective in high-traffic areas. Quick and inexpensive to produce, a half-dozen posters can efficiently bring attention to the event.

Posters are more eye-catching than handbills because they are larger and individually produced to include more design elements. Once a handbill layout is completed, enlarge it onto poster board (available at art supply stores) using paint or felt markers. Add more design motifs by painting them or adding felt or paper cutouts.

As with handbills, always ask for permission to place the poster, and let the merchant know when it may be removed.

Benefiting from local media

Besides purchasing advertising in local newspapers and spots on local radio and televi-sion stations, consider some of the many low-cost or even no-cost methods of spreading the word about your bazaar.

Contact the features editor of the local newspaper about the bazaar. If your fund-raiser is of general community interest, the newspaper may run a feature story.

An editor may send a reporter or photographer to cover preliminary events, such as setting up the bazaar. Or the paper may run a story about the organization for which the bazaar is being held. Be sure to request an entry about your fund-raiser in the newspaper's calendar of community events.

Local radio and television stations also may have community calendar features, and they may publicize the event free of charge.

With sufficient advance knowledge, a station also may present one or more representatives from the bazaar on a segment of a talk show. Be-

cause these events are planned several weeks in advance, especially if the bazaar occurs near a holiday, the more time you give the station, the better your chances of being included.

Local cable television networks often have at least one channel that is devoted to community events. Some channels feature a list of events that scrolls across the screen; others feature live or taped local news events and feature stories.

Still another option is public-access channels. Most often the local cable network provides equipment and expertise to produce a news or feature segment of general interest to the community.

When working with members of any media, it's a good idea to have specific projects from a variety of booth operators to show or talk about. (Or, arrange for an interview with a booth operator.) Unusual products that will be available at the bazaar or events such as raffles or door prizes are natural ways to get conversation started about the bazaar and to build enthusiasm for the event.

Whatever media you choose to publicize your bazaar, be sure to notify media people well in advance so information about the bazaar is not slighted by coverage of other events, but not so far ahead that the media—and the public—forget about the event.

PUBLICITY

With some simple materials and willing hands to help, publicity can pay off—and be great fun besides!

Bradstreet Bear, *above,* is wearing a sandwich board to publicize an event. Make this bear slightly larger than the original (on page 114) to accommodate boards made from scraps of poster board and trims. Place the bears in store windows or high-traffic areas. After the bazaar, give the bears as prizes to booth operators with the highest sales or the most effective displays.

For flyers like those *above right,* photocopy the headlines and important words on page 34. Flower-shaped memo pads, *opposite,* are available at school supply outlets. Jot pertinent information on each sheet of paper of the pad and use the sheets as handouts.

The eye-catching banner, *near right,* is based on the pattern for the carving shown on pages 6 and 7. Use it or another illustration to make a banner to highlight the bazaar.

Instructions for these publicity projects begin on page 34.

PUBLICITY BEAR

Shown on page 32.
Finished bear is 25 inches tall.

MATERIALS

Materials for Bradstreet Bear, shown on page 114 (see *Note* below)
Scraps of poster board, ribbon, rickrack
2-inch-high letter cutouts (designed for bulletin boards and available from educators' supply outlets; see the "School Supplies" listing in the Yellow Pages)
Artificial flowers
Glue

INSTRUCTIONS

Note: Bear shown is an enlarged version of Bradstreet Bear, shown on page 114; pattern and instructions begin on page 119. Enlarge pattern 25 percent; instead of transferring pattern to 1-inch squares, transfer pattern pieces to 1¼-inch squares. (*Note:* For an even larger bear, transfer patterns to 1½-inch squares; finished bear will be about 31 inches tall.) Adjust materials required and cut out pattern pieces. Assemble and clothe bear, eliminating pocket trim and watch on vest.

For signboard, cut two 9½x10-inch pieces of poster board. Plan message for front and back panels. Lay out letters on board; glue in place. (*Note:* If desired, substitute letters cut from plain paper for the purchased ones, or simply draw letters freehand onto poster board with felt-tip markers.) Edge board with rickrack or other trim. Conceal raw edges of rickrack at corners with an artificial flower or a decorative sticker.

Position boards on front and back of bear. Cut ribbon scraps to serve as shoulder straps; glue or tape to back sides of boards. Slip sandwich board assembly over bear's head; secure ribbon straps with a straight pin inconspicuously at shoulder, if necessary.

PRINTED FLYERS

Shown on pages 32–33.

MATERIALS

Type or printed words for message
Typing paper
Ruler
Paper cement
Marker

INSTRUCTIONS

To create flyers like the ones shown, use the assortment of printed words, *opposite*. Make a photocopy of page 34 to serve as the master; use as good a copier as is available so that subsequent copies will be clear and sharp.

Cut apart appropriate words from the master photocopy to convey message. To add dates, clip apart calendars for months and numerals. Look to other printed sources for remaining words, or simply add handwritten messages with a marker. For focal points on the flyers, use any clear black-and-white illustration, or use the illustrations intended for the gift tags on pages 184 and 185. (Use an enlarging or reducing photocopier to adjust the sizes of the drawings to the amount of space you have.)

Use a plain sheet of typing paper for the background. Arrange words, numbers, and drawings on the sheet to create a pleasing and effective design. Use a ruler to make sure that words are straight or centered. Affix elements to paper background with paper cement.

Have flyers printed at a local quick-print shop. Investigate the options available for printed material; colored papers and colored inks are often available for minimal additional cost.

APPLIQUÉD BANNER

Shown on page 32.
Finished size is 32x40 inches.

MATERIALS

1¾ yards light-colored solid fabric for banner background
Scraps of fabric in the following colors: dark red, rust, gold, light green, and dark green
Fusible webbing
Thread to match fabrics
Two 32-inch-long pieces of dowel or lath

INSTRUCTIONS

Enlarge pattern for wooden plaque shown on pages 6 and 7 (pattern is on page 17) so that motif is 26 inches wide. Cut fabric shapes to match pattern as follows: heart and outer petals of tulips are dark red; center petals and outer petals of smaller flowers are rust; remaining petals of smaller flowers and center leaf are gold; stems are light green; leaves are dark green. Cut pieces of fusible webbing to same shapes.

Cut two 33x44-inch panels for banner. (*Note:* This is for a lined banner. If banner is to hang against a wall, lining it is optional.)

Plan position of design roughly in center of banner. For letters, use words reproduced on an enlarging photocopier for patterns, or use letters from printed sources. Cut letters from any dark-colored fabric and also from fusible webbing.

If desired, add the dates and location of the bazaar to finished banner. Or, leave space for them and cut out additional information from adhesive-backed felt or paper. That way you can remove the letters and reuse the banners at another bazaar.

Following manufacturer's directions, affix fabric shapes to banner background with fusible webbing. Satin-stitch around edges of motifs and letters with matching thread.

Place banner front and back right sides together. Stitch around edges using ½-inch seams and leaving an opening for turning. Turn and press edges.

Fold top and bottom edges to back of banner and stitch, forming casings for dowels or lath. Slide dowels or lath into casings and hang.

PAINTED PAPER & WOOD

Getting the most from ordinary materials is the mark of a talented crafter. The unusual bazaar projects in this chapter may have humble origins, but crafts buyers will recognize them as fine examples of folk art executed in time-honored techniques.

Fraktur, which decorated Pennsylvania German family documents for generations, is the distinctive style of calligraphy appearing on the framed piece, *left.* Here, the alphabet is presented sampler-style, and is flanked by painted motifs. After mastering the pen strokes for the alphabet, reproduce it onto good-quality paper. Then add the checkerboard border, outline the motifs with a marker, and color the design with paints.

Borrow several of the design elements to decorate plain stationery or wooden boxes.

Instructions for projects in this chapter begin on page 42.

❖

These charming pictures recall Victorian silhouette portraits, but are simplified ink-on-paper designs.

The framed pictures, *above* and *opposite*, imitate this technique in a series of Victorian vignettes. First outline the designs on parchment paper with a fine-tip black pen, and then fill in the shapes with black acrylic paints. Or, highlight a section of the design by working a key element of the picture in color, as is done in the quilt picture, *above*.

"Shall we go for a stroll?"

Even the simplest wooden shapes can take on surprising character with different paint applications.

The rooster, *above,* derives its three-dimensional quality from layering the wings atop the body. An easy textural painting technique provides the country charm.

The sassy dolls, *opposite,* are constructed so that the legs are jointed. Each piece is painted, then the doll is assembled and dressed in a fabric apron and styled with yarn hair.

FRAKTUR DESIGNS

Shown on pages 36–37.
Finished size of framed fraktur picture is 9½x11½ inches.

MATERIALS

Good-quality paper such as parchment or watercolor paper
India ink; calligraphy pen with flat tip
Black fine-tip felt pen
Note cards; wooden boxes
Frame; clear matte varnish
Acrylic paints
Fine artist's brushes; pencil

INSTRUCTIONS

For the framed picture

Using a pencil, transfer the design, *opposite,* to paper; add two rows of squares across top and bottom to complete borders (see photograph).

Outline the checkered border and hearts and the rectangular sections with black felt-tip pen. Use India ink and a calligraphy pen to outline the letters and numbers.

Using acrylic paints, carefully paint the motifs; refer to the photograph for colors, or use colors of your choice. Paint the light colors first, then proceed to the dark ones. When dry, frame as desired.

For the boxes and note cards

Trace the motifs of your choice from the design, *opposite,* in pleasing arrangements onto greeting cards and wooden box tops and sides. Paint as desired. Finish boxes with varnish or oil.

continued

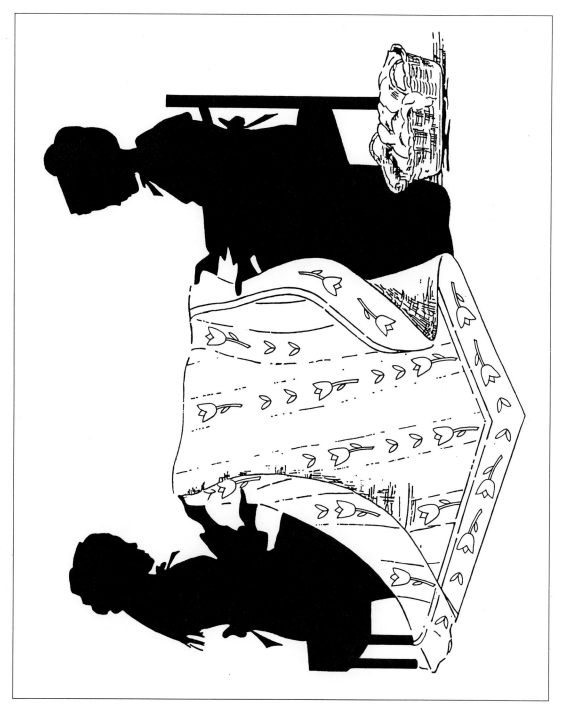

INK-ON-PAPER PICTURES

Shown on pages 38–39.

MATERIALS

Parchment paper
Black acrylic paint
Small artist's brush
Permanent fine-tip black pen
Tracing and carbon paper
Purchased frames

INSTRUCTIONS

Select the design of your choice, *right* or on page 43, and trace the full-size pattern onto tracing paper. Then, with carbon paper, transfer the design onto parchment.

Draw around the outline and the other small details with the fine-tip black pen. Paint the large areas with black paint, using a small artist's brush. Paint some areas of the design, such as the quilt in the pattern on page 43, in contrasting colors if desired.

When the paint is dry, frame picture as desired.

"Shall we go for a stroll?"

PAINTED CHICKEN

Shown on page 40.
Finished size is 11½ inches tall.

MATERIALS

One 12x15-inch piece (body and wings) and one 1½x12-inch piece (base) of 1-inch fir or pine
Acrylic paint in the following colors: ivory, rust, black, orange, and yellow
¼x1½-inch dowel pin
Antique glazing
Carpenter's glue; sponge
Jigsaw; drill with ¼-inch bit; black felt-tip pen
Sandpaper; carbon paper

INSTRUCTIONS

Trace the full-size pattern on pages 46 and 47 onto tracing paper. Match the A-B and C-D markings on the body with the A-B and C-D markings on the body/tail to make one pattern piece. Trace the wing to make a separate pattern. Cut out patterns and draw outlines onto wood; use carbon paper to transfer body details.

Cut body shape and two wings from wood. Sand all pieces, including the base.

Position chicken on base and mark placement for legs. Drill two ¼-inch holes in the base and in the bottom of the legs.

Refer to photograph to paint chicken, base, and wings. Outline facial features in black using felt-tip pen. With sponge, dab black paint on chicken and tail feathers as desired. Let dry; carefully apply antique glazing to all surfaces.

Glue wings to chicken. To attach chicken to base, put glue in holes in base; insert dowel pins. Put glue on bottom of both feet and in holes in legs. Place chicken over dowel pins on base.

WOODEN DOLLS

Shown on page 41.
Standing doll is about 9½ inches tall.

MATERIALS
12-inch length of 1x8-inch fir
Acrylic paints in assorted
   colors
Clear polyurethane
Artist's paintbrushes
Latch-hook rug yarn precut to
   3½-inch lengths (hair)
Scraps of plaid fabric (apron)
Jigsaw; sandpaper
Drill with ⅛-inch drill bit
Two 1½-inch No. 17 brads
Carbon paper; white glue

INSTRUCTIONS
DOLL: Enlarge the pattern, *right.* Transfer the outline *only* of the full-size doll body and two leg patterns to fir using carbon paper. Cut out body and leg pieces. Sand rough edges.

Drill a double row of randomly spaced holes around the outside edge of the head.

Transfer facial features and clothing details to the wood

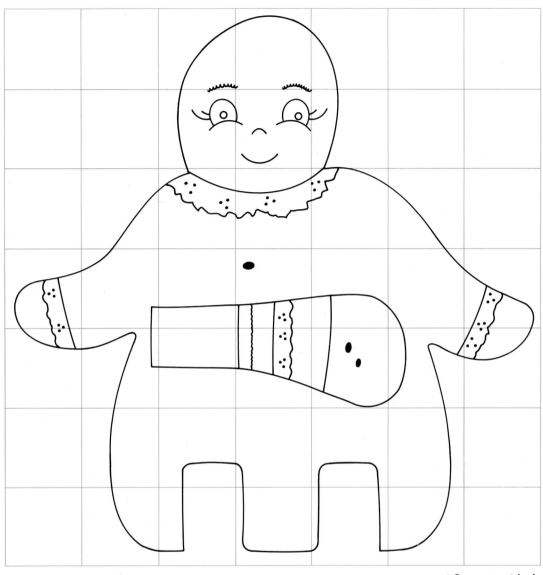

1 Square = 1 Inch

pieces. Paint design, referring to photograph for ideas. Seal with one coat of polyurethane.

Fold two strands of yarn in half. Using the end of an artist's paintbrush, poke the yarn tuft into one hole in the doll's head. Continue until all holes are filled; glue in place. Separate the strands in the yarn to give the hair a fluffy look.

Insert one leg into opening. Nail brad from outside of the body, through the leg, and into the body center. Repeat for second leg.

APRON: From plaid fabric, cut a 3x6-inch rectangle for skirt, a 1½x2-inch rectangle for bodice, a 1x27-inch strip for waistband, and two 1x5-inch strips for neck ties.

Round bottom corners of the skirt and top corners of bodice piece. Hem skirt bottom and sides; hem the bodice top and sides. Fold waistband strip in half; fold in half again. Topstitch long edge closed. Slightly gather top of apron skirt. Center waistband atop the skirt. Topstitch in place. Center bodice on waistband and skirt; topstitch in place.

Fold neck tie strips in half; fold them in half again and topstitch the long edge closed. Hand-sew strips to bodice top. Tie apron at waist and neck.

A

B

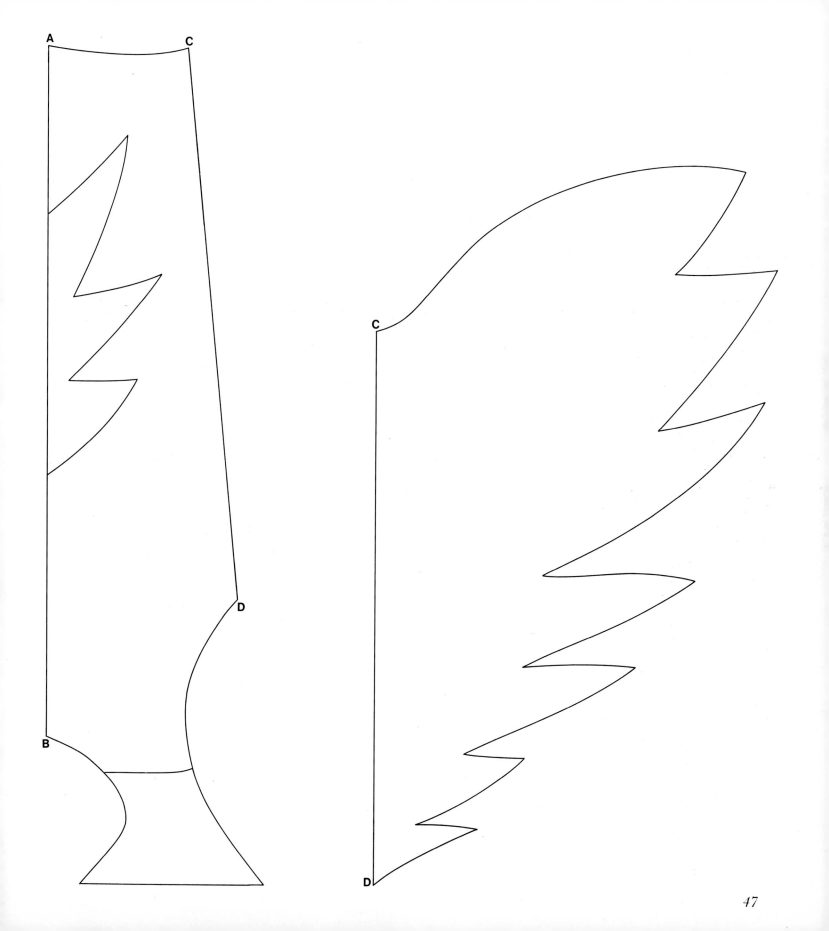

47

PATCHWORK & QUILTING

Smaller patchwork and quilted projects are more efficient money-makers than entire quilts, and they are just as appealing. The patchwork projects in this chapter will satisfy the most talented of quilters, but won't require weeks and weeks of effort.

Mixing patchwork styles is successful when patterns and colors complement each other. For example, the table accessories, *right*, reflect both traditional and contemporary patchwork. The pot holder and table runner feature a popular flower basket motif, and the place mats are simply strokes of color executed in fabric. Subtle colors used for all projects help to unite the styles.

Piecing the projects can be done by hand or by machine, but because the accessories are small, they can be quilted by machine.

Instructions for all patchwork projects in this chapter begin on page 54.

❖❖

Warm and inviting designs like these—
worked in pretty fabrics—are what make
patchwork and quilting so appealing.

The three-dimensional quality of the picture, *above*, comes from the tiny stitched-on pillows, flounced upholstery, and miniature crocheted anti-macassar. Use our full-size patterns to make the pieced pillow tops, *opposite*. They're traditional Schoolhouse and Ohio Star patterns, updated with pastel fabrics.

Beaming faces on the pillow dolls, *right*, are created with machine stitchery. The body shapes and costumes for the dolls are made from fabric scraps with machine appliqué in the conventional way. Then, touches of freehand machine embroidery are used to outline the features, emphasize the clothing details, and define the market baskets.

Vary the features, if desired, to make different expressions and personalities. Look to caricatures and illustrations for design inspiration.

When making patchwork projects like these, accumulate a variety of different prints of the same fabric weight, then sort them by color and scale.

FLOWER BASKET TABLE ACCESSORIES

Shown on pages 48–49.
Finished size of pot holder is 11 inches square; table runner is 15x39 inches; place mats are 12¾x18 inches; napkins are 16 inches square.

MATERIALS
For one pot holder, table runner, and four place mats and napkins
45-inch-wide cotton fabric in the following amounts and colors: ⅜ yard of medium blue; ¼ yard of navy; 1⅓ yards of medium brick red; ¼ yard of dark brick red; 2¼ yards of natural muslin
Wide, double-fold bias tape: 1¼ yards of navy and 9 yards of ecru
Polyester fleece
Cardboard or plastic for templates
Dark brick red sewing thread

INSTRUCTIONS
To make the best use of fabric, read all instructions and plan cutting sequence before cutting fabrics. Seams are ¼ inch wide.

Machine-quilt, using long stitches and dark brick red thread.

For one basket block
Trace the full-size diamond pattern, *right*, and transfer to plastic or cardboard to make a template for the "flower petals" in the basket. (The two center petals are medium brick red; outer petals are dark brick red.)

Then, using the flower basket block diagram, *right*, for reference, make templates for the remaining patterns.

Referring to the photograph for colors, cut pattern pieces from fabric, adding ¼-inch seam allowances.

To assemble the block, sew together a medium brick red and a dark brick red petal; make two pairs. Next, sew muslin square between tops of medium brick red petals; stitch smaller muslin triangles in place. Join petal assembly to larger navy triangle; set aside.

Sew smaller navy triangle to muslin rectangle; repeat with remaining navy triangle and muslin rectangle. Stitch these pieces to assembled basket and petals. Join larger muslin triangle to bottom of basket. Finish by stitching medium-blue triangles around the block.

For pot holder
Cut two 12x12-inch pieces of fleece and one of backing. Stitch on basket block; mark it for quilting, with diagonal lines spaced 2 inches apart. Sandwich double thickness of fleece between top and backing; quilt.

Round corners as shown in photograph. For tab, topstitch edges of a 5-inch strip of bias tape; pin to top corner. Bind edges of pad using bias tape.

For table runner
Make two basket blocks. Cut a 10½-inch square from medium brick red, ten 2¾x10½-inch muslin strips, and eight 2¾-inch navy squares. Also cut one 17x40-inch piece *each* from fleece and muslin.

Join two muslin strips to opposite sides of the medium brick red square. Stitch a basket block to each end of this strip, with flower petals pointing toward center (see photograph). Add a muslin strip to each end.

For the outer borders, join four navy squares alternately to three muslin strips (refer to the photograph); make two borders. Sew to long sides of the center of the runner.

To mark for quilting, find center of runner, draw a line; then, measure and mark 2-inch intervals. Sandwich fleece between top and muslin backing. Pin layers together; machine-quilt. Finish with bias binding.

For place mats and napkins
Cut muslin for top piece 13x19 inches; cut one 13x19-inch piece *each* from muslin backing and fleece.

Cut one medium-blue strip 1½x19 inches. Cut one navy strip and one dark brick red strip, each 1½x13 inches; sew together along one long edge.

Starting 3 inches from one short edge of place-mat top, mark quilting lines 2 inches apart. Sandwich fleece between top and backing. Pin to secure.

Turn under long edges of pieced red and navy strip. Pin to one end of place mat, so strip falls on line 3 inches from edge.

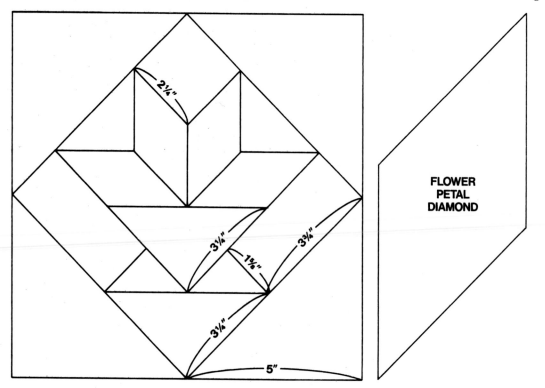

FLOWER PETAL DIAMOND

Topstitch in place. Stitch along remaining quilting lines. Then, turn under raw edges of medium-blue strip; topstitch along long edge of place mat, 2½ inches from edge.

Round corners of place mat and bind edges with bias tape.

For napkins, cut 17-inch squares of medium brick red fabric. Narrowly hem edges.

❖

PATCHWORK PILLOWS

Shown on page 51.
Pillows are approximately 16 inches square.

MATERIALS

Pastel fabrics (in colors of your choice) as follows: ¼ yard *each* of A, E, and F; ⅓ yard of B; ⅛ yard *each* of C and G; scrap of D
18x18 inches of backing fabric for each pillow; 16-inch-square pillow forms or fiberfill
½ yard of quilt batting
2 yards of cotton cording for each pillow
Cardboard or plastic for templates

INSTRUCTIONS

Trace patterns, pages 56 and 57, for each pillow, transfer to cardboard or plastic, and cut out pieces to use as templates. Trace around templates onto wrong side of fabrics for each design. Adding ¼-inch seam allowances, cut out pieces.

Following diagrams, pages 56 and 57, piece pillow tops.

To begin, join pattern pieces into small units or blocks, then sew units or blocks into horizontal rows. Use ¼-inch seams throughout.

Timesaving Tips—
Piecing Triangles into Squares

❖

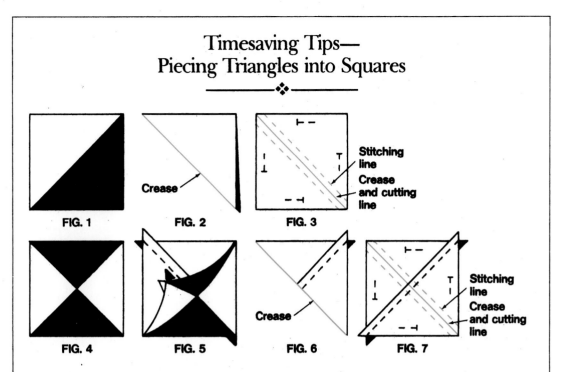

FIG. 1   FIG. 2   FIG. 3
Crease   Stitching line / Crease and cutting line

FIG. 4   FIG. 5   FIG. 6   FIG. 7
Crease   Stitching line / Crease and cutting line

Here's a fast, accurate method of piecing triangles, to use whenever you need a unit of right-angle triangles to form a square (Fig. 1, *above*). Or, use this technique for two units of right-angle triangles, to form a larger square (Fig. 4, *above*), as in the patchwork pillow shown on page 51.

For a one-unit square (with two triangles)
Cut one dark and one light square from fabric, tracing around a precisely cut cardboard template on the straight grain of the fabric. To determine the size of the squares, add ⅞ inch to the size of your *finished* (seamed) piece.

For example, if you need a triangle unit 2 inches square when stitched, cut the squares 2⅞ inches square. This allows ¼-inch seams and extra for the technique.

Next, place the two squares with right sides facing and fold in half on the diagonal (Fig. 2). Make a firm crease on the fold with your fingers. This crease is the stitching and cutting *guide.*

Lay the squares flat again, pinning them to keep edges even and secure. Using the crease as a guide, stitch ¼ inch away from it along both sides (Fig. 3). Cut fabric pieces apart on the crease line for a two-triangle unit. Press seams to one side.

For a two-unit square (with four triangles)
Cut one dark and one light square from fabric, tracing around a precisely cut template on the straight grain of the fabric. To determine the size of the squares, add 1¼

inches to the size of the *finished* (seamed) unit.

For example, for a triangle unit 2 inches square, cut the squares 3¼ inches square. This allows for ¼-inch seams, plus extra for the technique.

Then, follow directions for the one-unit (two-triangle) square, *above.*

Next, place two triangle units together (right sides facing), alternating the colors and matching seams (Fig. 5).

Fold in half on the diagonal, making a firm crease with your fingers (Fig. 6). Using the crease as a guide, stitch ¼-inch seams on both sides, pinning edges to avoid shifting (Fig. 7). Cut apart on the crease line; press.

Finally, stitch rows together and add borders to top, bottom, and sides to complete the pillow top.

Baste pillow top to a layer of quilt batting; quilt along design lines (see photograph).

Cover cording with bias strips of fabric, then baste binding along seam line of top.

Cut pillow back to match front. With right sides facing, sew back to front. Clip corners, turn, and stuff with fiberfill. Stitch opening closed.

———— ❖ ————

SOFA PICTURE

Shown on page 50.
Picture is approximately 16x20 inches.

MATERIALS
½ yard of striped fabric (wallpaper); ⅔ yard of print fabric (sofa); scraps of print and solid-color fabric (pillows)
7-inch-diameter doily (antimacassar)
1½ yards of narrow cording
¾ yard of polyester quilt batting
Graph and tracing paper
Cardboard
Water-erasable pen

continued

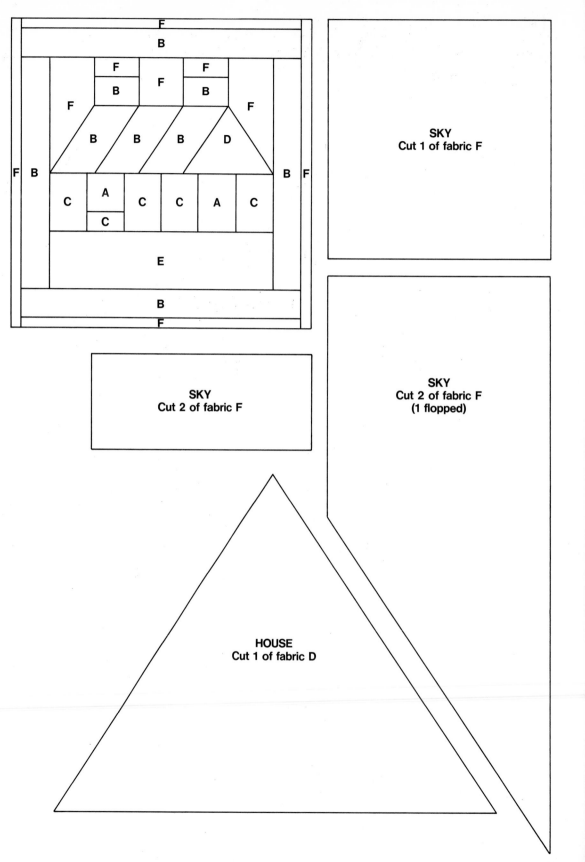

SKY
Cut 1 of fabric F

SKY
Cut 2 of fabric F

SKY
Cut 2 of fabric F
(1 flopped)

HOUSE
Cut 1 of fabric D

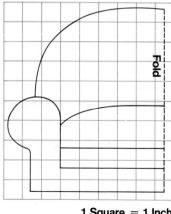

Fold

1 Square = 1 Inch

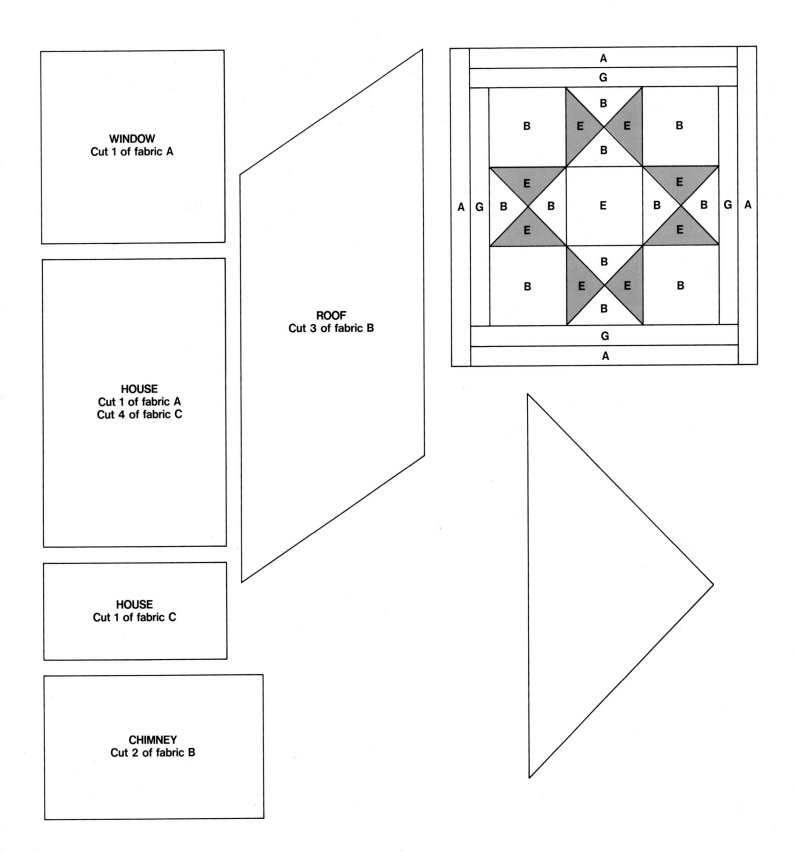

WINDOW
Cut 1 of fabric A

HOUSE
Cut 1 of fabric A
Cut 4 of fabric C

HOUSE
Cut 1 of fabric C

CHIMNEY
Cut 2 of fabric B

ROOF
Cut 3 of fabric B

INSTRUCTIONS

Enlarge pattern, page 56, then transfer pattern onto the print fabric using a water-erasable pen. Cut out sofa, adding ½-inch seam allowances. Baste sofa to quilt batting and machine-quilt around outlines of armrests and sofa cushion. Machine-sew along outer lines of sofa. Cut batting ⅛ inch beyond machine stitching; turn under raw edges and baste.

Cut and piece 1½ yards of 1-inch-wide bias strips from print fabric; cover cording. Sew cording around edge of sofa.

For the ruffle, cut a 3x28-inch strip of sofa fabric. Sew ½-inch hem along bottom and sides; gather top to fit bottom of sofa; baste in place. Cut doily in half and hand-sew to sofa.

Back striped fabric with batting. Baste sofa (centered) atop striped fabric. Sew sofa in place along piped edges. Tack top of ruffle to striped fabric.

Cover two ⅜-inch-diameter cardboard circles with a bit of batting and circles of fabric; gather edges of fabric and draw to back of cardboard. Sew one "button" to center of each sofa arm (see photograph). Stitch, stuff, and tack three small throw pillows to sofa.

Mount finished design on cardboard. Frame as desired.

PILLOW DOLLS

Shown on pages 52–53.
Dolls are 14 inches tall.

MATERIALS
For one doll
½ yard of fabric (main body
   pieces, bottom inset)
Scraps of coordinating fabrics
   (appliqués)

continued

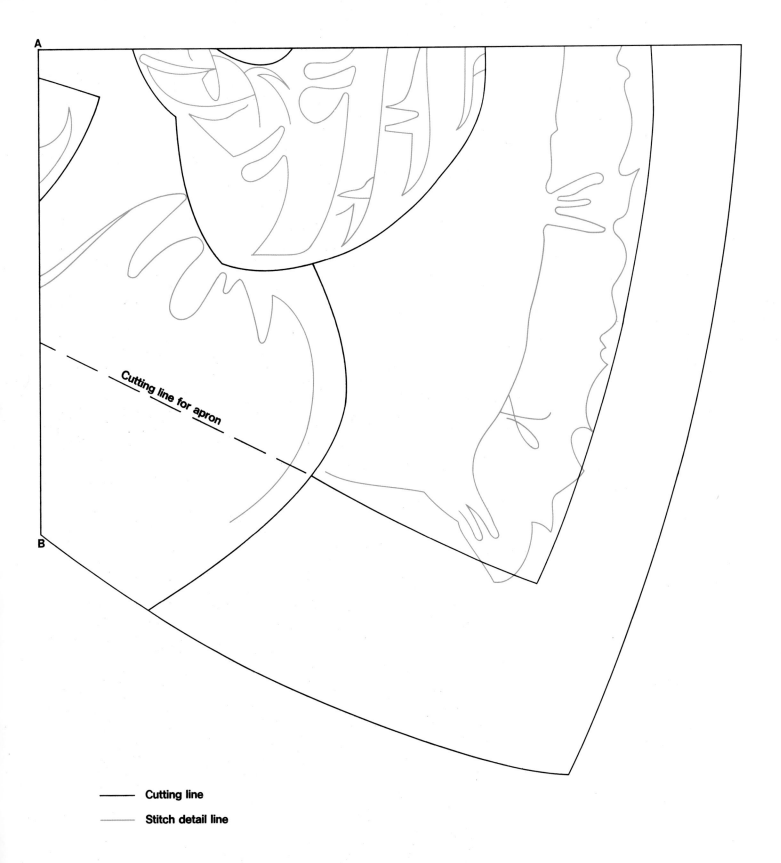

A

Cutting line for apron

B

——— Cutting line

——— Stitch detail line

59

Matching and contrasting
threads; fiberfill
Dressmaker's carbon paper
Tissue paper
14-inch square of tear-away
backing

INSTRUCTIONS

Trace the patterns, pages
58–61, onto tissue paper, joining left half of doll (pages 58
and 59) to right half of doll
(pages 60 and 61).

Note: All three dolls are made
with the same pattern pieces,
with a choice of two facial expressions. Flop the direction of
the dolls and change fabrics for
variety.

Transfer doll outline to fabric onto which appliqués will be
stitched. Transfer a second doll
outline to the backing fabric.
Add ¼-inch seam allowances
to both pieces. Do not cut out
the front piece until all appliqué on the doll is completed.

Transfer pattern pieces for
appliqués to fabrics; cut out.

Pin or baste pieces, referring
to the photograph for placement. With fabric atop tear-
away backing, sew around the
edges using narrow machine
satin stitches. (*Note:* Edges to be
covered by another appliqué or
stitched into a seam do not
need to be satin-stitched.) Remove tear-away backing.

Transfer detail lines to face
and clothing using dressmaker's carbon paper; machine- or
hand-stitch details.

To assemble dolls, sew front
and back together (right sides
facing), leaving bottom open.
Sew bottom inset in place, eas-
ing it to fit and leaving an opening for turning. Clip curves,
turn, and stuff. Slip-stitch opening closed.

——— **Cutting line**

Stitch detail line

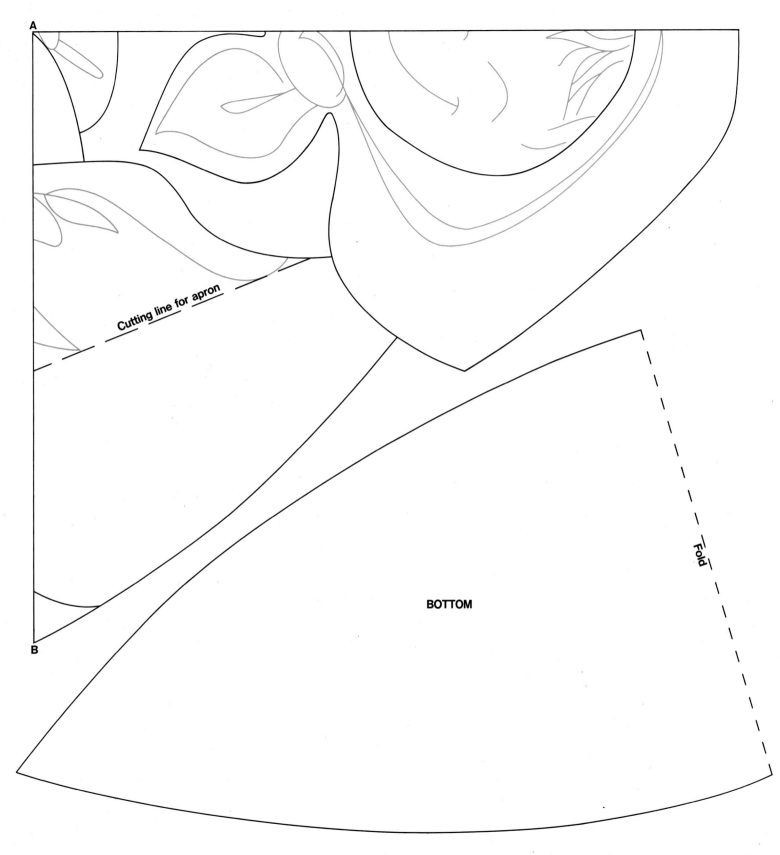

A

Cutting line for apron

B

Fold

BOTTOM

61

SEWING & STITCHERY

Stitchery projects are among the most sought-after bazaar crafts. The best projects feature good designs that are also showcases for the excellent stitchers in your group. This chapter contains practical and beautiful accessories sure to appeal to bazaar shoppers.

Anyone who knits or crochets knows the benefits of keeping needles and hooks together in one place. The quick-sew caddies, *right,* do just that. Bright fabric forms the background, and a piece of clear vinyl laid atop forms the pocket. Parallel rows of stitching create dividers to keep needles paired and hooks grouped by size.

The accompanying see-through storage envelopes are just right for containing small projects or managing elusive materials. An edging of grosgrain ribbon holds together the envelopes, which are closed with a snap fastener.

Small-scale motifs like these are ideal can-didates for creating by the batch because they work up fast and adapt to all sorts of finished items.

Working the flow-ers and lattice design for the handkerchief case and sachets on needlepoint canvas, *opposite,* is simplified because the back-ground is left unstitched.

Variegated pearl cotton thread adds color interest to the hardanger motif, *above.* Sell individual stitcheries, if desired, or affix them to the tops of purchased boxes.

Plan merchandising efforts at your booth around these colorful butterfly motifs for a springtime-fresh display.

Graceful butterflies worked in cross-stitches frame the mirror, *opposite*. Each wing is identical, so the pattern for one is reversed and repeated to complete the design. The larger butterflies are stitched over two threads of evenweave fabric; the motif attached to the potpourri jar lid is worked over one thread.

Old-fashioned pineapple crochet inspired the wings for the doily edging, *opposite*. Edge doilies as shown, or suspend single motifs from monofilament to hang in a sunny window.

The third butterfly design, *above*, is tatted from bright pearl cottons. The wings are basically circles with picots of varying lengths.

Tiny tatted flowers give the ordinary stationery, *below* and *opposite,* a dressed-up look. Use bits of leftover threads to work the simple flowers and glue them to purchased notes and blank calling cards. Color-coordinated inked borders enhance their elegant look.

Basic tatting skills and some plain paper products are all you need to create this outstanding stationery.

KNITTING & CROCHET CADDIES

Shown on pages 62–63.
Finished sizes of caddies are 12x16 inches and 7½x12 inches.

MATERIALS
For one of each caddy
½ yard *each* of polyester fleece and two fabrics for front and backing
1-inch-wide grosgrain ribbon (edges and ties)
⅓ yard clear vinyl; thread

INSTRUCTIONS
For crochet hook caddy
Cut 7½x12-inch pieces of fabric from the fleece, front, and backing fabrics.

Place the fleece between the fabrics; baste layers together. Cut a 3¾x12-inch vinyl pocket; bind top edge with ribbon. Place pocket atop caddy, having raw edges of pocket even with raw edges of caddy bottom. Channel-quilt every 1¼ inches through all thicknesses on the pocket only.

Cut a 26-inch tie from grosgrain ribbon; fold lengthwise and sew long edges. Knot ends.

Using ribbon, bind raw edges of caddy, mitering corners and catching center of tie in stitching along one 12-inch edge.

For knitting needle caddy
Adjust finished size to 12x16 inches; make vinyl pocket 8x12 inches. Channel-quilt and finish as for crochet caddy.

PLASTIC ENVELOPES

Shown on page 63.

MATERIALS
For four envelopes
1 yard of medium-weight clear vinyl; 4 heavy-duty snaps; 1-inch-wide grosgrain ribbon

INSTRUCTIONS
Make pattern for size of envelope front, as desired; cut from vinyl. Add rounded flap to top edge of pattern for back of envelope; cut from vinyl.

Press ribbon in half lengthwise; cut one length for top edge of front. Topstitch folded ribbon over front top edge.

Align front and back. Sew folded ribbon around all edges, beginning at bottom of one side. Fold flap over; mark center of flap and corresponding placement for snap on front of envelope; affix snaps.

HANDKERCHIEF CASE & SACHETS

Shown on page 64.
Finished size of case is 9x9 inches, without lace. Sachets are 3x3 inches.

MATERIALS
12x12-inch piece of 18-count interlock canvas; tapestry needle; fray retardant
DMC pearl cotton, Size 8: 1 ball *each* of white, No. 745 yellow, No. 518 blue, and No. 91 blue ombré
1⅓ yards of 1-inch-wide white pregathered lace

Two 9x18-inch pieces of pale blue crepe lining fabric
8½x17½-inch piece of lightweight quilt batting
1 yard of ¼-inch-wide pale blue satin ribbon

INSTRUCTIONS
Bind edges of canvas and baste center line. Refer to charts, *right* and *opposite*.

For handkerchief case
For outer border, use white to work 70x70 cross-stitches over two threads of canvas.

Work "handkerchief" in center in white continental stitches. (Leave canvas background unstitched; do not carry thread underneath from one letter to another.) Backstitch around letters with blue.

Using blue ombré thread, cross-stitch row of flowers above and below word; work each stitch over two threads of canvas. Work yellow centers. Work lattice background in white, working half cross-stitches over two threads.

Referring to chart, work flowers from upper left to lower right corner. For buds, work a single cross-stitch.

Steam-press canvas lightly on wrong side. Trim excess canvas to ¼ inch; treat edges with fray retardant. Topstitch lace trim around the edges of the cross-stitched border.

Fold each piece of lining fabric in half to form a square; press along fold. Open lining. Cut two 9-inch lengths of satin ribbon. With one lining piece right side up, mark a point on *each* long side 3 inches from short ends; place ribbons, right side up, across from point to point. Sew across ends of ribbon inside ¼-inch seam line.

With right sides facing, sew lining pieces together (¼-inch

continued

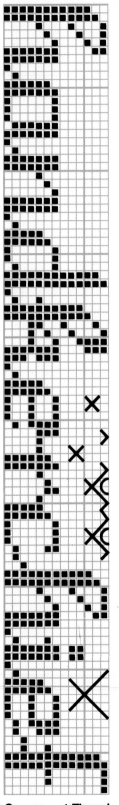

1 Square = 1 Thread

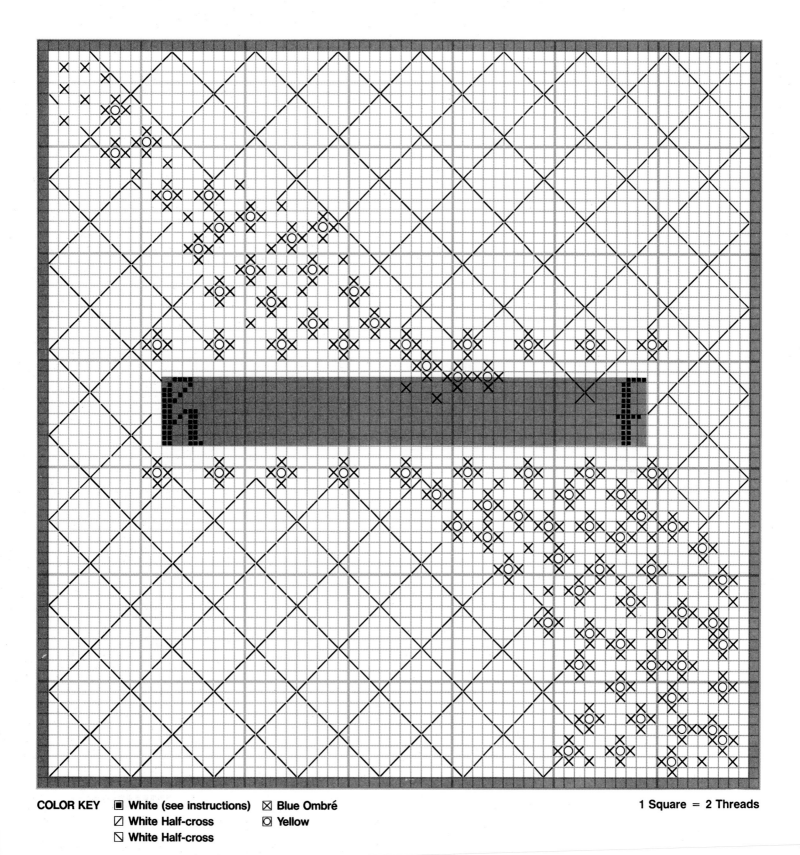

COLOR KEY ▣ White (see instructions) ⊠ Blue Ombré
⊿ White Half-cross ⦿ Yellow
◲ White Half-cross

1 Square = 2 Threads

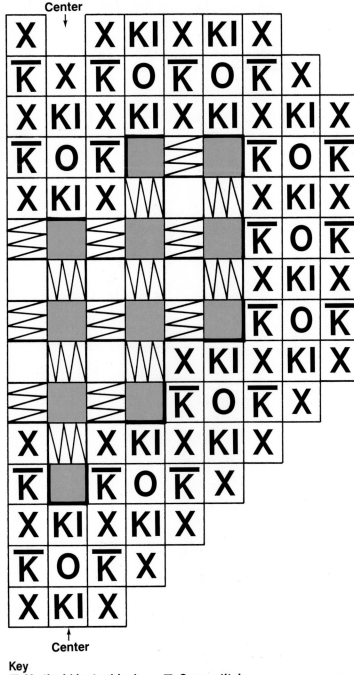

Center

Center

Key

- ⊠ **Vertical kloster block**
- ⊠ **Horizontal kloster block**
- ⊡ **Eyelet**
- ▨ **Cutwork**
- ⊠ **Cross-stitch**
- ▧ **Vertical bar**
- ▨ **Horizontal bar**
- ☐ **Unworked threads**

seam) around three sides; leave one short side open. Turn and press raw edges under ¼ inch. Work batting inside lining assembly. Sew opening closed. With ribbons to the inside, fold lining; press.

Stitch canvas to case, concealing blindstitched edge of case beneath lace trim.

For sachets

Mark 3-inch squares onto 18-count needlepoint canvas; do not cut out. Using blue ombré and yellow threads, cross-stitch flowers over two threads. Stitch flowers in rows or scattered randomly (see photograph).

Cut fleece to 3x6 inches; fold in half and sew two edges. Fill with potpourri; sew opening. Cut lining 3½x6½ inches; fold into a square and seam two edges. Insert potpourri; sew opening. Cut out canvas squares; sew atop filler. Tack lace atop raw edge of canvas. Add bows.

❖

HARDANGER BOX LID

Shown on page 65.
Finished embroidery is 2¾ inches.

MATERIALS

9x9 inches of white hardanger
  fabric; tapestry needle
DMC pearl cotton in the
  following sizes and colors: 1
  skein of Size 5 No. 99 rose
  ombré; 1 ball *each* of Size 8
  No. 745 yellow, No. 818
  pink, and No. 368 green
Wooden box with lid insert;
  scrap of foam core board
Scrap of dark lining fabric and
  white velvet tubing; white
  ribbon; polyester fleece

INSTRUCTIONS

FOR STITCHING: See chart, *left*, for position of foundation stitches, cross-stitches, kloster blocks, and eyelet stitches. Using green thread, work cross-stitches over two threads in the center of four threads.

Kloster blocks are satin stitches, worked uniformly. Using rose ombré, work five stitches over four threads, forming a square. Note the direction indicated on blocks; work adjacent blocks so that satin stitches are at right angles to each other.

Eyelet stitches are worked in yellow thread around the heart and between clusters of kloster blocks. Work them in the center of a group of four horizontal and four vertical threads.

To begin an eyelet stitch, slightly widen center hole in fabric with point of scissors. Bring needle up through hole and make a short vertical stitch at "12 o'clock." Continue around square, making satin stitches from center hole between each thread; pull thread taut with each stitch. When completed, there will be 16 stitches radiating from center.

FOR CUTWORK: Use sharp scissors with small blades to cut hardanger threads along black line of chart. Remove threads, using tweezers if necessary. Leave shaded squares on chart open. Work needle weaving in areas with zigzag lines.

FOR NEEDLE WEAVING: The open-thread bars (in groups of four) on the fabric are needle woven. Insert threaded needle from back to front in center of four threads.

Pull needle to the right and over two threads, around back of four threads and around to front, and over left-hand pair of threads and back through the center of group of four threads; then under two right-hand threads, around to front and back down through center of four threads. Continue in this figure-eight maneuver, pulling four threads snugly together.

TO ASSEMBLE: Press embroidery. Cut foam core board to fit lid insert; layer with fleece and lining. Wrap edges of embroidery around foam core; tape in place. Glue foam core to the lid. Trim with velvet tubing and ribbon bow.

MIRROR FRAME

Shown on page 66.
Finished size is 14x14 inches.

MATERIALS
18x18-inch pieces of fleece, backing fabric, and white hardanger
DMC floss in the following amounts and colors: 2 skeins of No. 336 navy, 1 skein *each* of No. 471 light olive green, No. 369 pale olive green, No. 745 pale yellow, No. 809 pale blue, No. 353 pale coral, No. 352 light coral, No. 963 pale pink, and No. 209 lavender
Felt pens in colors to match embroidery floss; graph paper; frame; mirror to fit frame

INSTRUCTIONS
Transfer the design, *right,* to graph paper using felt-tip pens. Reverse body and chart pattern for the mirror frame.

Begin cross-stitching at lower tips of wings, placed 4 inches from bottom and left edges of fabric. Stitch lower left butterfly first. Work design over two threads; stitch navy outlines first. Backstitch antennae. Align adjacent butterflies with the three outermost cross-stitches on wings. Leave 10 threads free between motifs. Press on wrong side.

To make the mirror frame, lightly mark cutout line. Machine-sew on line.

Pin stitchery (faceup) atop fleece. Stitch along cutout line. Pin right side of stitchery to right side of backing fabric. With fleece side up, stitch along cutout line again.

Stay-stitch the seam allowance through all thicknesses, pivoting at corners. Cut out all layers of cutout to ⅜ inch from stay-stitching. Clip corners. Pull the backing fabric through cutout to back; press. Topstitch through all layers along outer edge of stitchery.

Position stitchery atop mirror; frame as desired.

BUTTERFLY JAR LID

Shown on page 66.
Stitchery is 2¾ inches high.

MATERIALS
Scrap of white hardanger
DMC floss in colors for Butterfly Mirror Frame
Jar with screw-on lid (at least 3¼ inches in diameter)
Scraps of fleece, cardboard, lace, and ribbon; potpourri

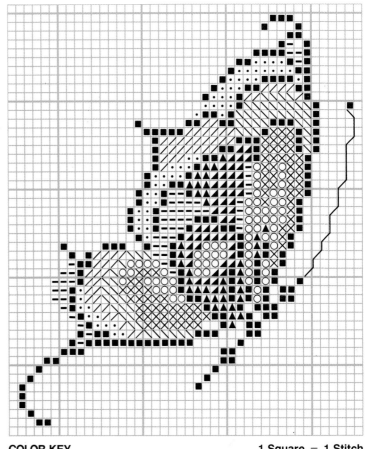

COLOR KEY   1 Square = 1 Stitch

■ Navy   ☑ Lavender   ▲ Light Olive
○ Pale Yellow   ☒ Pale Pink   ◩ Light Coral
⊟ Pale Blue   ◩ Pale Olive   · Pale Coral

INSTRUCTIONS
Referring to chart for Butterfly Mirror Frame, *above,* stitch the butterfly on hardanger. Work over one thread. Press.

Cut cardboard and two layers of fleece to fit jar lid. Layer fleece and stitchery atop cardboard. Tape edges to wrong side. Glue to lid. Trim with lace and ribbon; add bow.

TATTED BUTTERFLY

Shown on page 67.

MATERIALS
DMC pearl cotton, Size 8
2 tatting shuttles
Note cards; glue

Abbreviations: Page 74.

INSTRUCTIONS
For two butterflies, wind first shuttle with 5 yards of thread and second shuttle with 1 yard.
continued

TAIL: With first shuttle, R of 4, P, 4, Cl R. Grasp ring, wrap thread around little finger of left hand and with second shuttle, Ch 3; drop shuttle and lower left wing, with first shuttle, R of 2, 5 P separated by 2, 2, 1 L P, 12, P, 3, Cl R. With second shuttle, Ch 2 to shape body.

UPPER LEFT WING: With first shuttle, R of 3, join to last P of previous R, 2, 6 P separated by 2, 2, 3 L P (each progressively larger) separated by 2, 18, Cl R. With second shuttle, Ch 2.

HEAD: With first shuttle, R of 3, 1 extra-long P (about 3 inches, to be cut later for antennae), 3, Cl R. With second shuttle, Ch 2.

UPPER RIGHT WING: With first shuttle, R of 18, 3 L P separated by 2, 2, 6 P separated by 2, 3, Cl R. With second shuttle, Ch 2.

LOWER RIGHT WING: With first shuttle, R of 3, join to last P

of previous R, 12, 1 L P, 2, 5 P separated by 2, 2, Cl R.
BODY: With second shuttle, Ch 2 (knot takes the place of 1 D S); cut, leaving several inches to tie body threads to beginning tail threads. Tie and cut. Coat back of butterfly with thin layer of glue. Glue to cards.

❖

CROCHETED BUTTERFLY DOILY EDGING

Shown on page 66.
Finished size of butterfly motif is 3¼x5 inches.

MATERIALS
Coats & Clark "Big Ball" crochet cotton, Size 20: 2 balls of white
Size 11 steel crochet hook, or size to obtain gauge below
14x17-inch piece of white linen fabric

Abbreviations: See page 75.
Gauge: Total length of head, upper body, and lower body (excluding wings) = 1⅞ inches.

INSTRUCTIONS
Repeat these instructions to make 10 butterflies.

BODY: Ch 24. *Row 1:* Sc in second ch from hook, hdc in next ch, dc in next ch, hdc in next ch, sc in next ch—head completed; hdc in next ch, dc in next 3 ch, hdc in next ch, sc in next ch—upper body completed; hdc in next ch, dc in next ch, trc in each of next 7 ch, dc in next ch, hdc in next ch, sc in next ch—lower body completed. Fasten off. Do not turn.
Rnd 1: Joining to first sc of previous row, sc in same sc, sc

in next 3 sts, sl st in base of next sc, sc in next 5 sts, sl st at base of next sc, sc in each rem st cross, working 4 sc in last st; work sc in each ch along opposite side of foundation ch, and work sl sts opposite sl sts of other side; work 4 sc in last ch; sl st to first sc at beg or rnd. Fasten off.
Rnd 2: Ch for 1½ inches—first antenna made; sl st to top of head, sc in each sc around head and body, making sl sts over sl sts as before; ch for 1½ inches for second antenna. Fasten off.

WINGS: With head at left, join to fourth st from top of lower body.
Row 1: * Ch 5, sk 1 sc, sc in next sc. Rep from * 3 times, ending at base of head—4 lps made; ch 5, turn.
Row 2: **(3 dc, ch 3, 3 dc) in first ch-5 lp—shell made;** ch 4, sk 1 ch-5 lp, shell in next ch-5 lp; ch 1, shell in next ch-5 lp; ch 5, turn.
Row 3: Shell in center of first shell, ch 5, sk the ch-1 sp, shell in center of next shell, ch 3, 7 dc in next ch-4 lp, ch 3, shell in center of next shell; ch 5, turn.
Row 4: Shell in center of first shell, ch 3, dc in first of 7 dc, (ch 1, dc in next dc) 6 times, ch 3, shell in next shell, ch 4, sc in next ch-5 lp, ch 4, shell in next shell; ch 5, turn.
Row 5: Shell in center of first shell, ch 5, sc in next sc, ch 5, shell in center of next shell, ch 4, sc in ch-1 sp bet first and second dc, * ch 3, sc in next ch-1 sp. Rep from * 4 times, ch 4, shell in center of next shell; ch 5, turn.
Row 6: Shell in center of first shell, ch 6, sk ch-4 lp, sc in next ch-3 lp, * ch 3, sc in next ch-3 lp. Rep from * 3 times; ch 6 (3 dc, ch 3, 3 dc, ch 3, 3 dc) in center of next shell, ch 6, sc in

next sc, ch 6, shell in center of next shell; ch 5, turn.
Row 7: Shell in center of first shell, ch 6, sc in next sc, ch 6, sk ch-6 lp, shell in next ch-3 lp; ch 5, turn.
Row 8: 6 dc in center of first shell, 6 dc in center of next shell; ch 1, turn.
Row 9: Sc in each of the 12 dc. Fasten off. Do not turn—lower wing complete. Join in first ch-3 lp of Row 6.

UPPER WING: *Row 7*—Ch 5, shell in same ch-3 lp, ch 7, sk ch-6 lp, sc in next ch-3 lp, * ch 3, sc in next ch-3 lp. Rep from * twice; ch 7, shell in next shell; ch 5, turn.
Row 8: Shell in first shell, ch 7, sc in first ch-3 lp, * ch 3, sc in next ch-3 lp. Rep from * once, ch 7, shell in next shell; ch 5, turn.
Row 9: Shell in first shell, ch 7, sc in next ch-3 lp, ch 3, sc in next ch-3 lp, ch 7, shell in next shell; ch 5, turn.
Row 10: Shell in first shell, ch 7, sc in ch-3 lp, ch 7, shell in next shell; ch 5, turn.
Row 11: 6 dc in center of first shell, 6 dc in center of next shell; ch 1, turn.
Row 12: Work 1 sc in each of next 12 dc. Fasten off. Join in same place on opposite side of body and rep lower and upper wings.

TO FINISH: Arrange the 10 butterflies in an oval (or shape desired) on fabric, with the antennae toward the center and the wings of adjacent butterflies touching. Working from right side with sewing thread, sew the upper edge of wings, antennae, and head to fabric.

Working carefully from wrong side, cut away fabric extending beneath openwork of wings.

TATTING-TRIMMED CARDS

Shown on pages 68–69.

MATERIALS
Paneled flower with bud card
Purchased plain place cards or index cards cut to size
Size 70 tatting thread in pink
Fine felt-tip markers in pink and light green; ruler

Thank you notes
Embossed Thank You notes
Fine felt-tip markers in leaf green
Size 70 tatting thread in any flower color

Christmas holly card
Purchased plain place cards or index cards cut to size
No. 1 synthetic or red sable watercolor brush, or green felt-tip pen
Acrylic paint in green oxide and gold
Size 70 tatting thread in red

INSTRUCTIONS
For paneled flower with bud card
Note: For variety, use different-colored threads for the flowers and buds, with matching felt-tip pens. Or, trim all four corners of a card with flowers and leaves. Or, embellish a single corner with one flower and three leaves.

Wind shuttle with pink thread. For one full flower, work R of 1 D S, 8 P separated by 1 D S, 1 D S, Cl. Work a Sp. For a bud, work R of 4 D S, Sm P, 1 D S, L P, 1 D S, Sm P, 4 D S, Cl.

Alternate working flowers and buds until you have the number desired.

To decorate the card, mark off a ¼-inch margin on the card; go over the line carefully with a pink felt-tip marker. Referring to the diagram, *right,* and using a light green marker, draw three leaves in left top corner in a triangle (1). Leave space to glue the flower on the pink line so it is surrounded by leaves. In lower right corner, draw stem and leaves for the bud (2).

Using black ballpoint pen, draw veins in leaves and outline bud stem and leaves.

Carefully cut apart the tattos on the chain, separating flowers from buds. Using a toothpick, apply a fine line of glue to the flower. Press into place among leaves. Do the same for the bud, pressing it into bud casing and shaping the circle with the toothpick while the glue is wet.

For thank you notes
For three flowers (one in bloom, a partially opened bud, and an unopened bud), work a R of 1 D S, 7 P, Cl, Sp; R of 3 D S, Sm P, 1 D S, L P, 1 D S, Sm P, 3 D S, Cl, Sp; R of 7 D S, Cl, Sp. Repeat the entire sequence to make the desired number of flowers.

To decorate the notes, use a green marker and refer to the diagram, *bottom left.* Draw a long backward S curve (1) on note. Add more vine to top half of curve (2). Make leaves along the vine, leaving spaces for three flowers as indicated by heavy dots on vine. Draw line vine and veins in leaves using black pen.

Use partially opened flower for top, blooming flower for center, and unopened bud at the bottom. Line flowers with glue; press with toothpick to shape buds.

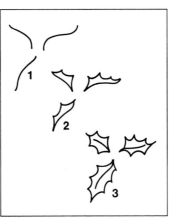

For Christmas holly card
To make three holly berries, work R of 8 D S, Cl, Sp. Tat as many as desired.

To decorate the card, load a No. 1 brush with green paint and make a curve (1), referring to diagram, *right.* Shape holly leaf with brush (2). Finish leaf on opposite side (3). Go over veins and upper half of leaves with gold outline. Using black ballpoint pen, emphasize veining and holly leaf outline.

Line the holly tattos with glue. Place holly in a triangle pattern among the leaves.

CROCHET ABBREVIATIONS

beg	begin(ning)
bl	block
ch	chain
cl	cluster
dc	double crochet
dec	decrease
dtr	double triple crochet
fol	following
grp	group
hdc	half double crochet
inc	increase
lp(s)	loop(s)
MC	Main Color
pat	pattern
pc	popcorn
rem	remaining
rep	repeat
rnd(s)	round(s)
sc	single crochet
sk	skip
sl st	slip stitch
sp	space
st(s)	stitch(es)
tog	together
trc	triple crochet
yo	wrap yarn over hook
*	rep from * as indicated
( )	repeat between ( )s as indicated
[ ]	repeat between [ ]s as indicated

BACK TO SCHOOL

Planning a booth around unusual—but practical—projects for school-age kids assures that it will receive plenty of attention.

Keeping up with the day-to-day activities of a busy household is a big task for most families. The handy message board, *opposite,* is sure to help out. The back portion of the board is cut from foam-core board, which is available at art supply stores or where framing supplies are sold. The message section is hardboard covered with slate paint.

Instructions and patterns for the projects in this chapter begin on page 88.

A bear cut from adhesive-backed vinyl decorates the top of the pencil box, *left.* It's just the right size for writing and drawing supplies, plus a surprise treat or two.

A snoozing, machine-appliquéd bear tops the nap mat, *opposite.* The mat is cut from quilted fabric and edged with bias tape. Letters cut from adhesive-backed, iron-on patching fabric are used for the Zs, and iron-on letters spell out "Do Not Disturb" on the sign hanging from the bear's foot.

Designed especially for overnight trips, the bag, *opposite,* will hold a child's favorite bed pillow inside the zippered opening. The flap on the front holds pajamas and a change of clothing; it is secured with a pair of ties slipped through plastic rings.

A pair of cushion insoles makes cutting the pattern for the slippers, *opposite,* almost foolproof. Use a sturdy washable fabric such as corduroy for the outer soles, and scraps of fabric left over from the overnight bag for the tops.

These charming preschoolers' accessories will make the time spent at nursery school, day-care centers, or kindergarten extra special.

Lovable pooches like these two are sure to be cherished throughout childhood. They are designed to hold kids' pajamas within the body, and feature a concealed zipper closure. Purchased plastic animal eyes fastened to the head and buckled dog collars add touches of realism.

Although these designs are shown as pajama bags, eliminating the zipper, stuffing the body with polyester fiberfill, and stitching the opening closed can turn the bag into an adorable stuffed animal. In either case, the animal heads can be posed slightly by tacking the side of the head to the body so that the dogs appear to be awake. To style a dog so that it sleeps at the foot of the bed, don't add plastic eyes, but embroider closed eyelids instead.

Choices of fabric can change the personalities of the toys. Consider substituting a woolen or corduroy for the fur shown.

School-age boys and girls will be quick to adapt these cuddly dogs to their bedtime routines. They're bags to keep nightwear clutter neatly contained, and can double as stuffed toys.

Brown-bag lunches are a thing of the past with these special sacks, *left*. They're patterned after paper bags, but are made from durable fabric so that they can be used over and over. Bright calico lines each bag, and a strip of nylon fastening material keeps the bags closed.

The cross-stitch designs applied to the front are stitched before the bags are assembled, using dressmaker's carbon to position and mark the stitches. As an alternative, eliminate the cross-stitch motifs, and affix iron-on initials or patches at the bazaar to customize the bags for customers.

A bright red apple decorates the back of the denim backpack, *opposite*. The pack is stitched from denim rectangles and features two straps to slip over a child's shoulders. A strip of nylon fastening tape keeps it closed.

These school sacks and backpack are nifty alternatives to purchased ones. Because the designs are simple and appealing to a wide range of tastes and ages, they're sure to sell quickly.

Begin each of these back-to-school wearables with a plain, bright-colored cotton sweatshirt or jersey.

Most schoolchildren already know the potato-printing technique used to decorate the sweatshirt, *left*. Slice a large firm potato in half to form the printing surface and then simply cut away unwanted areas of the potato surface until the design area is exposed—in this case, a heart. Using fabric paints or acrylics, stamp the motif across the front and sleeve of a sweatshirt. Other design possibilities are initials or your local school mascots.

The three sweatshirts, *opposite,* are embellished with machine appliqués. Each motif shape is cut from fabric and matching pieces of fusible webbing. After the fabric is affixed to the sweatshirt front, rows of machine satin stitches cover raw edges.

Decorating an inexpensive sweatshirt with special techniques turns an ordinary sportswear item into something special.

Monitor

Keyboard

Computer

Regardless of the age, purpose, or complexity of computers, they all share one basic element: the binary code that transforms letters and numbers we use into electrical impulses that machinery can understand. In the binary code system, each letter of the alphabet and each numeral is translated into a distinct eight-part code made up of an arrangement of 1s and 0s.

The binary code, when applied to patchwork, results in the wall hangings, *opposite* and *right*, and the pillow, *opposite*. Each horizontal row of the pattern represents a letter, with the pattern of dark and medium-colored triangles standing for a 1 or a 0. The dark narrow strip between groups of letters indicates breaks between the words.

For example, the wall hanging, *opposite,* announces "Genius At Work," and the pillow says "Super Kid." "Quiet, Please" is the message on the wall hanging, *right.*

These signs of the (high-tech) times are immediately comprehensible to kids who know about the binary code. Use the information in our instructions to devise all sorts of coded patchwork messages.

MESSAGE BOARD

Shown on page 76.
Finished board is approximately 12½x15 inches.

MATERIALS

9x10-inch piece of hardboard
Foam-core board
Crafts knife; metal ruler
White and red adhesive-back papers
Slate paint; yellow and black acrylic paints
¾-inch black adhesive letters
Black permanent felt-tip pen
Hot-glue gun, or crafts glue
18 inches of narrow ribbon

INSTRUCTIONS

Note: Use a crafts knife with a sharp blade when cutting foam-core board. A metal ruler is useful in cutting straight edges.

Enlarge the pattern for the board, *below,* and trace the window design, *opposite.*

Transfer the outline of the message board to foam-core board; cut it out and paint one side yellow (bus) and black (tires). The center portion will be covered with the slate and may be left unpainted.

Paint hardboard with two coats of slate paint.

Cut bumper from foam-core board; glue to bottom edge of bus, above tires. If desired, use a white pencil to mark tire treads according to pattern.

Transfer faces to white adhesive-back paper; affix to window on bus. Outline faces and window using black felt-tip pen; add pink to cheeks if desired.

From red paper, cut out stop lights. Affix to top corners of bus; outline with felt-tip pen.

Affix adhesive letters for "School Bus" under the window. Using glue gun or crafts glue, affix slate to foam-core board. Punch two holes in top of board. Thread ribbon through the hole; tie ends in a knot for a hanger.

PENCIL BOX

Shown on page 78.
Finished size is 2¾x5¾x9 inches.

MATERIALS

Purchased plastic pencil box
Scrap of silver adhesive-back Mylar
Scraps of solid and patterned adhesive-back paper
Permanent felt-tip pens in black, red, and desired colors

INSTRUCTIONS

Using pattern, *opposite,* trace scissor, bear, and crayon box. Referring to the photograph, transfer patterns to Mylar and adhesive-back paper. Using felt-tip pens, draw the crayons. Outline the bear, crayons, and oval on front of box with black felt-tip pen. Using red felt-tip pen, outline the crayon box.

Cut out pieces and affix to box, referring to photograph for placement.

NAP MAT

Shown on page 79.
Finished size is 34x46 inches.

MATERIALS

24x46-inch piece of quilted fabric; 2 packages of wide, double-fold bias binding
Fabric scraps for appliqué
Iron-on interfacing; fusible webbing (optional)
Jumbo rickrack
½ yard of grosgrain ribbon
Black pearl cotton floss
Scrap of black iron-on tape
1 package of nylon adhesive-back patches (for Zs)
1 package of ⅝-inch-tall iron-on letters

INSTRUCTIONS

To begin, round corners and bind edges of quilted fabric using bias binding. Next, trace patterns, pages 90 and 91, placing bear's arm in the position indicated. Cut out appliqués.

Cut out a 5x6½-inch piece for bear's sign. If necessary, back appliqués with iron-on interfacing so background color will not show through.

Pin pieces to background fabric; baste or fuse in place using fusible webbing. Machine satin-stitch appliqués to background; machine-stitch details on bear, except for face.

Trim sign with rickrack. Embroider bear's face using pearl cotton. Cut nose from black iron-on tape; iron in place. Outline-stitch the cord for the sign. using a double strand of pearl cotton.

Tack ribbon bow beneath bear's chin. Cut six Zs from nylon adhesive patches; apply to background, referring to photograph for placement. Using iron-on letters, spell "DO NOT DISTURB" on sign.

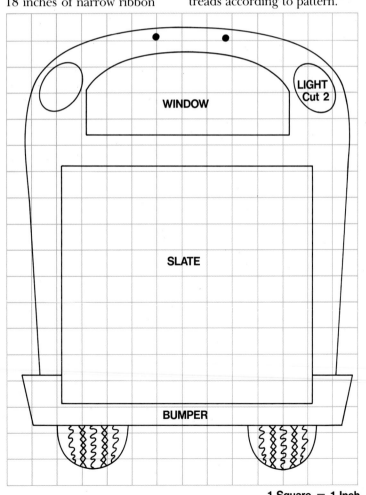

WINDOW

LIGHT
Cut 2

SLATE

BUMPER

1 Square = 1 Inch

Placement
for arm

A

B

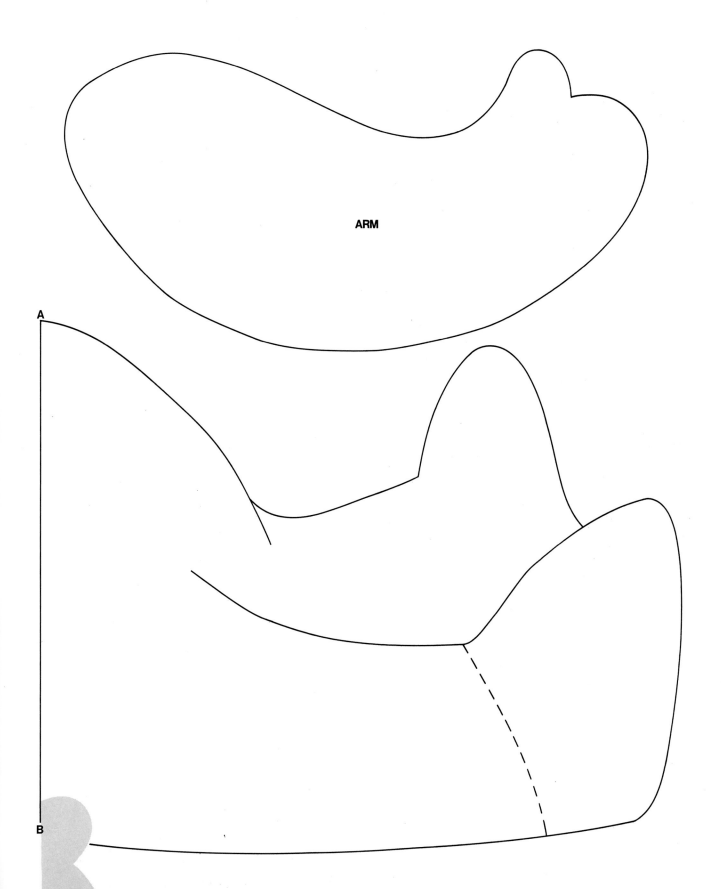

ARM

A

B

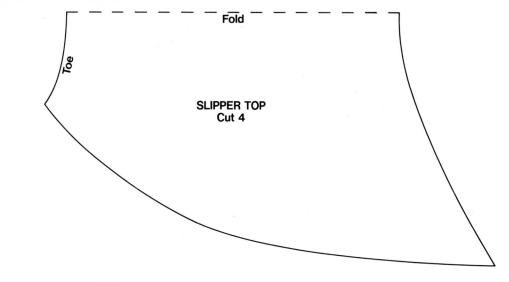

Fold

Toe

SLIPPER TOP
Cut 4

❖

SLIPPERS

Shown on page 79.
Size is based on woman's Size 5
insole. For larger sizes, adjust
materials accordingly.

MATERIALS

1 pair of foam insoles
⅓ yard of corduroy (outer
    soles); scraps of medium- to
    heavyweight fabric (tops)
Piping; double-fold bias tape
¾ yard of 1-inch-wide
    grosgrain ribbon

INSTRUCTIONS

Round off toe and heel of insole to fit child's foot. Trace insole onto a double thickness of
corduroy (right sides facing).
Stitch ¼ inch from drawn line;
leave opening at toe for turning. Trim and turn; slip insole
inside. Baste opening closed.
(Outer sole will be larger than
insole.) Make two.

Trace pattern, *above*. Cut out
slipper tops. (To adjust top for
other sizes, place paper pattern
over foot to check width and
length; add to pattern edges as
needed.) With right sides facing, sew pair of tops together at

toe curve, using ¼-inch seam;
clip curve.

Baste piping to right side of
one piece at top curve. Sew together, right sides facing; clip,
turn, and press. Machine-baste
side edges together.

Pin and sew slipper top
around front portion of sole.
Bind edges of slipper with bias
tape. Cut ribbon in half; tack
ribbon bows to slippers.

❖

OVERNIGHT
BAG

Shown on page 79.
Finished bag is 20x26 inches.

MATERIALS

1 yard of medium- to
    heavyweight fabric (bag)
½ yard of fabric (pocket, trim)
Scrap of felt (tag)
25-inch coat or sport zipper
Two 1½-inch plastic rings
Matching thread
Polyester fiberfill

INSTRUCTIONS

Note: Use ¼-inch seams unless otherwise indicated.

Enlarge patterns, *below* and
opposite, for pocket flap and tag.

Cut two 21x27-inch rectangles for the bag. With right
sides facing, machine-baste
across one long edge and down
4 inches on each side. Press
seam open.

Box corners by matching top
seam and side seam together,
right sides facing, forming a triangle. Two inches below the
point, sew a 4-inch seam across
the triangle. Trim excess point
½ inch from stitching.

Place zipper facedown over
top seam (approximately 2
inches will extend down on
each side). Hand-baste zipper
in place. With zipper foot, machine-sew zipper in place. Turn
right side out; remove basting.

For the pocket, cut contrasting fabric 13½x27 inches.
Turn under sides (short edges)
and bottom ½ inch; topstitch.
Turn under top edge ½ inch
twice; topstitch.

Make a 1½-inch pleat on
each end so pocket is 19 inches
long. Sew the pleat across top
and bottom to secure.

Make ties by cutting two
strips, each 1x12 inches. Fold
in ¼ inch on short ends and
long edges; press. Fold in half
lengthwise; topstitch. Tack center of ties to front of pocket 3¾
inches from bottom and 5½
inches from sides. Center pocket on one side of bag; sew to
bag along side and bottom
edges.

Cut two flaps from same fabric as bag. With right sides facing, sew around all edges, leave
an opening in bottom edge.
Turn, press, and topstitch all
around, ¼ inch from edge.

From pocket fabric cut two
3½x11-inch straps. With right
sides facing, fold each strap in
half lengthwise; stitch across
short ends and down long side
(¼-inch seam), leaving an
opening. Turn and press. Pin
straps vertically down front of
flap, placing each one 4⅝ inches from outside edge. Allow excess strap to hang off bottom
edge of flap. Stitch straps to
flap.

Slip loose end of strap
through a plastic ring. Fold end
of strap back; blindstitch to bottom edge of flap. Center flap
1¼ inches above pocket; topstitch in place.

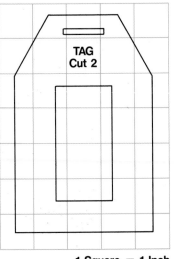

TAG
Cut 2

1 Square = 1 Inch

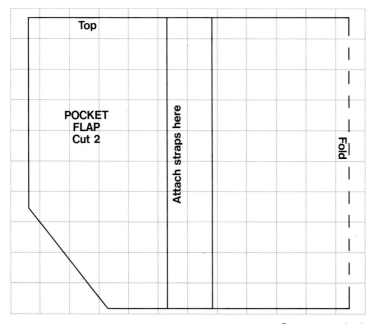

Top

POCKET
FLAP
Cut 2

Attach straps here

Fold

1 Square = 1 Inch

Cut two 4x12-inch handles; fold in half lengthwise, right sides facing. Sew as for straps; leave opening in center side. Turn and press. Sew across width of each handle, 1½ inches from end. Stuff center part firmly with fiberfill; blindstitch opening. Sew across stuffed portion of handle, 2 inches from previous row of stitching. Repeat for other handle.

To attach handles, pin flat ends of one handle to center top edge of case, ½ inch from zipper edge. Allow stuffed portion to stand up to form a handle; sew flat ends to bag. Attach other handle to opposite side of zipper.

Turn bag inside out and, with right sides facing, sew remaining sides and across bottom (½-inch seam). Form box corners same as for top.

Cut two tags from felt; sew together between dots (leaving angled area open). Topstitch around edges on *each* tag piece above dots. Cut cardboard to fit inside the tag; slip cardboard inside.

Make a strap by folding a 1x8-inch piece of felt lengthwise. Topstitch on both long edges. Insert strap through hole in tag and around handle; sew edges of strap together.

PAJAMA-BAG DOG

Shown on pages 80–81.
Finished size is 24x11 inches.

MATERIALS
½ yard of 60-inch-wide synthetic fur
Plastic dog eyes (size 21 mm)
Black embroidery floss
9-inch-long zipper
Fiberfill
Permanent black and light brown felt-tip markers
Long soft-sculpture needle
16-inch-long dog collar

INSTRUCTIONS
The nap and color of the fur used for the dog affect its appearance. Avoid furs with stiff sizing on the back. Curly furs make unclipped poodles. Long furs make Yorkshire terriers. *Note:* You may need to sew some furs by hand in places where four layers of fur meet— when sewing legs to body, for example.

Trace patterns, pages 95–97; match A–B, C–D, and E–F lines to complete the body. Trace patterns onto wrong side of fur, using a felt-tip pen; cut out pieces ½ inch beyond drawn line. Mark notches and location of eye. For opposite sides, lay marked pieces, wrong sides together, on back of fur. Cut roughly around the shape. Trim seams after sewing.

Because fur creeps, basting is important. Hand-baste all seams before machine-sewing them.

For the head, pin, baste, and sew front head sections. Then pin, baste, and sew back head sections. Join back and front units. Clip a small hole at the mark for the eye; insert plastic eyes. Set aside head.

There are *two* legs. Stitch pieces together; trim, turn, and stuff lightly with fiberfill. Sew closed across the top. Set aside.

Cut outer ears of fur and inner ears of cotton in a matching or complementary color. Sew ears, trim, and turn. Sew top.

For the zipper opening, place right sides of body section together and sew ends of top edge between large dots. Leave a 9-inch opening for the zipper. Hand-sew the zipper in place.

To assemble the body, baste legs and tail to right side of body (as shown in the diagram). Fold the other body piece over, so it is on top. Baste and sew all layers, leaving the neck and top edge open.

Pin, baste, and sew the head into the neck opening. Turn the dog right side out. Stuff the head only. Slip-stitch the top opening shut.

Trim the fur pile around the eyes. On light-colored fur, shade eye area with permanent felt-tip marker. If fur pile is long, trim around muzzle.

Position ears so top front corners are about 2 inches from eyes and 2 inches below back center head seam. Tack in place. Embroider nose (⅞ inch wide and 1 inch long) with six strands of floss, using long stitches. To finish, fasten dog collar around neck.

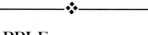

APPLE BACKPACK

Shown on page 83.
Finished size is 11x15 inches.

MATERIALS
½ yard of 60-inch-wide heavyweight denim
8-inch square *each* of batting and red sailcloth (apple)
Small fabric scraps of green (leaf) and brown (stem)
Matching thread
Tailor's chalk
2-inch piece of navy nylon fastening tape

INSTRUCTIONS
From denim cut a 14x20¼-inch rectangle for the front. With long edge at top and bottom, mark center point for placement of nylon fastening tape, 10⅛ inches from each short edge and 5⅜ inches from top. Place tape vertically over marking and sew in place.

continued

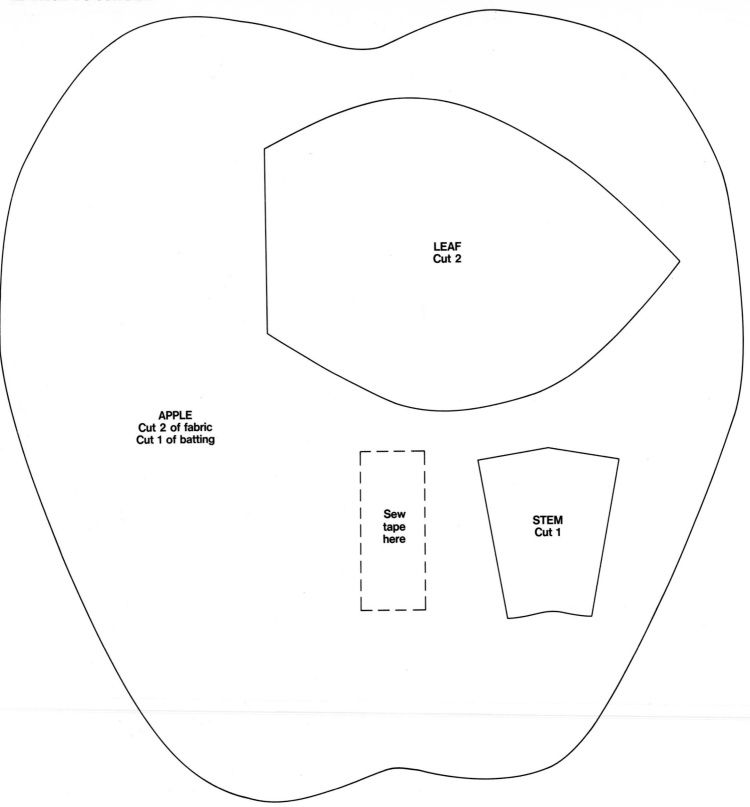

LEAF
Cut 2

APPLE
Cut 2 of fabric
Cut 1 of batting

Sew
tape
here

STEM
Cut 1

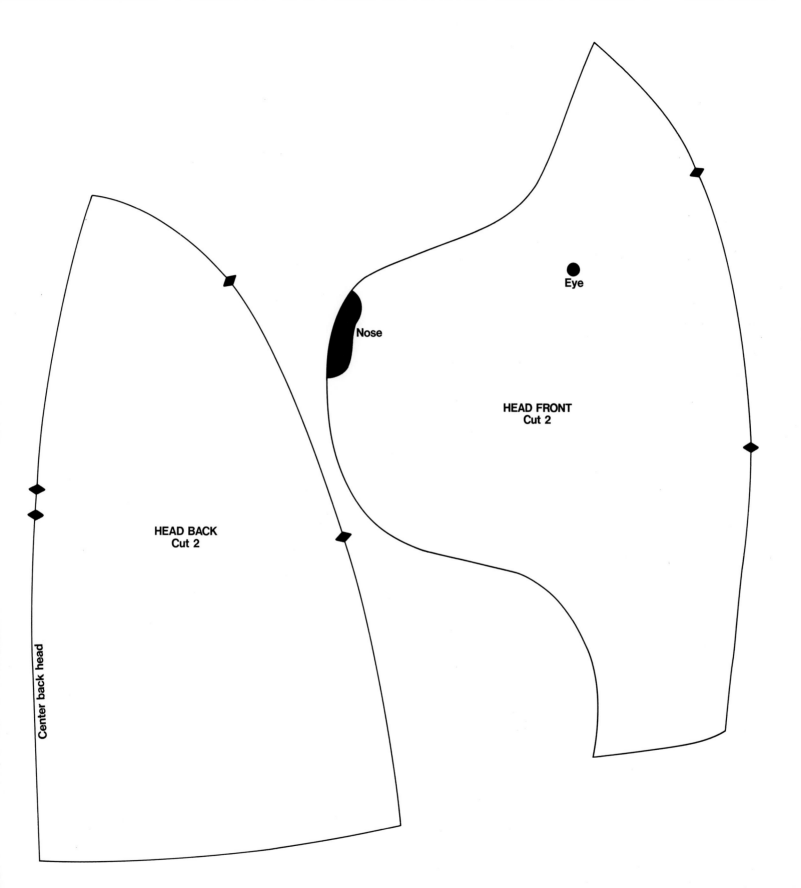

HEAD FRONT
Cut 2

Eye

Nose

HEAD BACK
Cut 2

Center back head

95

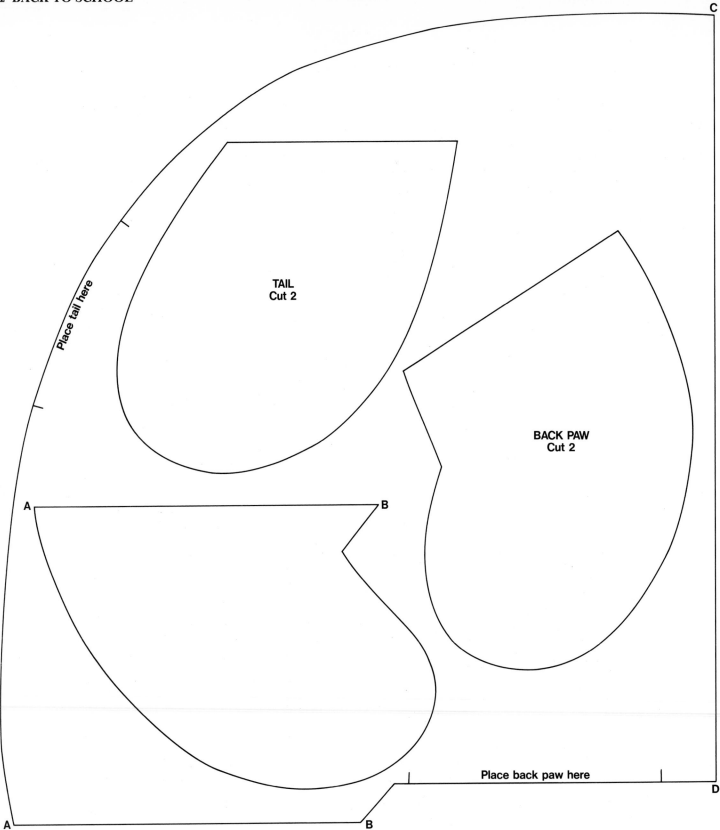

TAIL
Cut 2

BACK PAW
Cut 2

Place tail here

Place back paw here

A

B

C

D

A

B

96

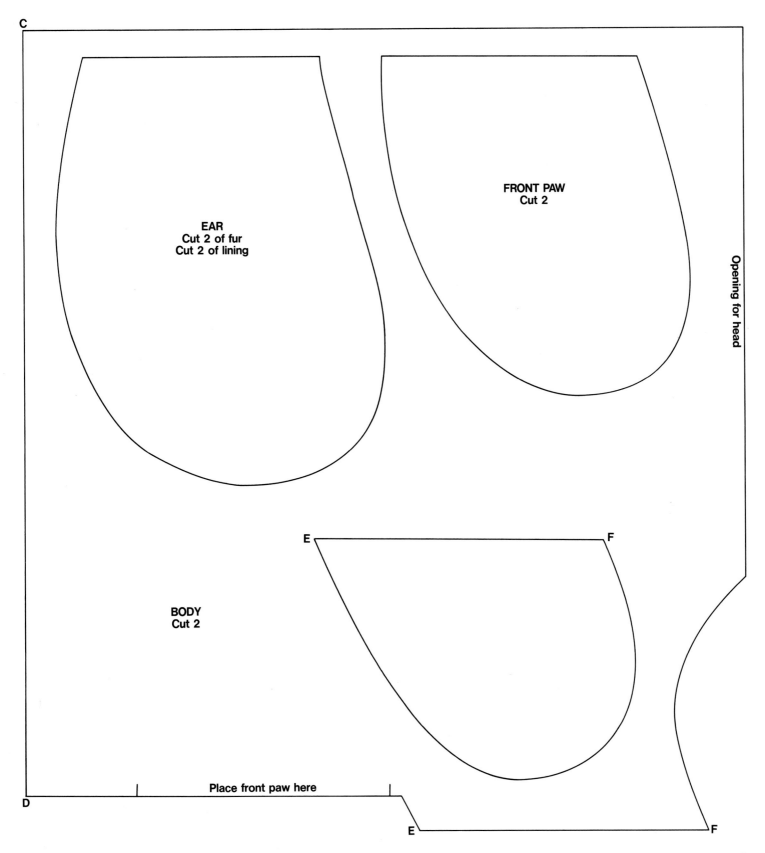

C

EAR
Cut 2 of fur
Cut 2 of lining

FRONT PAW
Cut 2

Opening for head

E   F

BODY
Cut 2

Place front paw here

D

E   F

97

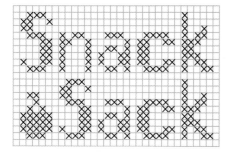 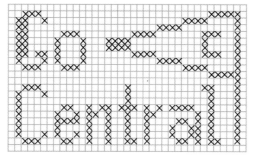 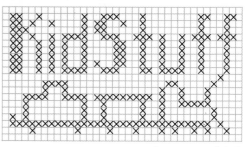

1 Square = 1 Stitch

Cut a 12x20¼-inch rectangle from denim for the back. With short edges at top and bottom, mark the placement of straps: 8 inches from top and 2¾ inches from bottom, 2 inches from each long edge. Also mark a dot 7½ inches from the top on each long edge for flap extensions.

Trace patterns for leaf, stem, and apple, page 94; cut from fabrics. Sew leaf pieces with right sides facing, leaving bottom open; clip and turn. Pleat bottom of leaf; baste.

Fold stem in half, right sides facing; sew, clip, and turn.

Sew fastening tape to one apple piece where indicated. Baste batting to the wrong side, ¼ inch from the edge; trim close to basting stitches.

Sew apple pieces together, right sides facing; leave an opening for turning. Clip curves, turn right side out, and sew the opening closed. Baste the leaf and stem to the back of the apple (see photograph).

On the front of the backpack, press under the top (long) edge on the flap. Press under again and stitch. On the back piece, finish the top edge of the flap in the same manner.

Cut two denim straps, *each* 4½x17¾ inches. Turn under long edges; press. Place folded edges together, wrong sides facing; topstitch ¼ inch from edge. Topstitch other edge.

To attach the straps to the backpack, pin straps so the wrong side is facing up and the end of the strap is on the placement line, with strap hanging down over the hemmed edge; stitch. Then, fold the strap back over itself and stitch ⅜ inch from edge to cover the raw edges. Finish the other end of the strap in the same manner.

Center the apple atop the flap, overlapping the flap approximately 2½ inches. Topstitch ⅛ inch around the entire apple.

With right sides of the front and back facing, sew the side seams. Trim the seams from the bottom to the dot only. Above the dot, turn the edges under ¼ inch and press. Press the entire side seam. Topstitch ⅜ inch from the side seam to cover the raw edges. Continue topstitching on the flap, hemming the sides of the flap at the same time.

Match the centers on the bottom of the backpack and pin. Fold the extra material on each side into a pleat, even with the edge. Baste bottom together.

Cut a 2¼x12⅞-inch binding piece from denim. Enclose bottom edges with binding.

❖

SCHOOL SACKS

Shown on page 82.
Finished size is 3½x7¼x14 inches.

MATERIALS
For one sack
⅓ yard *each* of medium-weight fabric (outside) and lightweight vinyl or cotton blend (lining is optional)
5 inches of 1-inch-wide nylon fastening tape
1 skein of embroidery floss of *each* desired color
Graph paper (5 squares per inch for Snack Sack, 8 squares per inch for others)
Sewing thread; masking tape
Embroidery hoop; needle
Ballpoint pen
Dressmaker's carbon

INSTRUCTIONS
Enlarge pattern, *right;* transfer to fabric and lining. (*Note:* ¼-inch seam allowances are included in the pattern.)

Transfer designs, *above,* to graph paper. Position atop dressmaker's carbon on sack front, referring to photograph for placement. Secure with masking tape. Trace stitches firmly with ballpoint pen.

With fabric in hoop, work cross-stitches using three strands of floss. Press on wrong side.

Cut out the sack on marked lines. Assemble sack and lining separately, using the following method: Sew bottom to front, bottom seam first, then side seams. Break stitching at angles. Sew back to bottom in same manner.

continued

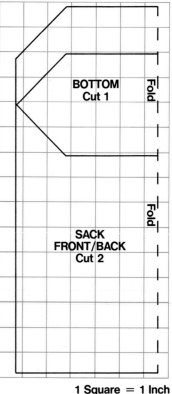

BOTTOM Cut 1

Fold

Fold

SACK FRONT/BACK Cut 2

1 Square = 1 Inch

99

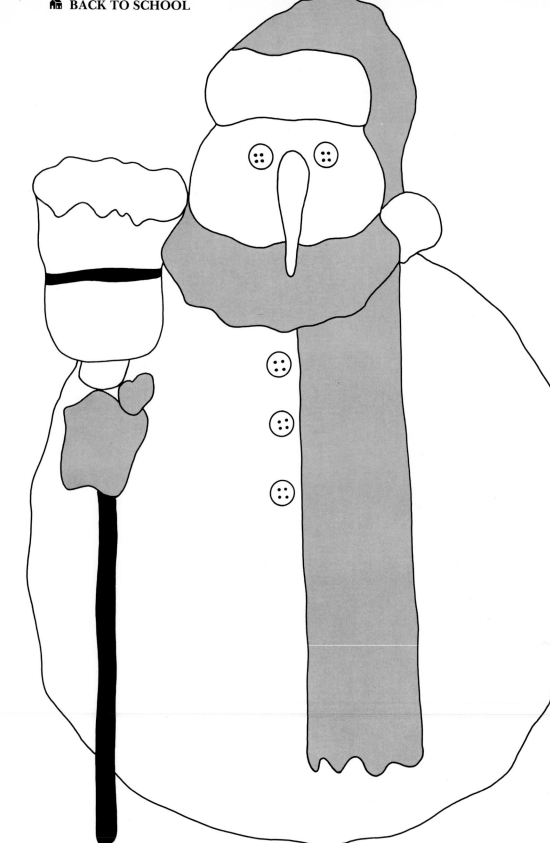

Fold and pin the sack in a straight line from corner to top, wrong sides facing. Topstitch ⅛ inch from fold. Repeat for each corner. Topstitch short sides of bottom in same manner. (For the lining, make tucks on wrong side of fabric.)

Sew side seams, right sides facing. Turn sack right side out.

Place the lining inside sack, wrong sides facing. Turn top edges under and pin, matching seams. Topstitch.

Center and sew hooked side of fastening tape along back top edge. Fold over to position soft side of tape; sew tape in place.

POTATO-PRINT SWEATSHIRT

Shown on page 84.

MATERIALS
Purchased sweatshirt
Black fabric paint or acrylic
   paint in tube
Large potato; paintbrush
Newspapers; pushpins
Water-erasable marking pen
Large sheet of cardboard
Small kitchen knife

INSTRUCTIONS
Wash and dry sweatshirt; press flat. Using water-erasable pen, draw a line across front and back at sleeve; draw a line across left sleeve to correspond. Trace heart, *opposite.*

Cover work area with newspapers. Cut potato in half and trace heart on smooth side. Using point of knife, cut along design line; cut away background to a depth of about ¼ inch.

Trim top of potato close to heart, leaving enough potato behind heart to act as a handle.

Paint a coat of fabric paint or acrylic on heart; practice printing on newspaper.

Slip a piece of paper inside shirt; smooth shirt and pin to cardboard. Beginning at center front of shirt, print one heart right side up. Continue row to each side, alternating right side up and upside-down hearts; keep spacing even. Allow to dry. (A hair dryer may be used to speed drying.)

Turn shirt over; pin to cardboard. Print back as for front; allow to dry.

Fold shirt so that center of sleeve is flat; print, allowing each section to dry before proceeding to next section.

When printing is completed, follow manufacturer's directions to set fabric paint. To set acrylics, iron each heart at medium setting for 5 minutes.

ANIMAL SWEATSHIRTS

Shown on page 85.

MATERIALS

Purchased sweatshirts
Fabric scraps in desired colors
½ yard *each* of medium-weight iron-on interfacing and fusible webbing (two sweatshirts)
Threads to match fabrics
Tissue paper; typing paper

INSTRUCTIONS

Wash and dry sweatshirts before stitching appliqués in place. Iron interfacing to backs of fabric scraps before cutting out appliqué shapes. Using tissue paper, trace around patterns on pages 99–101 for each shape to be appliquéd. Pin tissue paper pieces to desired fabrics and cut out; cut a matching piece of fusible webbing for each piece of fabric appliqué.

To fuse appliqués, slip the shaped pieces of fusible webbing between the sweatshirt and fabric appliqué pieces, then press the layers to the sweatshirt using a warm iron. *Note:* Slip paper towels between iron and fabric to catch stray wisps of the heated webbing.

To stitch, place a sheet of typing paper inside the sweatshirt under the area to be appliquéd. (This will keep the sweatshirt from stretching as you sew.) Using a wide, tight zigzag stitch, sew along raw edges of fabric cutouts, covering the edges completely with thread. Change thread colors in the machine to match the colors of the fabric.

BINARY DESIGNS

Shown on pages 86–87. Wall hangings are 16x24½ and 16x27½ inches. The pillow is 16x16 inches, without ruffle.

MATERIALS

For "Genius at Work" wall hanging
⅞ yard of light solid-color cotton
⅜ yard *each* of light print and dark print cottons
½ yard of 44-inch-wide fleece
Matching thread

For "Quiet Please" wall hanging
¾ yard of 44-inch-wide muslin
½ yard *each* of cotton print fabric and fleece
¼ yard of solid-color cotton
Matching thread

For "Super Kid" pillow
½ yard *each* of 44-inch-wide muslin and fleece
¼ yard of light print fabric
1 yard of dark print fabric
2 yards of narrow ecru piping
One 16-inch-square pillow form, or fiberfill
Matching thread

INSTRUCTIONS

Use ¼-inch seams throughout. Press seams toward darker fabric. Draw a right-angle triangle with 2-inch legs onto cardboard for a template. Adding seam allowances all around, trace triangles onto *wrong* side of fabrics according to specific instructions below.

Tips for Planning Your Own Patchwork Puzzles Using A Computer Code

Kids aren't the only people who love secrets. Even adults will be delighted with patchwork puzzles that contain hidden messages—and look beautiful besides. So next time you want to express some personal bit of wit, wisdom, or sentiment, tuck it into a piece of patchwork, using the computer code explained below.

Each of the designs shown on pages 86 and 87 is based on the binary code—a combination of numerals that represent letters that can be "read" by a computer. Each letter in the alphabet is represented by a sequence of zeros and ones.

We've translated each of the zeros and ones into squares made of two triangles. One triangle in each square is a neutral color, and the same neutral is used throughout the design. The color of the other triangle, however, changes according to whether it represents a zero or a one.

For example, the letter "Q" in the binary code is 0101 0001. In the "QUIET PLEASE" wall hanging, the blue triangles in the letter "Q" stand for zero and the pink triangles represent one.

Words in our patchwork puzzles are separated by narrow fabric dividers. (We don't want our secret messages to be *too* hard to read.)

If you want to make your patchwork piece more than eight squares wide, make it two or three words (16 or 24 squares) wide, and add fabric divider strips between the words to set them off.

Use the code below to spell any message in patchwork, encoding the numbers in the colors and fabrics of your choice. Just be sure to follow the binary code exactly so others can decipher it.

Need some suggestions for messages? How about "Home Sweet Home" on a wall hanging, or "Now I lay me down to sleep" on a child's quilt, or "Help Wanted" on a picture for the kitchen. You'll think of dozens of ways to use this code in projects you craft not only for bazaars but for family and friends as well.

Binary Code System

A 0100 0001	N 0100 1110
B 0100 0010	O 0100 1111
C 0100 0011	P 0101 0000
D 0100 0100	Q 0101 0001
E 0100 0101	R 0101 0010
F 0100 0110	S 0101 0011
G 0100 0111	T 0101 0100
H 0100 1000	U 0101 0101
I 0100 1001	V 0101 0110
J 0100 1010	W 0101 0111
K 0100 1011	X 0101 1000
L 0100 1100	Y 0101 1001
M 0100 1101	Z 0101 1010

For "Genius at Work"

Cut 96 triangles from light solid color, 44 from dark print, and 52 from light print fabric. (Or, cut squares of fabric and quick-stitch the patchwork triangles following instructions in the tip box on page 102.)

Following assembly diagram, *below,* form each horizontal row as follows: Sew triangles together on long edge to form squares; press. Sew squares together; press.

Sew the top six rows together. Sew middle two and bottom four rows together; press.

To make narrow fabric dividers that separate the words, cut two 1x17-inch pieces from the dark print fabric and fold lengthwise, wrong sides together. Baste raw edges of strips to raw edges of rows, following diagram. Join sections together in seams along edging; press.

For borders, cut two 2¼x17-inch pieces of dark print fabric. Stitch to the patchwork message at the top and bottom. Press toward borders.

Cut the backing fabric (solid light color) and fleece to measure 17x28 inches. Place fleece atop the wrong side of the patchwork. Place backing fabric atop right side of patchwork and sew around all sides, leaving a 6-inch opening at bottom. Clip the corners; grade the seams. Turn, press, and slip-stitch the opening closed.

Machine-quilt around triangles and borders next to seams, using even-feed foot. Make fabric loops or channel on back for hanging.

For "Quiet Please"

Cut 88 triangles from muslin, 56 from print, and 32 from solid-color fabric.

Following the placement diagram, *opposite,* sew triangles into squares, then sew squares together into horizontal rows.

Sew the five top horizontal rows together; press. Sew together the bottom six rows.

Make narrow divider according to instructions for "Genius at Work" hanging, *above.*

For borders, cut two 1¾x17-inch pieces of print fabric. Sew to patchwork top and bottom; press seams toward borders.

Cut fleece and muslin backing to 17x25 inches. Assemble, sew, and finish as for "Genius at Work" hanging.

For "Super Kid"

Cut 64 triangles from muslin, 39 from light print, and 25 from dark print.

Following the placement diagram, *opposite,* sew triangles into squares, then sew squares

together into horizontal rows.

Make narrow divider according to instructions for "Genius at Work" hanging, *above.*

Cut a 16½-inch square of fleece; baste to wrong side of patchwork. Next, machine-quilt around triangles along seams, using even-feed foot.

Using a zipper foot, sew piping to edges of patchwork; clip corners and overlap ends.

For ruffle, cut 4½-inch-wide bias strips of dark print fabric, piecing to 4 yards in length. Sew ends together and fold in half lengthwise; press. Gather raw edge to fit pillow; baste in place.

Cut a 16½-inch square of muslin for backing. With right sides facing, sew to patchwork; leave one side open. Clip corners, turn, and insert pillow form or fiberfill. Slip-stitch opening closed.

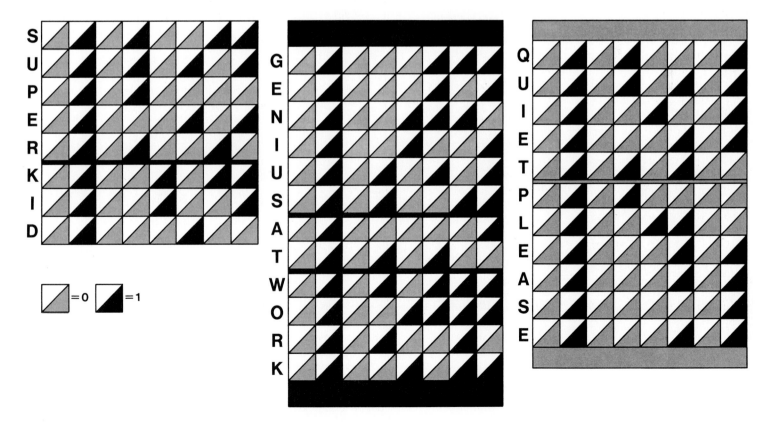

=0   =1

103

ENTERTAINMENT

The promise of a good time is the lure of the best bazaars. Here's how to make yours a stunning success.

A surefire way to make a bazaar memorable for buyers and sellers alike is to create an ambience that enhances the business at hand. A variety of entertainment ideas will establish a festive atmosphere and assure that the bazaar is a lively affair and a pleasure for all who attend.

Highlighting opening night

Many bazaars, especially those staged for charitable concerns, lend themselves to opening night events. This occasion can be an "invitation only" evening, with entertainment and special activities befitting the occasion.

If this type of evening is suitable, capitalize on it by inviting notable local residents, along with appropriate newspaper, radio, and television personnel.

Make the evening special by providing festive food and drink, and a pianist or small musical group. Consider several low-cost methods of staging a buffet; have all bazaar participants contribute a platter or two of party food, for example. If a college or university school of music is nearby, you may be able to hire some of the students to perform.

Staging drawings and raffles

Drawings for door prizes can serve two purposes—to entertain bazaar shoppers and, if prizes are specifically geared to

the merchandise or booths at the bazaar, to boost sales.

Many bazaars opt to have a drawing for one major prize. The prize can be a major crafts project from one of the booths (purchased with cash collected from each exhibitor, perhaps), or a project that everyone has helped to create, such as a quilt composed of blocks stitched by the bazaar participants.

The procedure for selecting the winner is simple: As patrons enter, encourage them to fill out cards with name, address, and telephone number.

At the close of the bazaar, select the winner's card and notify them of their good fortune.

Use periodic drawings throughout the bazaar to attract attention to certain areas, or to highlight certain designers. The value of each prize (when multiple prizes are awarded during the course of the bazaar) may depend upon how often one is awarded; the more prizes offered, the less expensive or valuable they are.

Unlike prizes given at individual booths, awards offered to all bazaar patrons should be

announced over a public address system or posted at entrances and exits as they are drawn. In either case, it's a good idea to have drawings scheduled at specific times, and to post the schedule or hand it out to interested shoppers.

You also can use drawings to attract business to specific booths. For example, each booth could contribute gift certificates toward dollars off a purchase as potential door prizes.

A raffle differs from a door prize in that chances or tickets for the prize are sold in advance of the bazaar. The best way to sell raffle tickets is by direct personal contact. Try door-to-door sales, word-of-mouth sales, and ticket booths in shopping malls or public spots. An added benefit of selling raffle tickets is that the sales effort helps to publicize the bazaar. (On bazaar handbills and posters you might mention the raffle—and the location of the ticket booth.)

Individual booth operators may stage drawings for specific prizes of their own. This is a good way to stop traffic at a booth and make personal contact with shoppers. Also, if the bazaar is an annual affair, you can use this effort to generate a mailing list that will be useful in future publicity efforts.

Local ordinances may dictate raffles and drawings be held in

a prescribed manner; check with officials beforehand.

Demonstrating and teaching crafts

With so many attractive, functional crafts on display, patrons invariably become interested in the techniques used to create the items for sale.

Capitalize on this interest by setting up demonstrations. These demonstrations can vary with the type of bazaar. For a country bazaar, for example, find local weavers, potters, or candle makers who can demonstrate their craft in an entertaining and informative manner.

In many regions there are guilds devoted to a particular craft. To encourage public interest in what they do, these groups often will stage demonstrations at no cost. ·

Teaching particular crafts techniques is another method of generating interest in handmade articles. Often, crafts retailers (and guilds) can provide

teachers and equipment (for little or no charge) to both large and small groups. Crafts stores are willing to do this, of course, to generate sales for their own supplies.

To be fair to booth operators, be sure that the accent is on learning a technique, not making finished items to compete with bazaar merchandise. Teach the *technique* of counted cross-stitch, for example, not how to make a hand-stitched Christmas ornament.

As with drawings for door prizes, it's a good idea to schedule these demonstrations at specific times and to make the most of them in your publicity.

Keeping kids occupied

Anyone who's taken young children shopping knows how soon their patience runs low. Design kids' entertainment to keep them happy and occupied, so parents are free to shop without concern.

● **Kids-only shopping:** For holiday bazaars, set aside a special area for children's purchases. That way, children can shop for parents and friends without spoiling the surprise. Price items appropriately to allowances, and if space permits, provide inexpensive gift-wrap materials and tools.

● **Paint-and-color areas:** You can amuse kids for hours with painting and coloring, especially as a group activity. Plan for a

large area, and keep equipment to a minimum.

Indoors, provide crayons or markers to simplify cleanup. Suspend sheets of paper on walls for drawing; use a theme or title on each page to inspire creativity. For example, label each large sheet with a letter of the alphabet with the specification that only things beginning with the appropriate letter be added to the sheet.

Outdoors, paint-and-color activities can be a little more adventurous. Using white paint, prime large appliance boxes to serve as portable, disposable canvases, or erect plywood easels with plain paper stapled to them. Keep the weather in mind, stabilize projects to avoid wind damage, and move activities to a porch or under a canopy if it begins to rain.

For small areas where large sheets of paper might be overwhelming, restrict activities to smaller items. Supply a stack of paper plates and string to make masks; give each child a plate and have him or her design a character or animal face. Have an adult or older child nearby to instruct and supervise activity, and to cut eye holes and staple string ties. Or, give each child a paper bag to color or paint as a simple hand puppet.

● **Face painting:** This activity is fun for both kids and adults. For best results, however, supply teens with equipment to

paint young children. Use nontoxic water-soluble paints, and limit designs to cheeks and forehead, away from eyes, nose, and mouth.

As a variation, use theatrical makeup (available from theatrical or dance supply outlets) to create clown, mythical creature, or animal faces. To complete the look, provide inexpensive hats, animal ears or noses, or other props fashioned from construction paper.

● **Dress-up areas:** Assemble a collection of costume components for kids to try on. A major benefit of this activity is that play can progress virtually unsupervised. Fancy party clothes (worn or out-of-style), athletic or professional uniforms, and specially made Halloween outfits are all good to use. Be sure to include a box of costume jewelry, a rack stocked with hats and headgear, and a large mirror so that kids can see their finished outfits.

ENTERTAINMENT

Kids—and grown-ups, too—can enjoy a day at the bazaar when you set aside a special area for children's games and toy making.

With some adult supervision, and some steps finished beforehand, children can complete the toys and favors *above*. The stick puppets are cut from paper shapes and assembled with paper fasteners. The horse has a candy cane head and a mane of knotted yarn.

The glittery star is made from cotton swabs; assemble it prior to the bazaar and let small children apply glue and glitter.

Painted crafts sticks are all you need for the toy plane, decorated with foil stars. Clown and bear paper cutouts sit atop a springy coiled chenille stick.

Few kids can resist hurling a beanbag at a target. Our colorful backboard is cut from sturdy foam-core board, available at art supply stores. Colored with permanent markers, the board has slots cut into it so it can slip into foil-covered ice-cream cartons embellished with stars.

Make coordinating beanbags from scraps of sturdy fabric in celestial star and planet shapes.

Instructions for all projects begin on page 108.

STICK PUPPETS

Shown on page 106.

MATERIALS
Red, white, and black
  construction paper
Glue
Paper punch
Small paper fasteners (brads)
Crafts sticks

INSTRUCTIONS
Use patterns, *opposite.*

For snowman, cut head and body circles, arms, and upper and lower legs from white paper; cut hat, bow tie (two triangles), and hands from red paper. Punch black paper and use circles for eyes and three buttons on front.

For Santa, cut body circle, arms, hat, and upper and lower legs from red paper; cut head, beard, and hands from white paper. Punch black circles for eyes and buttons as for the snowman.

Glue facial expression and hat to head; let dry. Glue head to body; let dry. Glue beard to Santa and bow tie to snowman; let dry. Glue hand circles to ends of arms. Glue each lower leg to a crafts stick, leaving about ½ inch of the upper leg exposed.

Pierce body and limbs at Xs on pattern. Fasten arms and upper legs to body with paper fasteners; fasten upper legs to lower legs.

Note: For smaller children, glue bodies to heads; add faces. Pierce pieces for assembly; let kids assemble puppets with paper fasteners.

CANDY CANE HORSE

Shown on page 106.

MATERIALS
Scraps of construction paper
Glue, yarn scraps
Small candy cane

INSTRUCTIONS
Use full-size pattern, *opposite;* trace horse and saddle.

Cut horse from paper and saddle from a contrasting color. Glue saddle to body and fold legs down along dotted lines. Punch holes at ends of body as indicated.

Cut seven 2-inch lengths of yarn and knot around cane just below curve to form mane. Insert end of candy cane into one of the holes. Cut five 2½-inch lengths of yarn for tail; knot and pull through other hole.

Note: For smaller children, glue horse/saddle assembly, knot yarn onto candy canes, and make tailpieces ahead of time. Then, let the kids fold down the legs, punch the holes, and insert head and tail into horse's body.

GLITTER STARS

Shown on page 106.

MATERIALS
Cotton swabs, glue
Red and green glitter

INSTRUCTIONS
Pour a small amount of each color of glitter onto a paper plate. Dip ends of two swabs into glue and then into red glitter; shake off excess and let each dry. Repeat with two more swabs and green glitter.

Glue the two red glittered swabs together at right angles at midpoint of swabs. Repeat with green glittered swabs. When dry, glue all swabs together at the center to form an eight-point star. Let dry.

Note: For smaller children, apply glitter to all swabs first and glue swabs into crossed pairs. Let the kids glue two pairs of swabs together.

AIRPLANES

Shown on page 106.

MATERIALS
Tongue depressors
Crafts sticks
Paint, glue, stickers

INSTRUCTIONS
Paint plane pieces in contrasting colors. Center and glue tongue depressor (wings) approximately 1 inch from (and perpendicular to) one end of crafts stick (fuselage). Decorate ends of wings.

Note: For smaller children, paint and assemble plane; let children add decorations.

JUMP-UP PARTY FAVORS

Shown on page 106.

MATERIALS
Pleated-paper nut cup
Scraps of construction paper
Paper punch
Glue
Chenille sticks
Masking tape

INSTRUCTIONS
Use full-size patterns, *opposite,* for teddy bear, gingerbread man (not shown in photograph), and clown.

For gingerbread man, reverse pattern along fold line to complete. Use bear pattern as given. Cut bodies from paper. Punch paper to form small circles and crescents; glue to bear and gingerbread man's bodies for faces and buttons. For clown, cut body, head, and hat shapes from paper; glue together, using dotted lines on pattern as placement guides. Glue circles (hands and feet) behind arms and lower edge of body. Add mouth. Glue on circles for eyes and polka dots on costume. Decorate hat.

Wind chenille stick around pencil, leaving 1 inch free at each end. Remove from pencil. Insert end into bottom of nut cup; tape on inside to secure. Straighten spring and tape figures atop.

Note: For smaller children, assemble figures, omitting faces. Assemble coil and base; let children decorate faces and attach figure.

BEANBAG GAME

Shown on pages 106–107.

MATERIALS
30x40-inch piece of foam-core
  board
Black and colored markers
3-gallon ice-cream cartons
Large oatmeal boxes
Foil, large paper fasteners
continued

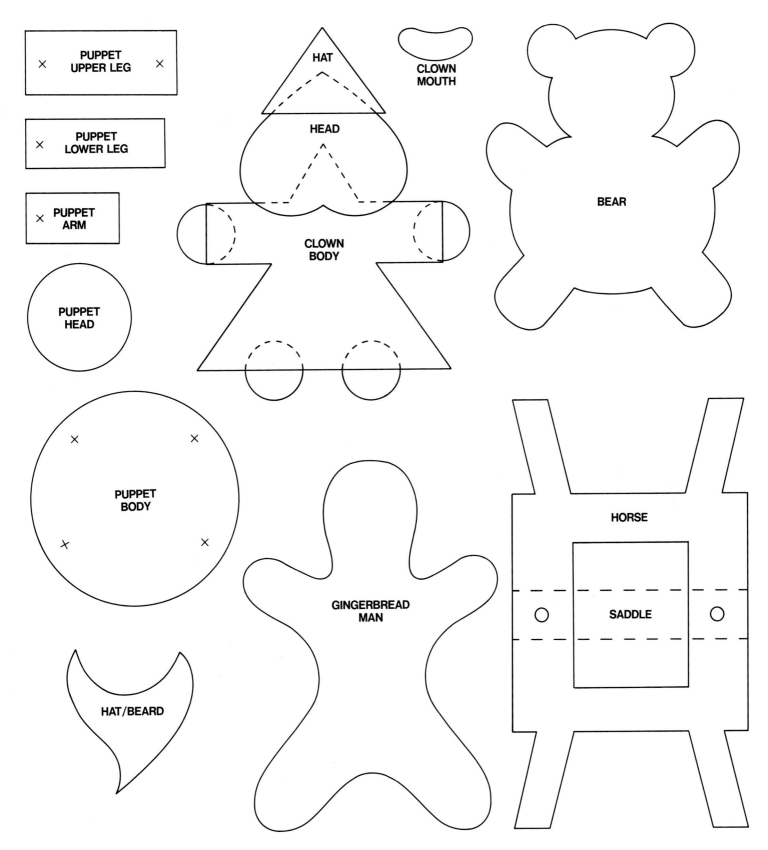

PUPPET UPPER LEG

PUPPET LOWER LEG

PUPPET ARM

PUPPET HEAD

PUPPET BODY

HAT/BEARD

HAT

HEAD

CLOWN MOUTH

CLOWN BODY

BEAR

GINGERBREAD MAN

HORSE

SADDLE

1 Square = 3 Inches

INSTRUCTIONS

Enlarge backboard pattern, *above*. Transfer to foam-core board, marking lightly with pencil. Outline bold lines of pattern with black marker; add shading to numerals to highlight them. Cut free-form stars from scraps of foam-core board to decorate fronts of larger containers.

Fill in remaining areas of design as desired, or use photograph on page 107 as a guide.

Decorate stars.

Cover containers with foil; secure with tape on inside. Fasten a star to front of larger cartons with paper fastener.

Slit bottom of board to receive each of the five target containers; slide containers up under numerals on the backboard, aligning the smaller containers under the larger point targets and placing the larger cartons in the center and at each end.

❖

BEANBAGS

Shown on pages 106–107.

MATERIALS
Sturdy fabric, beans

INSTRUCTIONS

For bag back, cut two 4½x8-inch rectangles; place right sides together. Stitch one long side, using ½-inch seams, and leaving a center opening. Press seams to one side.

Cut an 8-inch square for bag front. Trace pattern of star, *opposite*, or circle (use a salad plate for pattern) onto wrong side.

Pin front and backs together, right sides facing. Stitch shape twice. Trim ½ inch past outline; clip star points and around edge of circle. Turn and press.

Fill with beans. (Allow for ease; do not fill so that seams burst.) Slip-stitch closed.

BEANBAG

PLAYTIME PALS FOR KIDS

Handmade gifts and toys are cornerstones of almost every bazaar because dolls and animals are more precious when they're made by hand. The stuffed toys in this chapter are promising (and pleasing) candidates for new-found friends for every child.

Dressed in their mouse finery, the doll family, *right,* is ready for a birthday party. They're stitched from various types of gray fabric, and the tiniest scraps of calico, lace, and ribbon are sufficient for their clothing. Make them irresistible by adding tiny bead eyes, carpet thread whiskers, and spectacles created from fine wire.

Each adult and younger mouse is stitched from the same pattern, and the lengths of arms and legs are adjusted for the various "children."

Instructions for all projects in this chapter begin on page 118.

❖

Few toys are as appealing to kids—and grown-ups, too—as stuffed animals, such as this adorable teddy and pair of terriers.

essed for suc-cess, Bradstreet Bear, *above,* is a stalwart friend. He's stitched from a furry fabric and attired in an uptown vest (complete with pocket watch) and bow tie.

The terriers, *opposite,* are so lifelike be-cause the fabric used to make them closely resembles a dog's fur. Shiny black buttons are used for eyes, and each dog sports a bonny plaid bow.

One of the joys of making dolls is versatility; these delightful toys can range from elegant and proper to cute and cuddly.

Crisply attired for tea, the English maid doll, *above,* is every bit a lady. She's stitched from muslin and features an embroidered face.

The boy and girl, *opposite,* are simple rag dolls that any child will love to hug. Their heads are easy to fashion from fabric scraps.

MOUSE FAMILY

Shown on pages 112–113.
Finished size of Father Mouse is 12 inches tall; Baby Mouse is 6½ inches tall.

MATERIALS

⅜–½ yard gray fabric (bodies)
Scraps of pink satin (insides of ears)
Small black beads (eyes, nose)
Black carpet thread (whiskers)
Embroidery floss
Scraps of fabric (clothes); fusible webbing
Scraps of felt (bonnet, vest)
Scraps of lace, trim, and ribbons
Gray acrylic yarn (hair)
Permanent felt-tip pen
Polyester fiberfill
Safety pin; small snaps or hooks
Tracing paper

INSTRUCTIONS

Trace full-size pattern pieces, pages 120–123. Note which pieces include seam allowances. Cut out body and head pattern pieces from fabric, following the specific instructions below. For remaining pieces, draw around each pattern piece on a double thickness of fabric (right sides facing). Sew on drawn lines; cut out shapes ¼ inch from stitching. Turn.

HEAD: Using ¼-inch seams, sew the chin gusset to the head by matching D and C points on each side of the head. Next, sew together the front of the head from C to A. Insert the head gusset, matching A and B points on both sides of head. Leave neck open, clip curves, turn, and stuff.

Note: Baste each seam first; then, machine-stitch before continuing on to the next seam.

Cut ears from pink satin and gray fabric. Stitch together with right sides facing, leaving bottom open; turn. Turn under raw edges; blindstitch closed. Hand-sew ears to head, referring to photograph.

Sew beads for eyes and nose. For whiskers, pull three 4- to 6-inch strands of carpet thread through the tip of the nose. Knot on both sides to prevent thread from pulling out.

BODY: Using ¼-inch seams, sew one side seam, leaving open at markings. Turn under top and bottom edge ¼ inch; sew. Stitch remaining side together. Turn and stuff to within ½ inch of top.

Sew, then stuff arms; insert into arm openings. Blindstitch opening closed around arm. Sew, then stuff legs to within ½ inch of top. Insert legs into bottom of body; baste in place. Machine-stitch across bottom of body, securing legs.

Gather top edge of body. Insert neck; pull the gathering thread securely around neck. Adjust gathers and whipstitch body to neck. Stuff the body through side opening; hand-sew opening closed.

Trace tail pattern to include parts 1 and 2 for full length. (Baby's tail is Part 1 only.) Cut out tail; turn under all raw edges ⅛ inch. Fold in half lengthwise; sew turned edges together. *Note:* Adjust height of adult mice by shortening body and leg lengths.

For mice children, use smaller patterns and follow same procedure, *except* omit chin gusset on head. Instead, sew head pieces together from points D to A. Omit side opening in the baby; stuff body before adding

legs. Add the legs; sew bottom opening closed.

CLOTHING: For bloomers, sew front and back together. Turn under top edge and raw edges of legs ¼ inch; stitch. Add lace trim to legs. Beginning and ending at center front, thread a length of embroidery floss through the ¼-inch-wide waist casing. Slip the bloomers onto mouse; pull the floss to fit. Tie in a bow.

For blouse/shirt, turn under and stitch edges of center back (front) pieces. Sew pieces together at shoulder seam. Turn under raw edges of each sleeve. Sew sleeve and side seams. Finish bottom raw edge; add lace. For neck trim, sew lace ruffle or 1-inch-wide bias strip around the neck edge. Tack raw edge to inside. Add snaps or hooks, and tiny beads for buttons.

For the skirt, sew center back seam, leaving a 1-inch opening at top. Sew narrow hem; add lace. Gather skirt onto waistband, extending band ¼ inch beyond each side of skirt. Fold in ¼ inch; fold waistband in half. Blindstitch raw edge to inside. Add a snap.

For the apron, cut a 5x10-inch rectangle of fabric. Hem sides; sew ½-inch hem at bottom. Gather top edge to 1¼-inch-wide waistband. Finish same as waistband of skirt. Insert 7-inch-long fabric or ribbon ties on sides; tack in place.

For the shawl, cut an 8-inch square of fabric. Fringe edges; fold square in half diagonally.

For the diaper, fold a 5-inch square of fabric in half diagonally. Secure on the baby with a safety pin.

For the bib, fuse two pieces of fabric together using fusible webbing. Pink edges; add decorative topstitching, embroider

lazy-daisy stitches in bib center, and add ribbon ties.

For the bonnet, cut pieces from felt. Glue lace around brim; sew on ribbon ties.

For the pants, sew two pieces for *each* leg along side seam; sew from leg bottom up to X on center seam. Turn one leg right side out; slip inside other leg, lining up the center seam. Begin stitching at center back and leave small opening for tail just before center dot; continue stitching center front, stopping at dot. Add waistband same as for skirt.

Cut vest from felt. Sew pocket flaps to the front pieces. Sew fronts to back at shoulders; sew side seams.

To make the newspaper bag, trace around the pattern on a double thickness of fabric. Stitch on lines, cut out, and turn. Repeat for lining, making it ¼ inch shallower than bag at the bottom.

Put lining inside bag; turn under raw edges. Topstitch.

Fold in ⅛ inch on raw edges of 1x7-inch strip (for strap). Fold strap in half lengthwise; sew folded edges together. Tack strap ends to both sides of bag. Print "MEWS" on bag, using permanent felt-tip pen. Roll up tiny pieces of newspaper; place inside bag.

To make the pinafore, cut two straps; fold and press under the raw edges ⅛ inch. Fold in half lengthwise; sew along the folded edges. Cut out two pinafore bibs; pin together with right sides facing. Insert ends of straps between the bib pieces at Xs. Sew along sides and across top, catching straps in seams. Turn and press.

Finish skirt as for adult skirt. Sandwich the gathered skirt between the two long strips of waistband ties; allow approximately 6 inches to extend beyond each edge of the skirt. Stitch.

Sew bib to center front of skirt before flipping waistband up. Flip up bib and waistband ties. Turn under the raw edges of waistband ties ⅛ inch and stitch along these edges. Sew the front section of waistband through bib. When dressing child, crisscross the shoulder straps and slip ends into skirt. Tie waistband ties to hold shoulder straps in place.

SCOTTIE DOGS

Shown on page 115.
Finished size is approximately 17 inches long.

MATERIALS
For one Scottie
½ yard of long fur fabric
Scrap of pink felt for inner ears (optional)
1 black pom-pom
Two 15-mm black animal eyes, or ⅝-inch-diameter buttons
½ pound of polyester stuffing
Two 30-mm and one 55-mm doll joint (optional)
8x14-inch piece of medium-weight stretch fabric to match fur
Hairbrush; water-erasable pen
Thread; ribbon for bows

INSTRUCTIONS
Note: Two versions of Scotty dogs are given—one with a resting head and one with an erect head. Choose the pattern pieces (pages 124–127) for the dog desired.

Unless otherwise indicated, sew all seams with right sides facing. Seam allowances (⅜ inch wide) are included in all pattern pieces. Pin pieces together before sewing.

Trace pattern pieces, having nap of fur run in direction of arrows in pattern. On the body sidepiece, tape the patterns to match the A-B markings on pages 126 and 127 to make one pattern piece. Repeat these instructions for the bottom of the desired dog pattern.

Pin patterns to wrong side of fur and trace around pattern pieces with water-erasable pen. Carefully cut out through backing of fur only; avoid cutting fur. Cut the bottom of the dog from a scrap of stretch fabric suitable for the dog desired. Transfer markings. Use hairbrush to brush fur away from seams.

Sew the tailpieces together, leaving an opening at bottom. Trim, clip, and turn. Brush hair upward toward tail end. Stuff lightly; align side seams and baste opening closed.

Sew the center back seam on body sidepieces; trim and clip. Pin tail to marking on center back seam.

Sew back section to body, matching top dot to center back seam of body. Trim and clip curves.

Sew chest to front of body sides, matching large dot to center back seam of body; trim and clip curves.

Sew front legs together, leaving top open. Trim, clip, and turn. Stuff lightly.

Sew the front legs to the body, with large dot on front leg centered on seam joining chest to body sidepiece.

Pin bottom to body with narrow end of bottom toward front of dog; match large dots with seams.

Brush the fur away from the seam. Sew, leaving an opening for turning. Trim, clip, and turn. Brush fur, concealing all seams except center back.

Sew rear legs together, leaving them open where indicated. Trim, clip, and turn.

If you are using doll joints, poke a small hole where indicated on inside of each leg for joint placement. Insert a large stud from the 30-mm doll joint from the inside through the fur. Stuff legs lightly; sew opening closed. Poke small holes on inside of body at rear leg placement markings. Attach legs.

If you are not using doll joints, stuff body and sew opening closed. Then stuff the rear legs; hand-stitch them to body at markings.

Stitch center head seam. Secure eyes in place. Trim and clip curve. Sew head gusset to head, matching large dot to the center head seam at nose placement dot. Trim and clip curve.

Pin the head back to head front, matching large dot to center head seam and gusset seams to notches on head backpiece. Sew, leaving an opening; trim and clip curves.

If you are using doll joints, poke a small hole where indicated for head placement. (*Note:* For dog with erect head, make hole at dot on head gusset. For dog with resting head, make hole at dot on head back piece.) Insert large stud of 55-mm doll joint from inside through dot on head.

Turn, stuff firmly, and slip-stitch opening closed. Brush fur; hand-stitch pom-pom (nose) to end of center head seam. Set head aside.

Trim fur to ¼ inch long at center of *each* ear front piece. (If you are making a white dog and wish to have pink-tinted inner ears, cut two additional ear pieces from pink felt; baste to *wrong* side of front ear pieces.)

Brush fur from seam line; sew front and back ear pieces together, leaving opening at bottom. Trim, clip, and turn. Brush hair upward. Turn in bottom edge; blindstitch closed. Bend bottom edge forward; pin, then hand-stitch to head.

If using doll joints, poke a small hole on front of body for head placement. (For the erect head, make hole 1½ inches back from chest on center back seam. For the resting head, make hole as marked on chest.) Join head to body.

If you are not using doll joints, hand-stitch head to body at markings. Add a ribbon bow around the dog's neck.

BRADSTREET BEAR

Shown on page 114.
Finished bear is 19 inches tall.

MATERIALS
Bear
⅝ yard of 60-inch-wide fur fabric
Leather scraps (muzzle, footpads)
Two ½-inch black shank buttons (eyes)
1-pound bag of polyester fiberfill
No. 5 black pearl cotton
Carpet thread
Tracing paper
Soft-sculpture needle

Vest
⅓ yard plaid fabric
Three ½-inch gold buttons
Child-size bow tie
6-inch gold chain
Small dime-store pocket watch

continued

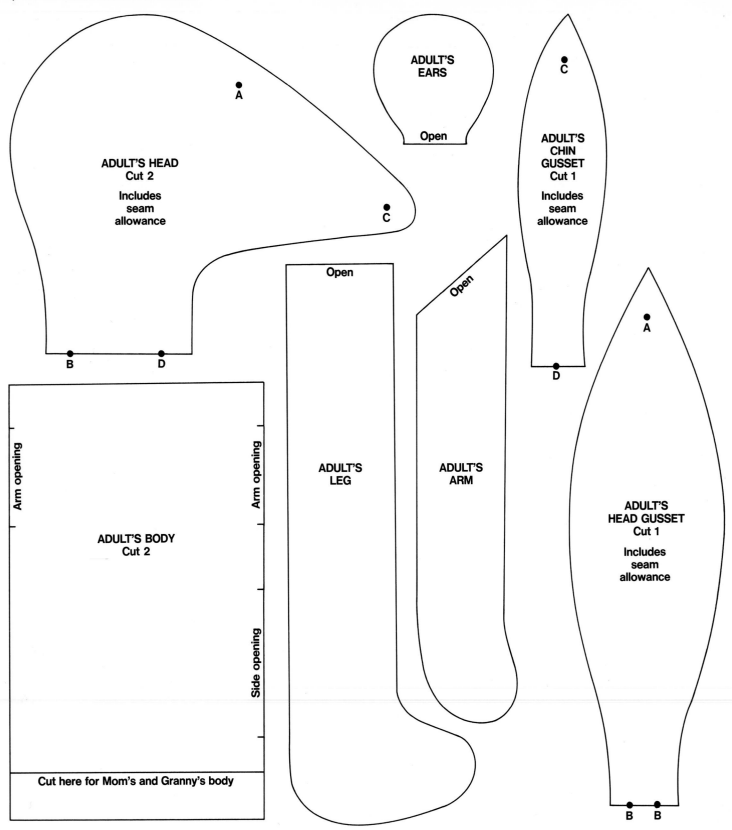

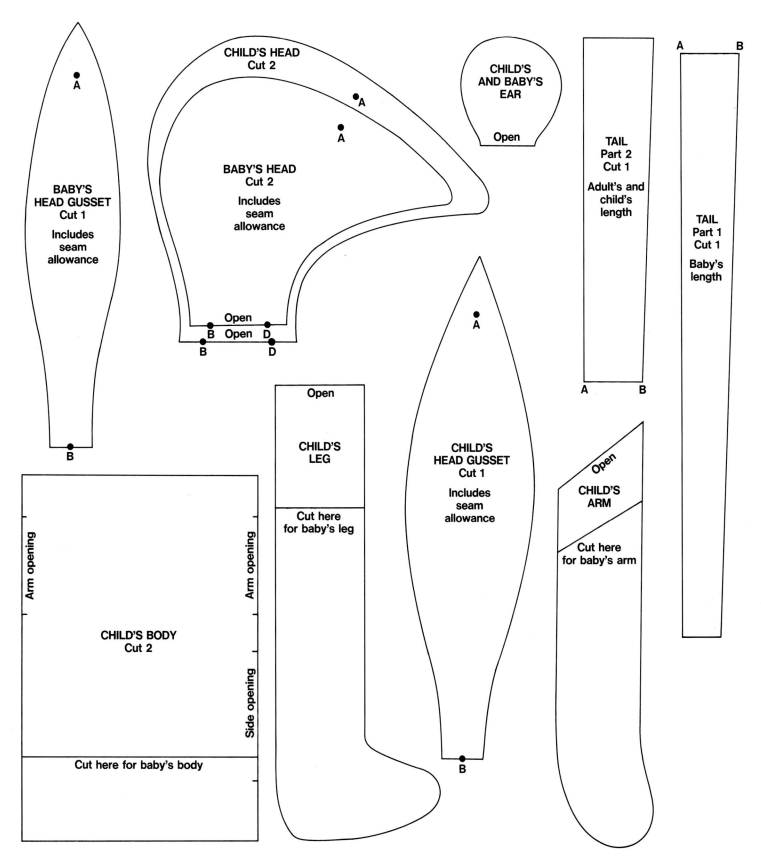

BABY'S
HEAD GUSSET
Cut 1

Includes
seam
allowance

A

B

CHILD'S HEAD
Cut 2

A

BABY'S HEAD
Cut 2

Includes
seam
allowance

A

Open
B Open D
B D

CHILD'S
AND BABY'S
EAR

Open

TAIL
Part 2
Cut 1

Adult's and
child's
length

A B

A B

TAIL
Part 1
Cut 1

Baby's
length

Open

CHILD'S
LEG

Cut here
for baby's leg

A

CHILD'S
HEAD GUSSET
Cut 1

Includes
seam
allowance

B

Open

CHILD'S
ARM

Cut here
for baby's arm

Arm opening

Arm opening

Side opening

CHILD'S BODY
Cut 2

Cut here for baby's body

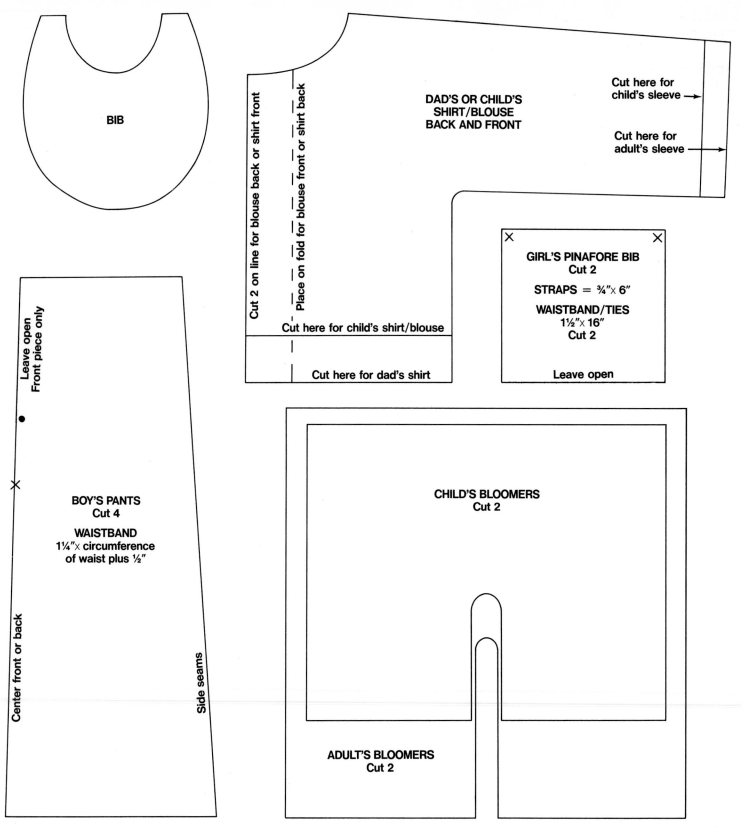

BIB

DAD'S OR CHILD'S
SHIRT/BLOUSE
BACK AND FRONT

Cut 2 on line for blouse back or shirt front

Place on fold for blouse front or shirt back

Cut here for child's sleeve →

Cut here for adult's sleeve →

Cut here for child's shirt/blouse

Cut here for dad's shirt

GIRL'S PINAFORE BIB
Cut 2

STRAPS = ¾"× 6"

WAISTBAND/TIES
1½"× 16"
Cut 2

Leave open

Leave open
Front piece only

Center front or back

Side seams

BOY'S PANTS
Cut 4

WAISTBAND
1¼"× circumference
of waist plus ½"

CHILD'S BLOOMERS
Cut 2

ADULT'S BLOOMERS
Cut 2

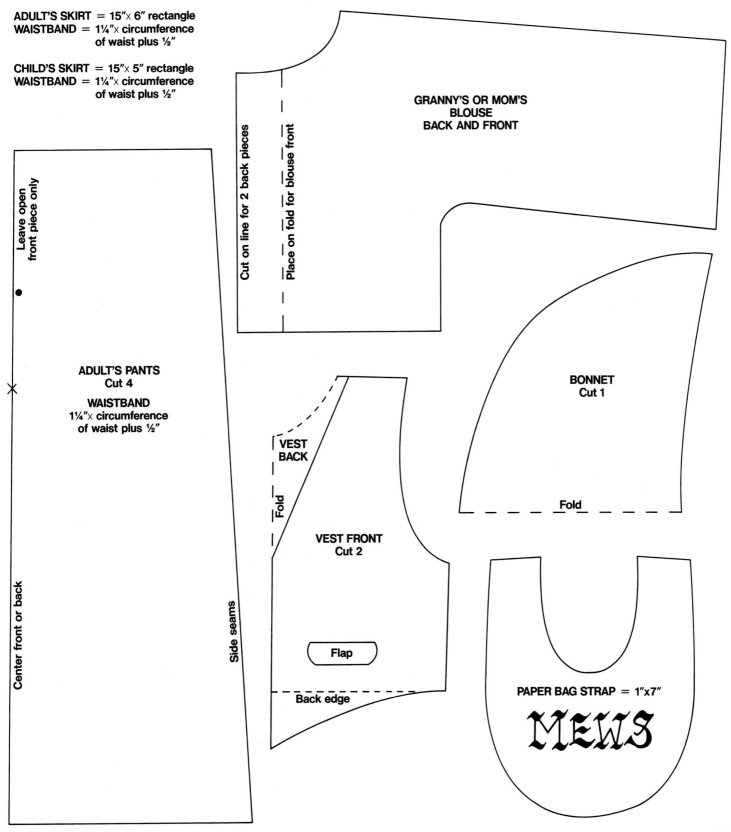

ADULT'S SKIRT = 15"x 6" rectangle
WAISTBAND = 1¼"x circumference of waist plus ½"

CHILD'S SKIRT = 15"x 5" rectangle
WAISTBAND = 1¼"x circumference of waist plus ½"

Leave open front piece only

Center front or back

ADULT'S PANTS
Cut 4

WAISTBAND
1¼"x circumference of waist plus ½"

Side seams

Cut on line for 2 back pieces

Place on fold for blouse front

GRANNY'S OR MOM'S BLOUSE
BACK AND FRONT

BONNET
Cut 1

Fold

VEST BACK

Fold

VEST FRONT
Cut 2

Flap

Back edge

PAPER BAG STRAP = 1"x7"

MEWS

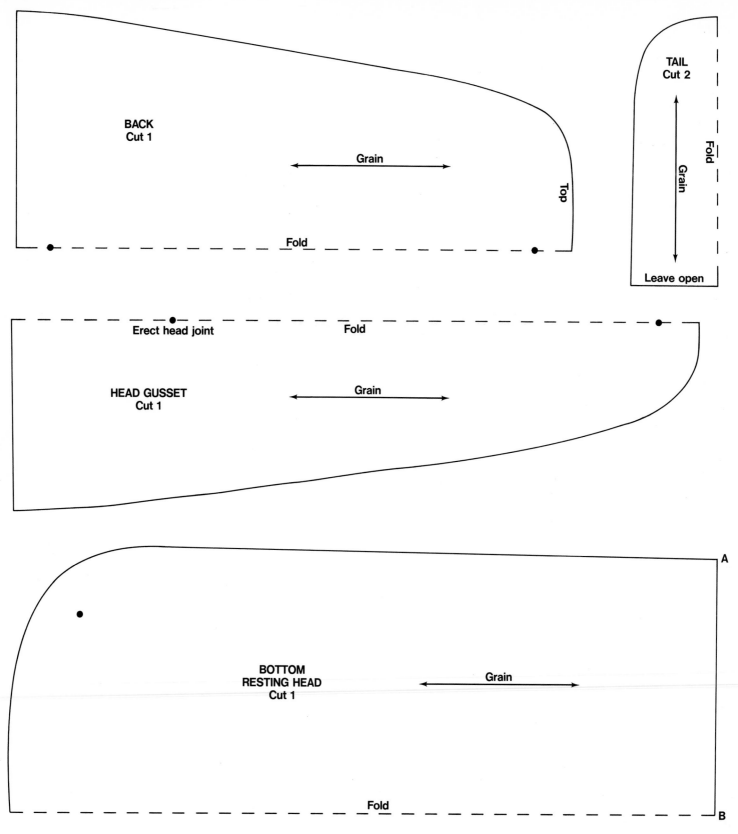

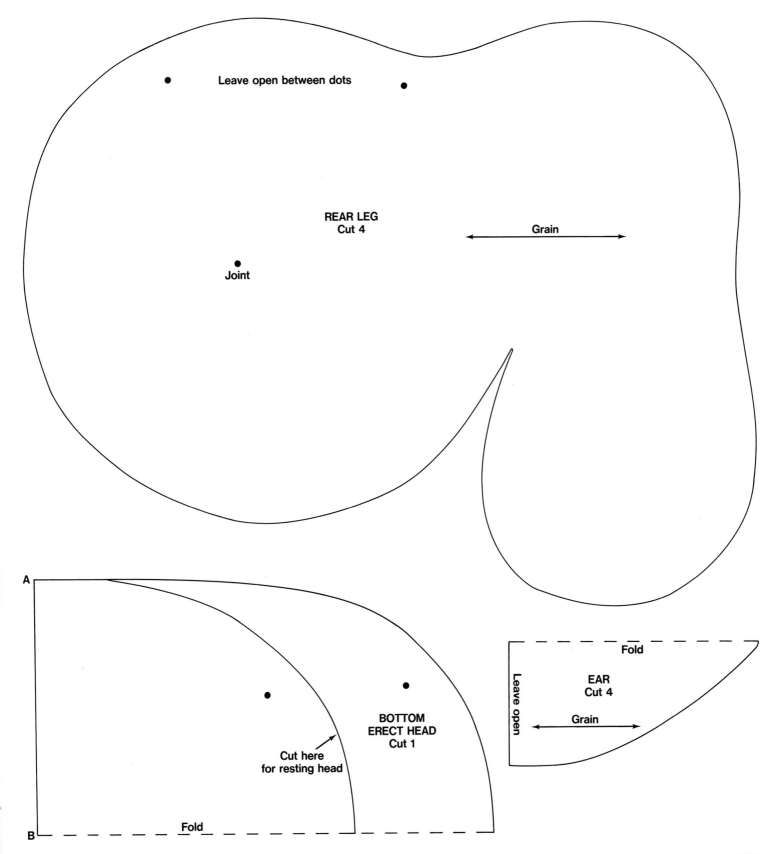

Leave open between dots

REAR LEG
Cut 4

Grain

Joint

A

Cut here
for resting head

BOTTOM
ERECT HEAD
Cut 1

Fold

B

Fold

EAR
Cut 4

Leave open

Grain

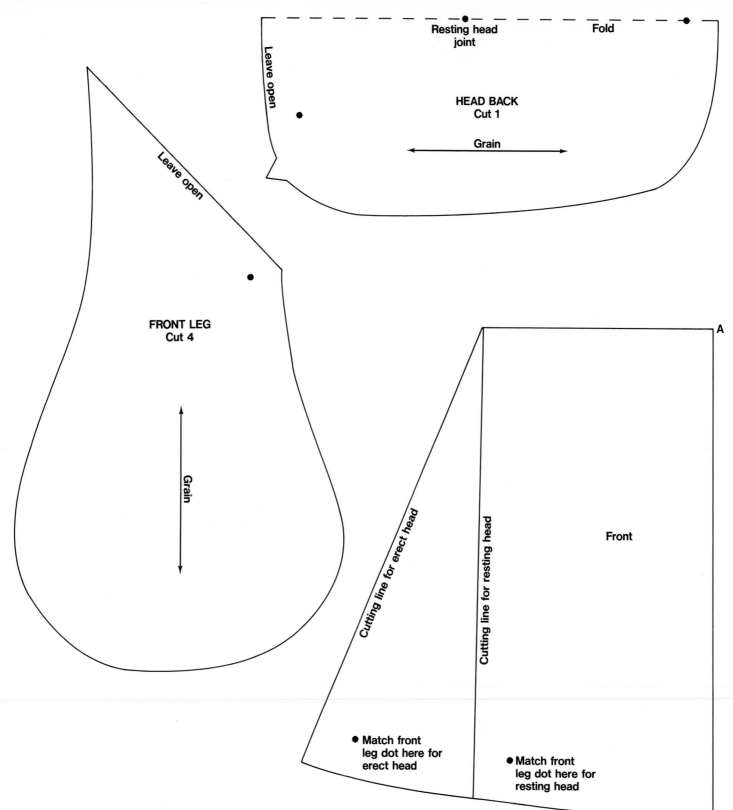

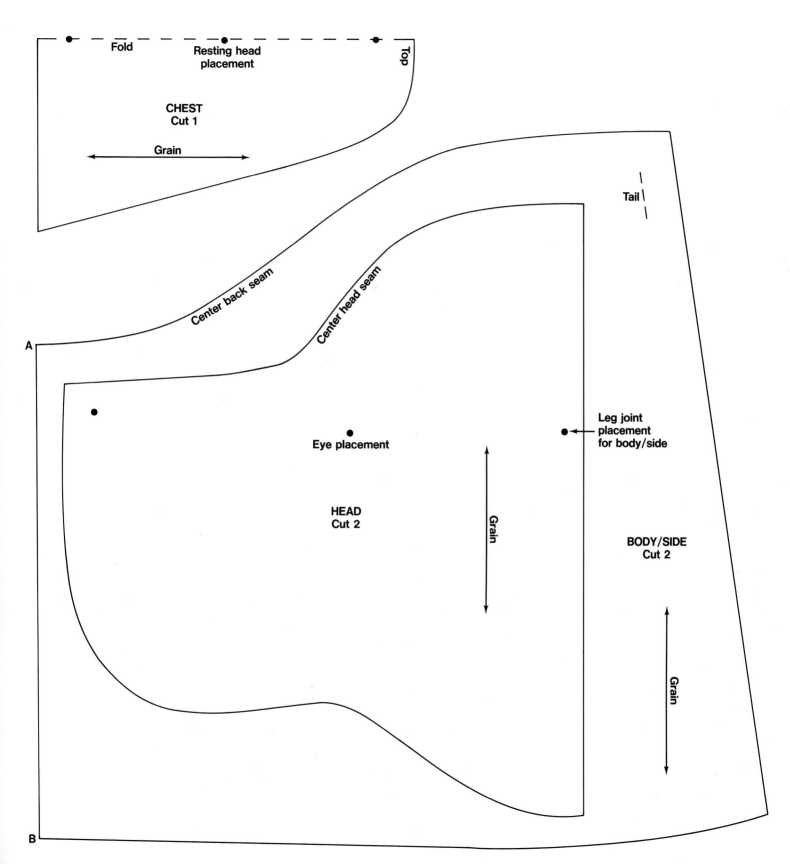

CHEST
Cut 1

Fold

Resting head
placement

Top

Grain

Center back seam

Center head seam

Tail

A

Eye placement

Leg joint
placement
for body/side

HEAD
Cut 2

BODY/SIDE
Cut 2

Grain

Grain

B

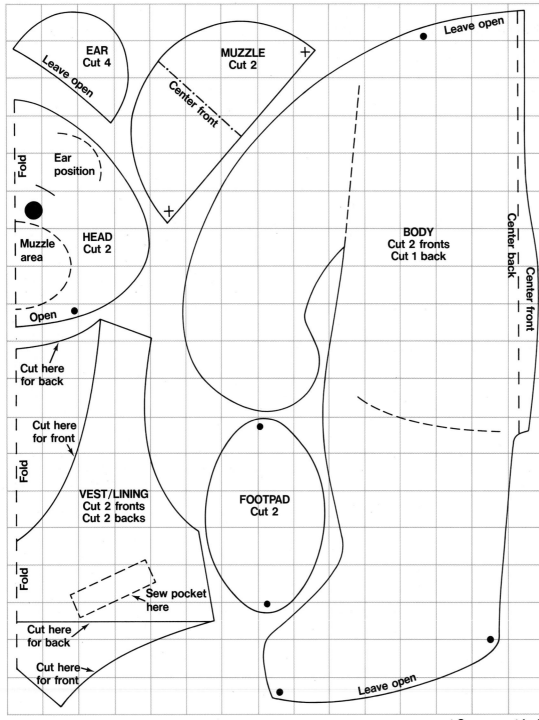

EAR
Cut 4

Leave open

MUZZLE
Cut 2

Leave open

Center front

Fold

Ear
position

Muzzle
area

HEAD
Cut 2

Open

Cut here
for back

Cut here
for front

Fold

VEST/LINING
Cut 2 fronts
Cut 2 backs

Fold

Sew pocket
here

Cut here
for back

Cut here
for front

BODY
Cut 2 fronts
Cut 1 back

Center back

Center front

FOOTPAD
Cut 2

Leave open

Leave open

1 Square = 1 Inch

INSTRUCTIONS

Note: When cutting the fur fabric, cut from back through backing only; avoid cutting fur. All pattern pieces include ¼-inch seam allowances, unless otherwise indicated.

For the bear

Enlarge the patterns, *left,* and cut out. From one layer of fur fabric, cut out body, head, and ears. Cut footpads and muzzle from leather.

Sew head front and back together with right sides facing; leave an opening for turning as indicated along chin on the pattern. Turn and stuff firmly. Hand-sew opening closed.

Bring straight edges of muzzle section together, matching Xs. Sew along straight edge, making a cone shape. Fold the cone so the seam lines up with center front (dotted line on pattern). Measure ½ inch from top of the point; sew straight across tip. Cut off excess fabric. Turn right side out. Turn under raw edge ¼ inch and baste.

Stuff muzzle; pin to front of head, centering seam on underside. Blindstitch in place.

With doubled pearl cotton, straight-stitch mouth atop seam (see photograph). Satin-stitch the nose right under the horizontal seam. Stitch eyebrows. Sew eyes in place.

Sew two ears together, in pairs, right sides facing, leaving bottoms open. Turn and stuff lightly. Stitch openings closed. Sew to head.

For body, sew fronts together on center seam. Stay-stitch between dots along top of body on front and back. With right sides facing, sew front and back together; leave open each foot bottom and top of body between stay stitches. Clip seam.

Sew footpads onto bottoms of feet, matching dots. Turn

bear right side out. Stuff legs and arms. Hand-sew along shoulders and hips (dotted lines on pattern). Stuff body firmly. Turn under raw edges at neck edge; sew closed. Sew head to body.

VEST: Cut out fronts and back from plaid fabric. With right sides facing, sew two front sections together, leaving shoulder and side seams open. Turn and press. Press under seam allowance at shoulder and side edges. Repeat for back of vest. Place front and back of vest on bear and blindstitch it to bear at shoulder and side seams.

Cut two 1¼x2¾-inch strips for pockets. Press all raw edges under ¼ inch; hand-sew to vest front. Sew buttons and watch chain in place.

❖

TEA PARTY DOLL

Shown on page 116.
Finished size is 16½ inches tall.

MATERIALS
Doll
6x7-inch piece of off-white knit fabric (head)
⅓ yard of muslin (body, arms); scraps of gray flannel (legs) and black fabric (shoes); embroidery floss in blue, brown, and rose
40 inches of brown wool roving (available from weaving shops), or yarn may be substituted (hair)
Fiberfill; powdered rouge
4 shirt-size flat buttons with 4 holes (arm joints)
White carpet thread; sewing thread; lightweight paper
Water-erasable marking pen

Clothing
Muslin scraps (bloomers, apron)
Small print or striped fabric scraps (blouse)
8x21-inch rectangle of black fabric (skirt)
Scraps of black knit fabric (gloves)
10 tiny black beads
½ yard of ⅛-inch-wide black grosgrain ribbon (shoes)
Purchased straw hat
Elastic thread; sewing thread
4 snaps; 5 tiny beads (blouse)

INSTRUCTIONS
For the doll
Enlarge pattern pieces, page 130, onto paper. *Note:* Pieces are sewn together with right sides facing.

HEAD: Trace around head pattern on double thickness of knit. Open up fabric; machine-stitch on outline. Turn to right side. Place stitched outline over pattern; trace facial features using a water-erasable marking pen.

Fold the fabric over again, with drawn features to inside. Stitch over previously stitched outline. (*Note:* Place lightweight paper under fabric while stitching to prevent puckering; tear away paper after sewing.)

Trim and clip seam; turn. Stuff head and neck area with fiberfill, keeping the head egg-shaped.

To shape the chin/neck area, use the pattern as a guide and work short backstitches with doubled carpet thread; sew from one seam to another through all thicknesses. Pull thread firmly to create a slight indentation. End by wrapping thread across back of neck; insert needle into opposite side seam; pull firmly and knot.

FACE EMBROIDERY: To embroider, use two strands of floss unless otherwise indicated. Begin and end all threads at back of head.

Satin-stitch the eyes using blue floss. With brown floss, outline-stitch upper eyelid; use one straight stitch under the eyes for lower lids and two straight stitches for each eyebrow; use one strand to make two tiny straight stitches for the nostrils. With rose floss, satin-stitch upper and lower lip. Add cheek color with powdered rouge.

BODY: Cut out body and mark Xs for button positions. Turn under ⅛ inch on top and bottom edges; stitch. Sew button securely with carpet thread to inside of body on each side where indicated, making an X with the thread on the outside of the body. Stitch back seam, leaving opening.

LEGS: Sew an 8x4-inch strip of flannel to a 4x4-inch strip of black fabric. Fold in half, lengthwise, with right sides facing. Place leg pattern on fabric, matching pattern seam line and fabric seam. Draw around pattern. Repeat for other leg. Stitch on drawn lines, leaving tops open. Cut out, clip, turn, and stuff. Slip legs into bottom of body; stitch across.

With doubled carpet thread, run a gathering stitch across the top edge of the body. Insert the head/neck, allowing ½ inch of neck to extend; pull gathering thread until body fits snugly around neck. Stuff the body through center back opening; sew closed.

ARMS: On a double thickness of fabric, draw around the arm pattern; repeat for other arm, flopping pattern. Sew button where indicated on inside section of each arm only, in the same manner as for body. Sew arms, leaving opening; trim, clip, and turn. Stuff and sew closed. Tack elbow joint from seam to seam as indicated on pattern. Backstitch divisions for fingers.

To attach the arms, use a long needle and double carpet thread. Loop thread through X on body (avoid catching fabric). Pull tightly on loop; slip needle and arm snugly against body.

Repeat, pulling through to other side; attach other arm in same manner. Run needle back through body to first side, pulling second arm tightly against body; knot thread under arm.

HAIR: Cut a ¾-inch muslin strip, long enough to encircle the head. Pull out five 8-inch lengths of roving; line them up across strip. Sew in place; trim away excess muslin. With muslin facing toward top of head and roving hanging down over the face, wrap the muslin strip around head, placing it forward on front of head. Hand-stitch to the head.

Pull the back section of hair to top of head; roll ends under and stitch. Pull front and sides together to top; twist ends into knot and stitch in place. With pin, pull wisps of hair down at sides.

For the clothing
All seam allowances for the clothing are ¼ inch and pieces are stitched together with right sides facing, unless otherwise indicated.

BLOOMERS: Cut out; hem bottom edges. Stitch seam A.
continued

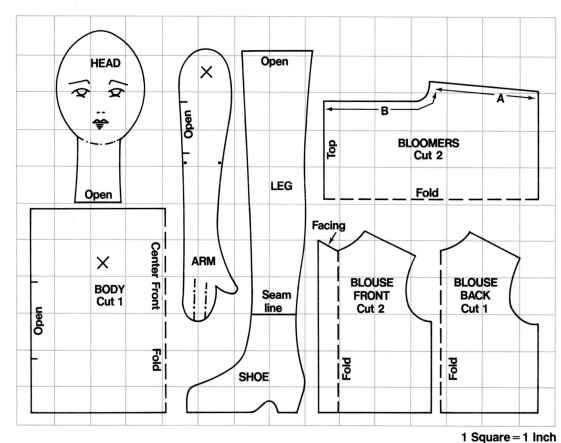

1 Square = 1 Inch

Turn one leg right side out and insert it into the other leg, lining up seam B. Sew the legs together along this seam. Turn inside out. Turn ⅜ inch to inside on waist edge, making a casing for the elastic; stitch. Run elastic thread through casing; pull to fit snugly and knot.

BLOUSE: Cut out pattern pieces; stitch the shoulder seams. Press seams open, then press front facings under.

With right sides facing, sew 1¼ x 5-inch collar strip around neck, extending the collar ½ inch on each side beyond the neck edge. Press under ¼ inch on the remaining raw edge of the collar. Fold the ½-inch extensions toward the collar. Then, fold the collar in half and stitch it in place. Cut two 6-inch squares for sleeves. Gather one edge to fit blouse armhole; sew sleeve to armhole. Repeat for the other sleeve.

Turn under narrow casing at the bottom edge; hem. Run elastic thread through the casing; pull to fit wrist and knot to secure.

Next, stitch the side and sleeve seams. Hem the lower edge of the blouse. Sew three snaps to the front. For buttons, sew five tiny beads down one side of front edge.

SKIRT: Seam the short ends to within 2 inches from the top edge. Stitch a narrow hem at the bottom edge.

Cut out a waistband 1½ inches wide and long enough to encircle the waist, then add 1 inch to the band length. Gather the skirt to fit the waistband, allowing ½ inch to extend on both sides of the opening. Turn under ¼ inch on the raw edge of the waistband; fold extensions toward band. Fold waistband in half; stitch to skirt. Sew on snap.

APRON: Cut a 7x14-inch piece from muslin. Sew narrow hems on the 7-inch sides and along the bottom edge. Gather the top edge to 4½ inches. Cut a 1½x18-inch strip for the waistband/tie. Center and sew the apron to one edge of the band. Press under ¼ inch on remaining edges of the waistband/tie. Fold in half; sew entire length and across ends.

GLOVES: Cut two 1¾x2-inch pieces of knit fabric. Fold in half widthwise; stitch and turn. Slip one glove onto one hand, allowing fingers to ex-

tend beyond glove. Tack glove to hand between thumb and fingers. Repeat for the other glove.

SHOES: Sew five beads for buttons to each shoe; tie narrow ribbon around top.

FINISHING: Decorate purchased hat with black grosgrain ribbon, if desired. To make the shawl, knit or crochet a triangle. Or cut and fringe a fabric square; fold on the diagonal.

❖

RAG DOLLS

Shown on page 117.
Finished size of girl doll is 14 inches tall; boy doll is 11 inches tall.

MATERIALS
For the dolls
⅔ yard of peach-color fabric
½ skein of gold yarn (hair)
Red embroidery floss
Black felt scraps (shoes, eyes)
Stiff cardboard; thread
Glue gun (optional)
Polyester fiberfill

For the girl's clothing
⅓ yard of solid-color fabric (dress)
¼ yard of print fabric (pinafore)
6 inches of print fabric (pantaloons)
Scrap of gray felt (spats)
⅔ yard of ½- or 1-inch-wide ruffled eyelet (pantaloons)
Bias tape (dress and pinafore)
Eight ¼-inch black buttons with shanks (shoes)
Snaps
1 yard of 1-inch-wide grosgrain ribbon (hair)
½ yard of ¼-inch-wide satin ribbon (pinafore); thread
⅔ yard of ⅛-inch-wide elastic

For the boy's clothing

¼ yard of striped fabric

Two ⅝-inch buttons
(trousers)

6 inches of print fabric (shirt)

4 tiny pearl buttons (shirt)

¼ yard of ⅝-inch-wide satin
ribbon (bow tie)

Thread; snaps

INSTRUCTIONS
For the dolls

Trace the pattern pieces for doll bodies, pages 132–135. Add ¼-inch seam allowances to pieces; cut pattern pieces from fabrics.

When stitching, sew all pieces together with right sides facing and using ¼-inch seams, unless otherwise indicated.

Trace bottom half of the leg pattern (up to the broken line) for the shoe pattern; cut four from black felt for each doll.

Embroider the face and attach the eyes as indicated. Stitch the head pieces together, leaving an opening for turning. Clip curves, turn right side out, press, and stuff.

Sew the arms, leaving an opening for turning. Clip fingers, turn arms right side out, press, and stuff lightly. On boy doll, machine-stitch the fingers. Hand-sew the arms closed.

Pin the wrong sides of the shoes atop the right side of the leg (foot) pieces; stitch across the top edge of the shoes. Then sew the leg fronts and backs together. Pin soles to shoe bottoms; stitch, clip, and turn right side out. Stuff legs to within ½ inch of the top.

Matching the front and back leg seams, pin the legs (facing upwards) onto the body front;

stitch across. Place right sides of body pieces together and sew, leaving an opening at bottom, where legs are attached. Clip curves, turn right side out, and press.

Stuff the body and hand-sew the opening closed. Hand-sew the arms to the body.

Hand-sew the head to the body placing the chin along the dash lines on front of body. For the girl's hair, wrap yarn around a 4x10½-inch piece of stiff cardboard. Holding the bundle firmly, slip it off the cardboard and stitch across the center to make a part and to secure hair. Tack the hair to the head. Attach grosgrain ribbons to each side of the head.

For the boy's hair, wrap yarn around the length of a 3x7-inch cardboard. Slip yarn off the cardboard and tie it around the middle with another piece of yarn; cut open all loops. Glue or tack the yarn to the head. Trim the hair on front and sides. (See the photograph for reference.)

For the girl's clothing

Trace all pattern pieces. Add ¼-inch seam allowances, and cut pattern pieces from fabrics. Cut a 4⅜x21-inch rectangle from printed fabric for the pinafore and a 5¼x21-inch rectangle from solid fabric for the dress skirt.

PANTALOONS: Turn under the bottom edges of the legs; stitch the ruffled eyelet atop fold. Sew the inner leg seams. Turn one piece right side out and slip it inside the other; stitch the crotch seam; clip curves, turn right side out.

Turn under the top (waist) edge, creating a casing for elastic, and stitch; leave a ½-inch

opening. Cut elastic to fit the doll's waist. Insert the elastic into the casing and knot securely at the ends; blindstitch opening closed.

DRESS: Gather the top edge of the skirt. Beginning at the bottom, sew the center back seam for 2½ inches. Turn under ½ inch on the bottom edge; sew a narrow hem.

Turn under the edges of the back opening. Stitch bias tape to the neckline; clip, turn, and tack tape to the inside.

Gather the top edge of the sleeves. Join the sleeves to the bodice, gathering to fit.

Stitch the underarm and bodice side seams. Turn under the bottom edges for elastic casings; stitch, leaving an opening. Cut elastic to fit the doll's wrist. Insert the elastic, pull tight, and knot securely. Blindstitch opening closed.

Adjust gathers and sew the bodice to the skirt. Sew snaps to the back.

PINAFORE: Hem the sides and bottom of the skirt; gather the top edge.

Hem the bottom edges of the pinafore sleeve ruffle and gather the top edge to fit the bodice sleeve opening between dots. Adjust the gathers and stitch in place. Turn, press, and topstitch.

Hem raw edge back of bodice top. Sew bias tape to neckline, right sides facing. Clip curves, turn to inside, and tack in place. Stitch the underarm seams.

Pin the bodice to the skirt, adjusting gathers; stitch. Tack ribbon to the back neckline of the bodice for a tie.

SPATS: Use spat pattern to mark placement for buttons on outside of shoes. Sew four buttons *each* to the sides of the girl's shoes only. Button spats over shoes.

For the boy's clothing

Trace all pattern pieces. Add ¼-inch seam allowances, and cut pattern pieces from fabrics. Make the shoe pattern same as for girl's shoe; cut from fabric.

SHIRT: Sew fronts to back at shoulders. Hem the sleeve bottoms, then sew the top edge of the sleeves to the shirt; sew the underarm seams.

Join the collar pieces, leaving the inner edge open. Clip the curves, turn, and press; baste the open edge together.

Sew the collar edge to the wrong side of the neckline; clip the curves, turn right side out, and press. (The raw edge will be underneath the collar on the right side of the shirt.) Edgestitch the seam allowance to the body of the shirt.

Sew snaps to the shirt front, then sew buttons in place.

TROUSERS: Hem the bottom edges. Sew the inner leg seams. Turn one piece right side out and slip it inside the other; stitch the crotch seam; clip curves, turn right side out. Pleat pants where indicated on pattern; hem the top of the trousers.

Sew straps, leaving an opening for turning. Turn right side out and topstitch ⅛ inch from edges. Attach the straight short edges of the straps to the wrong side of the center back. Cross straps and attach with buttons to front, over pleats.

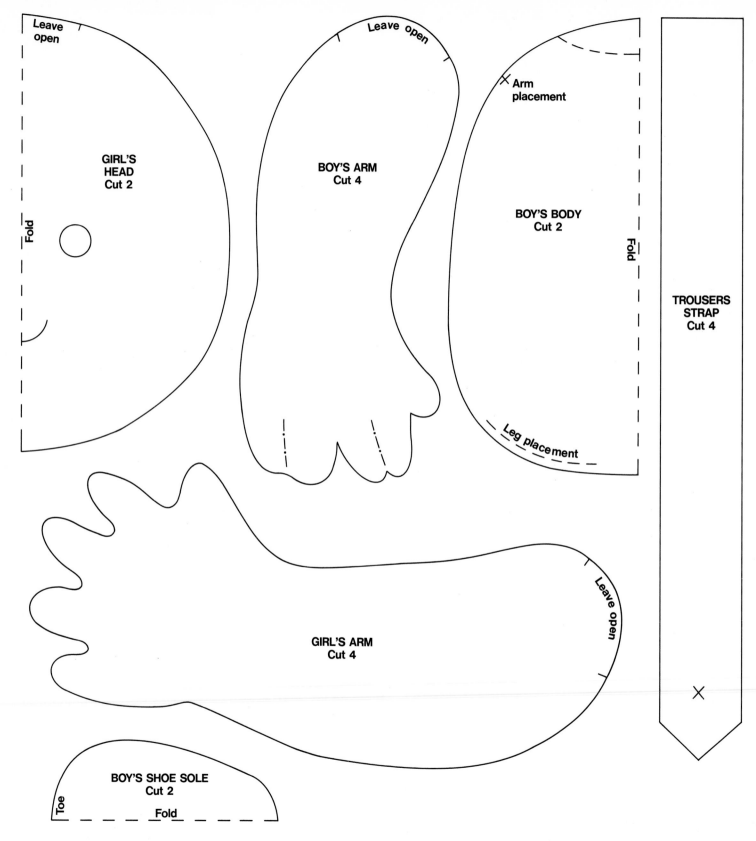

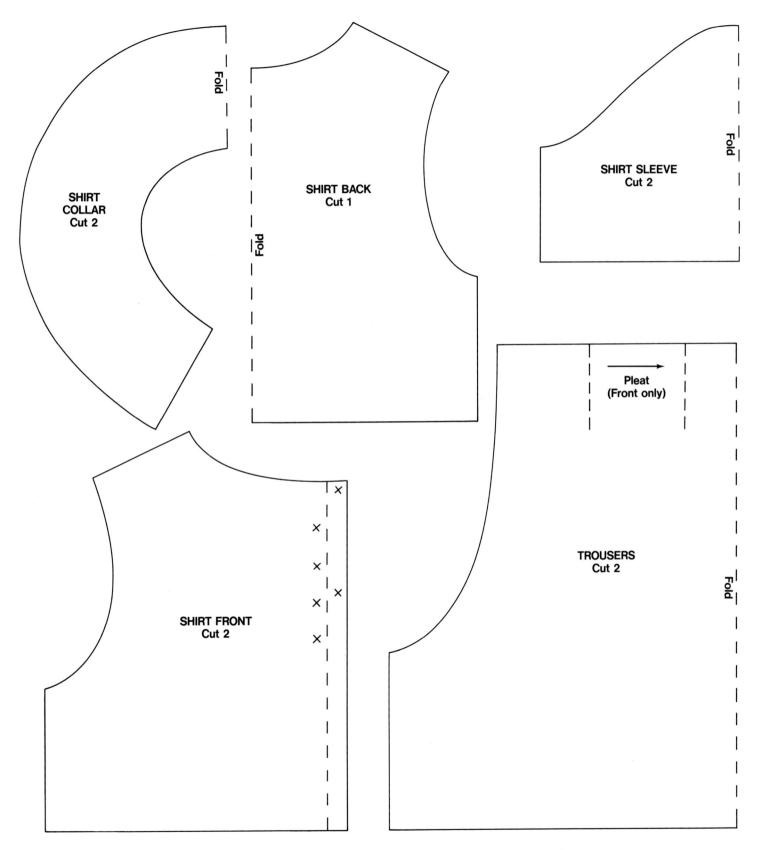

SHIRT COLLAR
Cut 2

Fold

SHIRT BACK
Cut 1

Fold

SHIRT SLEEVE
Cut 2

Fold

Pleat
(Front only)

TROUSERS
Cut 2

Fold

SHIRT FRONT
Cut 2

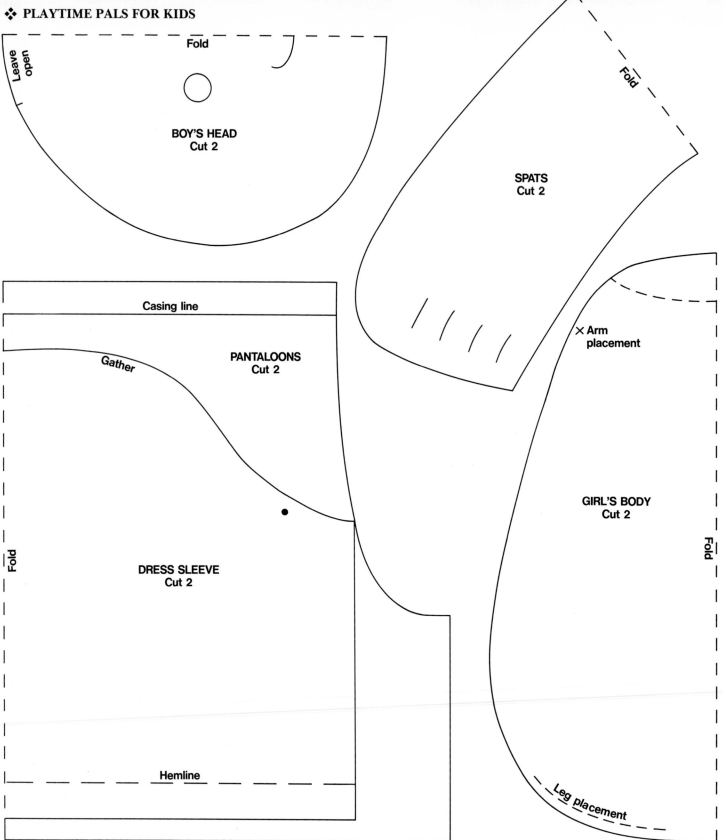

Fold

Leave open

BOY'S HEAD
Cut 2

Fold

SPATS
Cut 2

Casing line

Gather

PANTALOONS
Cut 2

✕ Arm placement

Fold

DRESS SLEEVE
Cut 2

GIRL'S BODY
Cut 2

Fold

Hemline

Leg placement

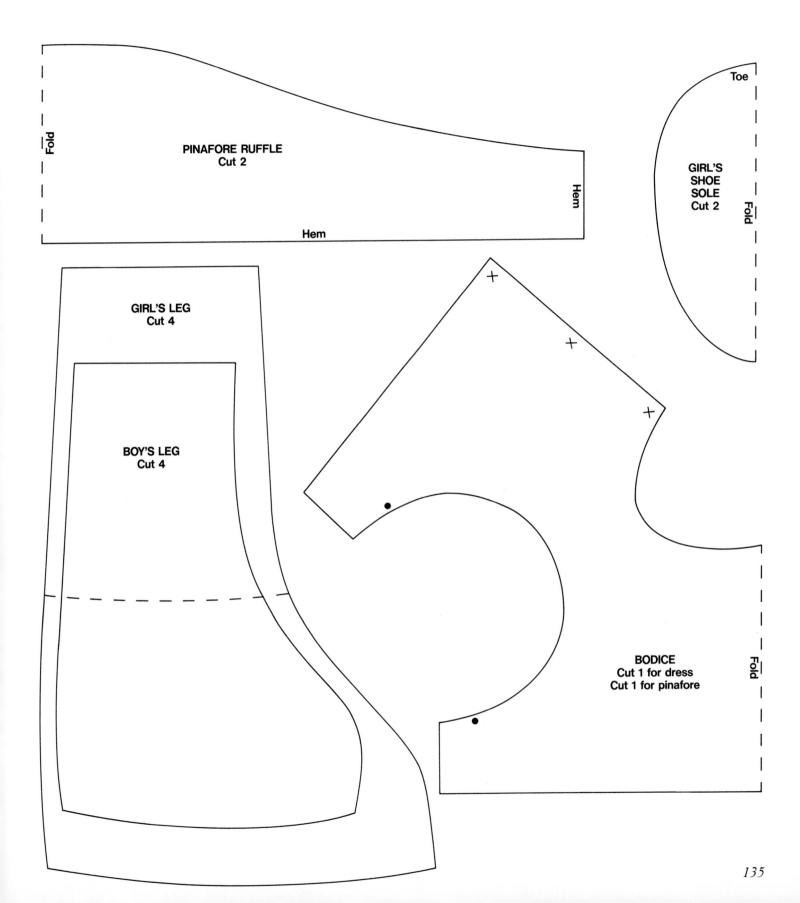

PINAFORE RUFFLE
Cut 2

Fold

Hem

Hem

GIRL'S
SHOE
SOLE
Cut 2

Toe

Fold

GIRL'S LEG
Cut 4

BOY'S LEG
Cut 4

BODICE
Cut 1 for dress
Cut 1 for pinafore

Fold

135

GIFTS TO MAKE FOR BABIES

It's easy to see why baby gifts are among the most popular items at any bazaar. Good designs for pretty and practical infant accessories are easy to find, and demand is high for handmade gifts for friends' latest arrivals and for new family members.

Our collection of baby items is based on the machine-appliquéd crib quilt, *right.* The whimsical motifs are designed to complement a hand- or machine-embroidered alphabet, and can be stitched from scraps.

The accompanying tote—for baby's "safaris"—features four of the animal designs used on the quilt, here stitched together to form a handy pocket. It's large enough to easily carry a newborn's necessities.

More designs adapted from this quilt appear on the following four pages. Instructions for the quilt, along with full-size patterns for the motifs, begin on page 142.

❖

These projects are suitable for either a baby's room or that of an older child.

Inspired by the motif for the letter I, the ice-cream cone hangup, *above*, is perfect for window or wall. Begin with a real cone, preserving it with polyurethane. Then, add a foam plastic ball frosted with acrylic modeling paste.

The picture frames, *right*, are made from strips of pine and are appliquéd with hardboard cutouts.

Machine stitching simplifies the steps in making these cheerful nursery accessories and stuffed toys.

Choose motifs representing edible things for the bibs, *above*. Use scraps from the sashing and backing for the bibs' ties.

Large enough to be really useful, the pincushion, *above*, features a pair of mice and a multicolored label.

Enlarge the rabbit pattern to make the toys, *opposite*, which also feature floppy ears lined with calico.

❖━━━━━━━❖━━━━━━━

ALPHABET QUILT

Shown on pages 136–137.
Finished size is 41x46 inches.

MATERIALS

⅜ yard *each* of pastel pink, yellow, blue, and green cotton

10x10-inch square of yellow print cotton

14x14-inch square of green print cotton

1½ yards of coral pink striped cotton

1 yard of gray print cotton

1¼ yards of 45-inch-wide cotton print (backing)

Scraps of brightly colored cotton (appliqués)

Black embroidery floss; sewing thread

Crib-size quilt batting

Tracing paper; dressmaker's carbon paper

INSTRUCTIONS

Note: Cutting directions include ½-inch seam allowances.

FOR THE SQUARES: From pastel cotton fabrics, cut 5x5-inch squares as follows: 6 pink, 7 yellow, 7 blue, and 6 green.

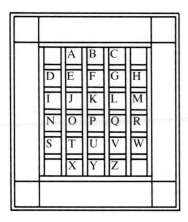

Using tracing paper, trace designs for alphabet squares, pages 142–148.

Using dressmaker's carbon, transfer designs for letters A, C, J, L, T, and V to pink squares. To yellow squares, transfer designs for D, F, H, N, P, R, and Y. To blue squares, transfer B, I, K, M, S, U, and W. To green squares, transfer E, G, O, Q, X, and Z.

Hand- or machine-embroider letters on squares using satin stitches and two strands of black floss or sewing thread.

Referring to the photograph for colors, cut out animals and other design motifs; do not add seam allowances to the pieces. Using thread to match appliqués, machine satin-stitch designs to the squares, fitting the elements in the patterns together in the same way that jigsaw puzzle pieces fit. Hand-embroider features and details.

TO ASSEMBLE TOP: Cut four 5x5-inch squares of yellow print cotton. Cut 25 strips, *each* 2¼x5 inches, from coral striped cotton. Referring to the placement diagram, *below, left,* assemble squares into vertical rows, with sashing strips in between. For example, the first row starts with a blank square, followed by squares for the letters D, I, N, and S, and another blank square (with sashing strips between the squares). The second row consists of squares A, E, J, O, T, and X, with sashing strips in between. Continue, following diagram.

Cut six 2¼x32-inch strips of coral fabric. (Measure length of rows of squares before cutting, to verify dimensions; adjust as necessary.) Referring to the assembly diagram, sew vertical rows together with long sashing strips in between.

continued

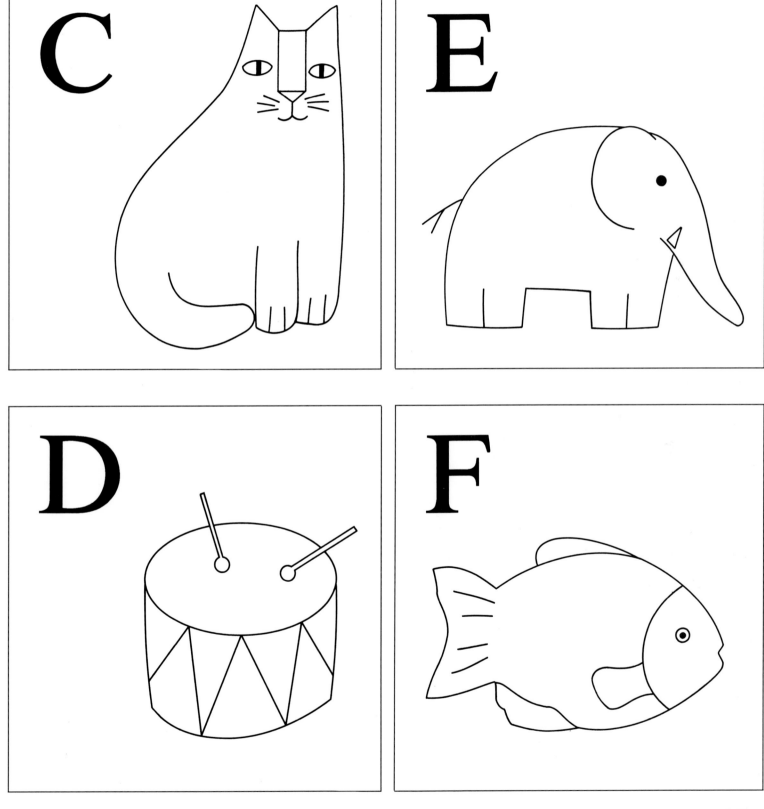

K

M

L

N

Cut two 2¼x29-inch strips of coral fabric; stitch to top and bottom of squares.

Next, cut sashing strips for borders. Before cutting these strips, measure the quilt center carefully; adjust length of borders as needed. Cut four 7x7-inch squares from green fabric. From gray fabric, cut two border strips, each approximately 7x29 inches; stitch a 7x7-inch square to each short end. Sew border to squares along the top and bottom of the quilt center. From gray fabric, cut two borders, each approximately 7x34 inches; stitch to sides of center.

TO ASSEMBLE QUILT: Layer the backing, batting, and top together; stitch around outside edge. Trim excess backing and batting.

From coral fabric, cut two 2¼x43-inch and two 2¼x48-inch strips; bind outer edges, mitering corners.

Machine-quilt on seam lines around each letter square and along border strips.

BABY'S TOTE BAG

Shown on page 136.
Finished size is 5x13½x15½ inches.

MATERIALS

⅝ yard of 60-inch-wide denim or canvas
⅝ yard of coordinating fabric (lining and pocket edging)
11⅝-inch square of lightweight canvas (pocket backing)
Four 5-inch squares of pastel fabrics (appliquéd blocks)
Scraps of fabric and fusible webbing (appliqués)
⅛ yard of coordinating print (sashing strips for pocket)
⅓ yard of coordinating fabric (strap covering, optional)
3¼ yards of ⅞-inch-wide webbing (straps)
Black embroidery floss
Thread to match fabrics
5x14-inch piece of cardboard (optional)
Tracing paper
Water-erasable marking pen

INSTRUCTIONS

Use ½-inch seams, unless otherwise indicated. Cut canvas as follows: two 14½x16¼-inch pieces (front and back), two 6¼x14½-inch pieces (sides), and one 6¼x16¼-inch piece (bottom). Cut lining fabric to correspond.

TO SEW POCKET: Select and trace four designs from the alphabet quilt. Referring to the photograph for colors, cut appliqué pieces from fabric scraps and fusible webbing. Using an iron, fuse pattern pieces to pastel blocks.

Using narrow machine zigzag stitches and contrasting thread, satin-stitch edges of appliqué pieces. Hand-embroider French knots for eyes, using two strands of floss.

Cut one 1⅜x10¼-inch and two 1⅜x5-inch sashing strips. Join top two blocks at center with a short strip; repeat for bottom blocks. Press seams open. Join top row to bottom row with the long strip; press seams open.

Cut two 1⅜-inch-wide strips of lining fabric (pocket edging) equal to the side length of assembled pocket. Join to each side; press seams open.

Cut two 1⅜-inch-wide strips equal to the length of the top and bottom of the assembled pocket; sew in place and press seams open.

Place pocket piece atop lightweight canvas, right sides facing. Sew ½-inch seams, leaving open at bottom. Clip corners, trim seams, and turn. Press; blindstitch opening closed. Finished pocket should measure 10¼ inches square.

TO ASSEMBLE BAG: Using a water-erasable marking pen, mark placement of pocket on canvas front, 1¾ inches from bottom edge and 3 inches from side edges.

Sew bottom of canvas bag piece to bottom of front and back, ending stitches ½ inch from ends. Extend lines marking width of pocket along bottom and back of bag.

Cover strap with fabric, if desired. Starting at the *bottom* of the bag, pin the outer edge of the strap along the marked line (pocket covers straps in front).

Pin strap to pocket front, extend it for the handle, then pin down the front again, across the bottom and up the back of the bag. Extend it for the handle again, and down the back of the bag to the starting point. Topstitch in place, ending all stitching 1 inch from the top of the bag. Pin and stitch pocket over straps on front, matching bottom of pocket to marking.

Sew sides to bag, breaking stitches at corners. Press seams open. Turn and crease seams. Edge-stitch sides of bag for a crisp finish.

TO FINISH: Place the cardboard in bottom of bag. Sew lining as for bag, omitting pocket; leave opening at bottom. Insert canvas bag inside lining bag, right sides facing; move straps out of the way of top edge. Stitch tops together; turn, stuffing lining into bag. Topstitch edge. Stitch straps to top of bag.

PINCUSHION

Shown on page 138.
Finished pincushion measures approximately 5½x11 inches.

MATERIALS

¼ yard *each* of chintz, muslin, and fleece
Scraps of fabric and fusible webbing (appliqués)
Purchased piping or 1⅛ yards *each* of ⅛-inch- and ¼-inch-diameter cording and sufficient yardage in two prints to cover cording
Embroidery floss (letters)
Water-erasable marking pen
2 packages of bird grit
Sewing thread in matching and contrasting colors
Tracing paper

INSTRUCTIONS

Cut two 6½x12-inch pieces *each* from chintz and muslin. Trace mouse design, page 145, twice (once reversed) and letters for "PINS" from the quilt. Tape the designs to a window; trace outlines of letters and mice to chintz front, referring to photograph for placement.

Trace mouse shapes onto appliqué fabric; cut out. Cut shapes from fusible webbing; fuse mouse shapes atop chintz front. Pin chintz front atop fleece. Using narrow machine zigzag stitches, satin-stitch around raw edges and tail. Change thread color and satin-stitch detail on ears and mouth.

Using one strand of floss and changing color for each letter, embroider letters. Using two strands of floss, make French knots for eyes on mice.

On chintz front, baste two rows of cording along ½-inch seam line, placing the narrow cording next to chintz front.

continued

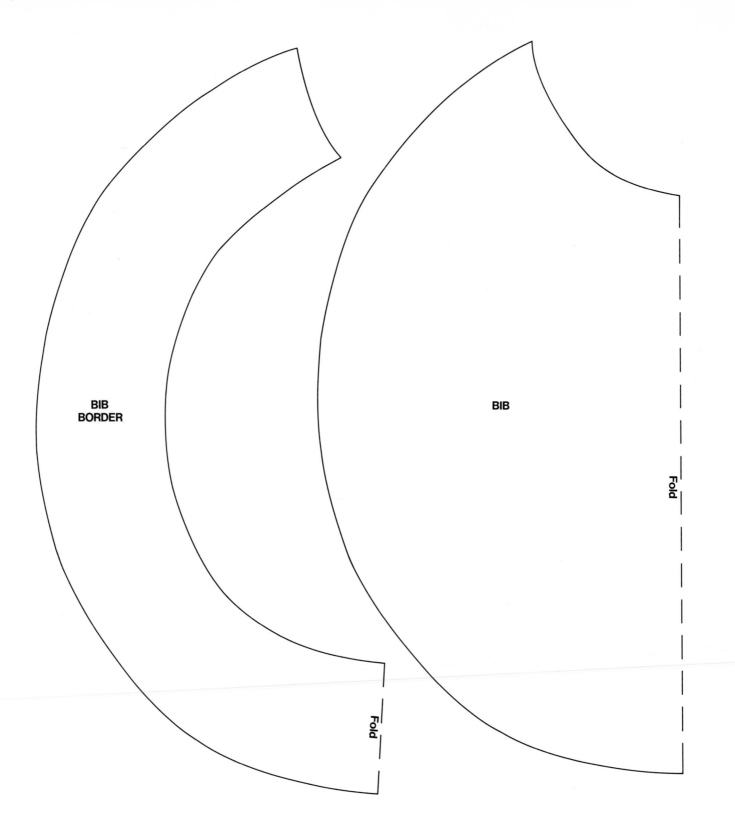

BIB
BORDER

BIB

Fold

Fold

Cut backing fabric to 6½x15 inches; cut in half widthwise and finish one short edge on each piece. (Pincushion cover is like a pillow sham.) Baste right side down atop chintz front, with the finished edges overlapping at center and raw edges matching. Stitch on seam line; clip corners and turn.

For inner bag, sew muslin pieces together with right sides facing, leaving an opening for turning. Fill with bird grit; sew opening closed. Insert bag into pincushion cover.

BABY BIBS

Shown on page 138.

MATERIALS
For one bib
9-inch square *each* of pastel cotton, coordinating cotton print, and terry cloth
1⅓ yards of bias trim
Cotton scraps (appliqué)
Tracing paper

INSTRUCTIONS
Trace the patterns, *opposite*. Without adding seam allowances, cut bib from pastel fabric and border from print. Using the appliqué pattern of your choice, pages 142–148, cut pieces from fabric scraps.

Machine-appliqué the design to the bib front. Pin border to bib with outer edges even; satin-stitch inner border curve to the bib.

From terry cloth, cut out bib back. Place behind front; sew together ¼ inch from edges.

Make or use purchased bias trim to cover outer edge of bib. Center and stitch a 28-inch piece of bias to neck edge, sewing to ends of tie extensions. Tie knot at each end.

BUNNY TOYS

Shown on page 139.
Small bunnies are 8 inches tall; large bunny is 11½ inches tall.

MATERIALS
⅓ yard of pastel chintz for large bunny; ¼ yard of pastel chintz for *each* small bunny; ¼ yard of contrasting print (ears)
Yarn (pom-pom tails)
⅓ yard of polyester fleece
Polyester fiberfill
Water-erasable marking pen
Tracing paper; cardboard
Sewing thread
Narrow ribbon (bow)

INSTRUCTIONS
Trace the pattern from the rabbit quilt block, page 146. Enlarge the pattern to the desired size. (The large bunny is four times the size of the original; the small bunny is three times the size of the original.)

Cut main pattern piece along body lines, omitting ears and tail. (Cut ears separately.) Trace body pattern onto wrong side of chintz; add ½-inch seam allowance and cut out. Cut backing and one layer of fleece to correspond. Tape body pattern to a window; tape fabric for body front atop pattern. Using a water-erasable pen, trace pattern details.

Pin body front atop fleece. Using narrow zigzag stitches and contrasting thread, sew all details *except* whiskers. Hand-sew long stitches for whiskers.

Draw around ear pattern on wrong side of chintz for ear backs; add ½ inch for seams. Cut ear fronts from contrasting fabric. Cut one layer of fleece for *each* ear.

Place ear fronts atop fleece and sew with ¼-inch seams to

backs, right sides facing. Leave lower edge open. Trim seams, clip curves, and turn. Fold side edges ¼ inch toward center at bottom; baste to secure.

Baste ears to body front. Sew body front to back, right sides facing; leave an opening at bottom. Trim seam, clip curves, and turn. Stuff lightly; sew opening closed.

To make pom-pom for tail, cut a piece of cardboard 2½x3 inches. Wind yarn around the 2½-inch width for small bunny and around the 3-inch width for large bunny. Hand-stitch pom-pom securely to body.

Add narrow ribbon bow to bunny's neck.

ICE-CREAM CONE HANGUPS

Shown on page 140.
Cones are 5¾ inches high.

MATERIALS
Purchased sugar cones (bases)
Foam balls 2 to 2½ inches in diameter
Modeling paste (from an art supply store); knife
Polyurethane; paintbrush
Acrylic paints in white and ice-cream or sherbet colors
Paper clips; crafts glue
High-gloss acrylic spray
Pastel ribbons

INSTRUCTIONS
Apply six or seven coats of polyurethane to inside and outside of sugar cones. Dry thoroughly between coats. Using crafts glue, glue a foam ball to each cone; dry. Using a knife, spread modeling paste atop foam ball as if you were frosting a cake.

Cut paper clips in half (making U shapes). Add glue to ends of wire and insert the U into the top of each ball; allow modeling paste to dry.

Mix acrylic paint with white to obtain pastel color of your choice; paint ball. Tie ribbon through wire atop ball and hang as desired.

PICTURE FRAMES

Shown on page 141.
Inside dimensions (picture areas) of frames shown are 6x6 inches, 5x7 inches, and 11x15 inches.

MATERIALS
1x2-inch lengths of pine; 1x4-inch lengths of pine
Wood glue; hot-glue gun
Semigloss paint in colors of your choice (frames)
Picture hangers
Scraps of ¼-inch-thick hardboard (appliqués)
Acrylic paints (appliqués); paintbrushes; gesso

INSTRUCTIONS
Frames may be any size. Once you've decided on the inside dimensions of the frames you want to build, cut 1x2-inch or 1x4-inch lumber to the desired sizes, mitering corners and rabbeting the inner edges. Glue pieces together and paint when dry. Add picture hangers.

For wood appliqués, select patterns from those used on the alphabet quilt. Cut shapes from hardboard, prime with gesso, and paint with acrylics.

Mount designs on frames using a hot-glue gun. Embellish frames with additional motifs, such as the tail on the kite, if desired.

CHRISTMAS TONIGHT

Holiday shoppers every-where rely on Christmas bazaars as sources for unique handmade gifts for family and friends.

Clement Moore's classic Christmas poem has delighted children for generations, and a memorable line from the poem inspired the embroidered picture, *left.* The sleeping child is covered with a patchwork quilt designed as a sampler of embroidery stitches. A variation of the lazy-daisy stitch appears as a garland to frame the design. Easy satin stitches are used for the remainder of the design, and touches of gold embroidery thread add sparkle.

Although this embroidery is framed as a wall decoration, it also would work as a pillow front or album cover.

Instructions for projects in this chapter begin on page 164.

Holiday treats and toys adorn the front of one of the stockings, *left*, which can be machine-stitched in a jiffy. The other stocking features an embroidered pocket intended to hold real candy canes. Cuffs embroidered to resemble eyelet are used for both of the stockings.

More embroidery motifs appear on the fanciful ornaments, *opposite*. Accents of machine appliqué can be used to highlight the rocking horse, teddy bear, and Father Christmas designs, and a ruffle made from pindot fabric edges each.

Scraps of pine and bright paints are all that you need to make the heart and star ornaments, *opposite*. The shapes are easy enough to cut out with a jigsaw and are ideal projects to make by the dozen.

Simple but striking designs such as these are the kind of attention-getting projects that are featured at every successful Christmas bazaar.

Inspired by the embroidered picture shown on pages 152 and 153, the doll and her bed and linens, *opposite,* are sure to capture a young girl's heart. She's stitched from cuddly knit fabric and dressed in a flannel nightgown, nightcap, and slippers. The stretchiness of the knit fabric allows you to sculpt the head into a realistic shape as you embroider the face.

Purchased wood finials are attached to uprights cut from a closet pole to form the legs for the doll's bed. Use pieces of hardboard for the head- and footboard. Bed linens are easy to stitch from scraps of fabric and lace.

More adaptations from the embroidered picture are the star-face bear and pillow, *right.* Assemble the bear from corduroy, adding felt paws and features. (A smaller, simpler version of the bear sits at the foot of the bed, *opposite.*) The pillow is sized for a single bed, and features a border and ruffle in festive red and green fabrics.

Dolls and teddy bears are popular gifts year-round. When tied to Christmas merchandising, they're irresistible. Our doll is patterned after the girl in the embroidered picture, with her very own teddy bear, too.

Although Christmas traditions vary from region to region, the Advent calendar is one that's universally cherished. Our wooden version is quick to build with just the simplest of materials.

Lengths of lattice strips built into a basic box shape make this calendar. (Use short pieces of lattice for the ends.) Divider strips cut to the same size as the box ends are spaced inside the box to create the hiding spots for each day's treat.

Inexpensive gold-tone upholstery brads—centered and tacked gently into the top of each section of the box—become the buttonlike fasteners for the felt flap "doors." The adhesive-back numerals and letters that are used on the flaps can be purchased from art or office supply stores.

Perched across the calendar are bear ornaments sewn from scraps of calico. Assemble the body in one piece, then sew the arms and legs separately and tack them on.

To give the ornaments individual personalities, create simple costumes from scraps of felt, lace, and ribbon. For example, a circle of fabric edged in lace becomes a grandmother bear's nightcap, a strip of gathered tulle forms a ballerina bear's tutu, and a New Year's Eve bear sports a top hat and tuxedo shirt.

Because the gold- and pearl-tone beads used for the tree trims, *left,* are sold in convenient lengths (and already strung), making these showy ornaments is a snap. Apply a coating of glue to cover half of the surface of a plastic foam ball and simply spiral the beads around until the glue is covered. When dry, repeat for the uncovered surface of the ball.

Skills used to work a counted cross-stitch pattern on even-weave fabrics are adapted to create beaded stitcheries like the snowflake ornaments, *opposite.* As each half cross-stitch is begun, thread a white seed bead onto the needle before the half cross-stitch is completed. Then tack the bead down as you finish the stitch.

This pattern for a six-point snowflake also can be stitched with embroidery floss or pearl cotton.

Beads have been popular materials for ornaments since Victorian times. Today, you'll find a variety of inexpensive beads for spectacular ornaments.

Roses are an elegant touch at holiday time and the two rose designs, *left*, are hand-crafted versions of this favorite flower.

The rose cross-stitch design can be assembled into an ornament or a package tie-on. The white rose is shaded with four colors of floss, and is flanked by holly leaves, berries, and delicate violets.

The crepe-paper-like foil used for the unusual metallic roses is silver on one side and gold on the other. The paper's texture enables the petals to remain stable once they are gracefully shaped. Leaves can be fashioned from foil paper or purchased in craft and hobby shops.

Simple stuffed hearts made from velveteen take on an air of Victorian elegance with small bouquets attached to the tops. Use silk flowers for the bouquets. And for proper proportion, include just a few large blossoms surrounded by buds, tiny leaves, and tendrils made from loops of narrow metallic ribbon.

Sumptuous materials like the glittery foil, rich velveteen, and silk flowers used for these ornaments needn't be expensive and aren't hard to find.

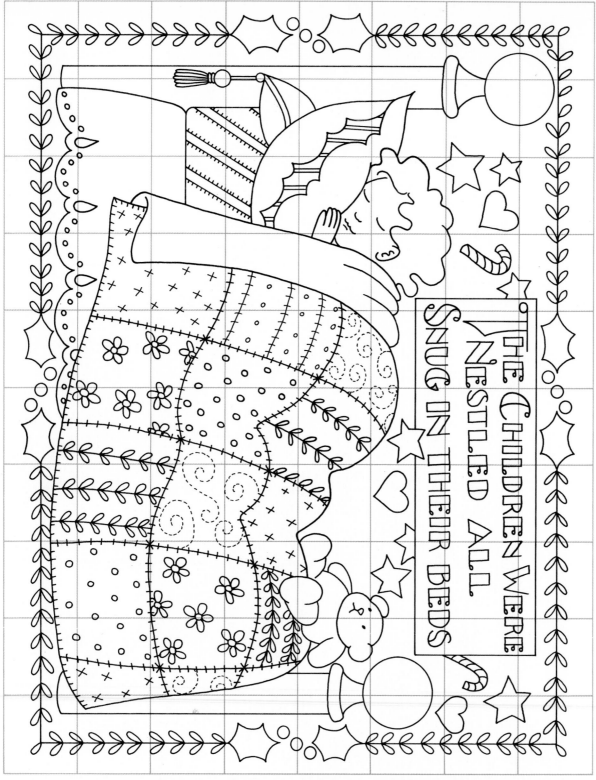

Embroidered Picture: Use Full Size   Embroidered Pillow: 1 Square = 2 Inches

164

EMBROIDERED PICTURE

Shown on page 152.
Finished size, framed, is 9½x12 inches.

MATERIALS
16x18 inches of white fabric
DMC embroidery floss and metallic threads in colors of your choice (see photograph)
Embroidery hoop; needle
Fine black felt-tip pen
Water-erasable marking pen
Tissue paper
Purchased frame

INSTRUCTIONS
Using a fine black felt-tip pen, trace the full-size pattern, *opposite*, onto tissue paper. (Disregard the grid; enlarge the pattern only for the pillow design shown on page 157.) Tape the design to a well-lighted window, then tape white fabric atop the pattern (centered).

Using a water-erasable marking pen, trace the design onto the fabric. Mount the fabric in an embroidery hoop.

Stitch the design, using one strand of metallic thread and two strands of embroidery floss. Refer to the photograph for color and stitch ideas.

(To add interest and texture to the embroidered design, use couching, outline, straight, satin, lazy-daisy, and running stitches, backstitches, and French knots.)

After embroidery is completed, press carefully on wrong side. Frame as desired.

EMBROIDERED & APPLIQUÉD STOCKINGS

Shown on page 154.
Finished size of stockings is 24 inches tall.

MATERIALS
For both stockings
Scraps of red and green fabrics for appliqués
¾ yard *each* of white fabric (stocking front and back) and lining fabric
25x28-inch piece of fleece for *each* stocking
⅓ yard of red piping for *each* stocking
White, red, yellow, green, and brown embroidery floss
Embroidery hoop and needle
Tiny red buttons; brown buttons; 3 yellow star buttons (optional)
Dressmaker's carbon paper; tissue paper; thread

INSTRUCTIONS
Enlarge the cuff and stocking patterns, page 166, onto tissue paper, adding ½-inch seam allowances all around.

FOR CUFFS: Transfer cuff pattern onto red fabric using dressmaker's carbon paper; do not cut out. Mount the fabric in a hoop, and embroider the design, using two strands of white floss. Cut out the cuff; cut a matching lining from red pin-dot fabric. Set aside.

For embroidered stocking
Enlarge the pattern on page 166 and transfer it to white fabric using dressmaker's carbon.

On the stocking front, using three strands of green floss, work backstitches for circles, or sew red buttons in place. Backstitch garland stems and work lazy-daisy stitches for leaves.

Transfer the toe and heel patterns onto red print fabric, adding ¼ inch for seams; cut out. Turning under the raw edges, appliqué the toe and heel in place, then embroider the inner edges with double rows of yellow backstitches (see the photograph).

For pocket, transfer rectangle pattern (with saying) onto green print fabric, adding ¼-inch seam allowances; do not cut out.

Using three strands of embroidery floss, backstitch the pocket outline with yellow. Work yellow running stitches just inside the outline; backstitch the letter outlines in red. Fill the letters with yellow satin stitches.

Cut out pocket and a matching green lining. With right sides facing, sew pocket front to back, leaving an opening for turning. Turn, press, and sew opening. Sew star buttons in place. Sew pocket to stocking.

For appliquéd stocking
Transfer the pattern, page 168, onto white fabric.

Cut apart the stocking design for appliqué patterns. Cut the appliqués from desired fabrics without adding seam allowances. Machine-satin-stitch appliqués in place. Using brown floss and satin stitches, embroider bear's eyes and nose; outline-stitch the mouth. Sew small brown buttons in place for elbow and leg joints.

TO ASSEMBLE: Cut out the stocking front and back. Cut two stocking shapes from fleece. Baste fleece to wrong side of stocking front and back; trim fleece.

Sew lining pieces together, right sides facing, leaving the top edge open. Trim seams and clip curves.

Sew piping to stocking front. Sew front to back with right sides facing, leaving top edge open. Clip, turn, and press.

Sew together the short ends of embroidered cuff; repeat for lining. Leaving straight edge unstitched, sew cuff to lining (right sides facing). Clip curves, turn, and press.

With right sides facing, slip cuff inside stocking lining; sew straight edges together. Trim seam, turn, and press.

Insert lining/cuff into stocking, wrong sides facing. Turn under seam on stocking top; sew stocking to lining. Turn cuff to outside of stocking. Add loop for hanging.

WOODEN STAR & HEART ORNAMENTS

Shown on page 155.
Finished ornaments are 3½ inches tall.

MATERIALS
Scraps of 1-inch pine
Band saw; sandpaper
Acrylic paints in white, red, and yellow; monofilament
Artist's paintbrushes

INSTRUCTIONS
Transfer patterns, page 167, to pine; cut out and sand.

Prime ornaments with white acrylic; let dry. Paint; let dry. Tape monofilament to the back side for hanger.

1 Square = 2 Inches

THE
STOCKINGS
WERE HUNG
BY THE
CHIMNEY
WITH CARE

1 Square = 2 Inches

EMBROIDERED ORNAMENTS

Shown on page 155.
Finished ornament, including ruffle,
is 5¼ inches in diameter.

MATERIALS
White fabric (for front and
   back)
DMC embroidery floss in
   desired colors
DMC gold and silver metallic
   threads
Embroidery hoop and needle
Fabric paints (optional)
Red and green calico fabrics
   (for ruffle)
Monofilament or ⅛-inch-wide
   ribbon (for hangers)
Polyester fiberfill
Tissue paper; compass
Black felt-tip marking pen
Water-erasable marking pen

INSTRUCTIONS
Using felt-tip marking pen,
draw three 4½-inch-diameter
circles onto tissue paper; add
¼ inch for seam allowances.

Using felt-tip pen, center and
trace the full-size horse, Santa,
and bear patterns, *opposite*, inside the circular patterns.

Lay white fabric atop the tissue paper pattern. Using a water-erasable marking pen, trace
designs onto the fabric.

Paint the designs, if desired.
Mount the fabric in a hoop and
embellish with embroidery
stitches, using two strands of
floss and one strand of metallic
thread.

Cut out embroidered fronts
and matching backs.

For the ruffles, cut 1x28-inch
strips from red or green calico
for each ornament. Sew short
ends together to form tube.
continued

Fold

Fold strip in half lengthwise, with wrong sides together. Run a gathering thread ¼ inch from raw edge. Gather and pin strip to fit around the ornament. Sew ruffle to the front.

With right sides facing, sew front to back; leave opening for turning. Clip curve, turn, and stuff lightly with fiberfill; sew opening closed. Attach monofilament or ribbon loops for hangers.

---❖---

CHRISTMAS DOLL

Shown on page 156.
Finished doll is 16 inches tall.

MATERIALS
For the doll
⅓ yard of off-white T-shirt knit fabric
One 25-mm wooden bead
White carpet thread
DMC embroidery floss in black, blue, and peach
Approximately 77 yards of tapestry yarn, or a similar substitute
Fiberfill; long needle
Powdered rouge; white glue
Tissue paper
For the clothing
½ yard of print flannel
Scrap of white flannel (bodice)
12-inch square of white cotton (cap)
1 package *each* of red and white baby rickrack
1¼ yards of ¾-inch-wide pregathered eyelet
4 tiny buttons; 3 snaps
13 inches of ⅜-inch-wide elastic
Elastic thread; cardboard
2 white pom-poms (slippers)
Red and gray felt squares
White glue

INSTRUCTIONS
Use ¼-inch seams throughout, unless otherwise indicated. Trace full-size patterns, pages 170 and 171, onto tissue paper; cut out.

For the doll
BODY AND LEGS: Trace body pattern onto *double* thickness of knit fabric. Stitch on line, leaving top and bottom open; restitch the seam for added strength. Trim the seam and clip curves. Leave body wrong side out.

Draw around leg pattern on double thickness of knit. Sew on line, leaving top and bottom opening; also leave an opening in the back seam. End stitching at the dots on the bottom of the foot. Trim seam. Cut out foot sole; baste and stitch to bottom of foot, matching dots. Turn. Make two legs.

Slip legs into body, feet first, lining up raw edges of legs and bottom of body. Pin, then sew across bottom edge of body, encasing legs in seam. Turn.

Stuff hands and arms to dotted line indicated on pattern (shoulder). Sew through body along line. Continue to stuff the body and neck, adding extra stuffing to tummy and buttocks area.

Using a double strand of carpet thread, sew finger divisions. Turn under raw edges of neck ¼ inch; baste.

Working through the opening in the back seam, stuff feet and legs firmly. Sew leg openings closed. Using carpet thread, gather each ankle. Begin at the center front seam and work around to one side (see dotted line on pattern), then back to the center front and along the opposite side of the ankle. Pull gathers to form the ankle; secure the thread end in the seam.

HEAD: On *single* thickness of knit, draw around pattern. Stitch on line. Do not cut out. Draw eyes and mouth on fabric.

Embroider the face, using two strands of black floss to outline-stitch around the eyebrows and eyes. Satin-stitch the eyes, making black pupils and blue irises; work white French knots for the highlights. Using one strand of black floss, embroider straight stitches for eyelashes.

Place head front atop knit fabric, right sides facing. Sew on the previously stitched line, leaving top section open for turning. Trim, turn, and stuff.

If the wooden bead has a hole in it, place stuffing in the hole; wrap a bit of fiberfill over the top of the bead.

To shape the nose, slip bead into the head, placing it in the nose position. Apply glue to back of bead, using a long skewer. Sew opening in head closed.

Using three strands of peach floss, insert needle from back of head to front; bring needle out at corner of mouth. Outline-stitch along mouth line. Tie off thread by pushing the needle to the back of the head and knotting it.

Using one strand of black floss, sew two tiny stitches under bead nose for nostrils.

TO ASSEMBLE HEAD AND BODY: Pin neck to back of head where indicated on the pattern. Hand-sew bottom of neck to head. If necessary, add more stuffing to neck before stitching top of neck to head.

HAIR: Cut six strands of yarn, each 64 inches long; lay strands together. Fold strands in half and slip a pencil through the looped end. In one hand, hold the loose ends firmly and tautly. With the other hand, twist the pencil clockwise, so strands of yarn twist around each other.

When the yarn is tightly twisted, bring the loose ends up to the pencil end so the two halves of yarn wrap around each other. Remove the pencil and tie a short length of yarn around the end, 3 inches from the end. Cut the loops at this end only, to match the rest of the loose ends.

Following the steps above, make seven skeins.

Pin five skeins across top of head on seam between Xs on pattern. Allow loose ends to hang over face for bangs. Sew five skeins in place, using one strand of yarn. To make a curl, tie two fat knots, about 1 inch apart, in each of the bundles. Tack knots to head.

Tack looped ends of remaining two skeins to the center top of head across the bangs. Allow each skein to hang down on both sides of the face. Tie two knots in each skein, allowing the loose ends to remain free. Tack knots to side of face. Tie ribbons around the loose ends. Trim bangs.

Powder cheeks, knees, and hands with rouge.

For the clothing
BODICE: Cut bodice front and back from white flannel. Stitch the shoulder seams. Sew rickrack and eyelet trim down both sides of center front.

SLEEVES: Cut two 6x12-inch rectangles from flannel. Pin sleeve to armhole, gathering between dots on armhole; sew. Turn under raw edge of sleeve. Zigzag-stitch elastic thread on wrong side of sleeve, ½ inch from edge. Pull ends of elastic to fit wrist. Sew side seam and sleeve, catching ends of elastic in seam.

Turn under 1/8 inch on raw edge of center backs; stitch. Fold back each side 1/2 inch; press.

NECKBAND: Cut a 2x11-inch strip of flannel. With right sides facing, pin band around neck, allowing about 1/2 inch to extend beyond each corner of neck; sew. Fold short ends in; fold band in half twice. Sew in place.

SKIRT: Cut 8x36-inch piece of print flannel. Join short ends (1/2-inch seam), stopping 1/2 inch from the top. Press open. Gather top edge to fit bodice, matching seam to the center back edges. (Front is shorter than back.) Sew skirt to bodice.

Topstitch red baby rickrack around waist. Hem skirt. Sew snaps to back opening and buttons down center front. Tack rickrack bow at waist.

CAP: Cut a 10 1/2-inch-diameter circle from white cotton fabric. Turn under 1/8 inch on raw edges; stitch. Sew eyelet atop the edge. Using elastic thread, gather 1 inch from the outside edge of eyelet. Gather circle to fit around head; secure.

PANTALOONS: Enlarge the pattern on page 171, and cut from fabric. Join two pantaloon legs at center front and center back. Turn under raw edge on leg bottoms. On wrong side, zigzag-stitch over elastic thread, 1/2 inch from bottom edge of leg. Pull elastic to fit leg. Repeat for other leg.

Stitch front and back inside leg seams, catching ends of elastic in seam. Turn under 1/2 inch on top edge; stitch, leaving a 1-inch opening. Run 3/8-inch

elastic through casing. Overlap ends of elastic 1/2 inch; sew together. Sew opening closed.

SLIPPERS: Cut soles from cardboard. Glue gray felt sole to one side of cardboard sole. Cut slipper top from red felt. Place cardboard sole, gray side down, atop slipper top. Match center fronts. Extend 1/4 inch of slipper top over cardboard side of sole; glue. Add rickrack to slipper top. Cut out red felt sole; glue to bottom of cardboard sole. Attach pom-pom.

❖

DOLL BED COVERLET AND PILLOWS

Shown on page 156.

MATERIALS
1x11 3/4 x19 3/4-inch piece of foam (mattress)
Sewing thread
For the fitted sheet
20x27 3/4-inch piece of striped fabric
For the dust ruffle
13x21 1/4-inch piece of white fabric
1 1/4 yards of 4 1/2-inch-wide pregathered eyelet
For the top sheet
25 1/4x26 3/4-inch piece of red flannel
For the square pillow
6x6-inch piece of green fabric
22 inches of decorative piping
Green DMC floss (tassel)
Polyester fiberfill
For the bed pillow and pillowcase
1/4 yard of pinstripe fabric; fiberfill
17x24-inch piece of white fabric
17 inches *each* of piping and 1-inch-wide eyelet

For the coverlet
1/2 yard *each* of red, green, and yellow calico
18 1/2x24 1/2-inch piece of white fabric (lining)
Two 18 1/2x24 1/2-inch pieces of batting
Yellow DMC embroidery floss

INSTRUCTIONS
For the fitted sheet
Fold the corner of the striped rectangle on the diagonal, right sides facing, so that one short side meets one long side. On the folded edge, measure 5 3/4 inches from the folded corner point. From that point stitch 1 inch toward raw edges, then diagonally for 3 1/4 inches, stopping 3/4 inch from the edge and 6 1/4 inches from corner. Turn under 3/8 inch twice for hem.

For the dust ruffle
Turn under 1/4 inch, then 3/8 inch on short sides of white fabric; stitch.

Cut the eyelet into two 21-inch lengths. Turn under 1/4 inch twice on each end of the eyelet and hem.

Sew eyelet to the long sides of the dust ruffle, using a 5/8-inch-wide seam.

For the top sheet
For the long sides, turn under 1/4 inch, then 3/8 inch; stitch. For the bottom hem, turn under 1/4 inch, then 3/4 inch; stitch. For the top hem, turn under 1/4 inch and then 1 1/2 inches; stitch.

For the square pillow
Stitch piping to the right side of one square. With right sides facing, stitch the squares together, leaving an opening for

turning. Trim seams, turn, and stuff. Slip-stitch the opening closed.

Make a tassel 3 1/2 inches long from embroidery floss; attach to corner of the pillow.

For the bed pillow
Cut two 8x12-inch pieces of pinstripe fabric. Using 1/2-inch seams, sew together with right sides facing; leave opening for turning.

Trim seams, turn, and stuff. Sew opening closed.

For the pillowcase
Baste piping and lace together; trim seam to 1/4 inch.

Fold white fabric in half, with right sides facing (12x17 inches); slip piping/lace piece inside fold, with raw edge of piping/lace piece meeting fold. Sew 1/4 inch from the folded edge; turn.

Fold pillow in half, *wrong* sides facing; match piping/lace edges. Stitch, using a 1/4-inch seam allowance; turn.

With *right* sides facing, stitch 1/4 inch from previous seamline. Sew the end seam, trim, and turn.

For the coverlet
Cut calico fabrics into 3 1/2-inch squares (this measurement includes 1/2-inch seam allowance). Cut 48 squares.

Stitch squares together, assembling eight rows with six squares in each row.

Place coverlet top, right side up, atop two layers of quilt batting. Place right side of lining atop coverlet. Stitch together, using 1/4-inch seams; leave an opening for turning. Trim and turn; sew opening closed.

Tie at the corners of each square, using six strands of embroidery floss.

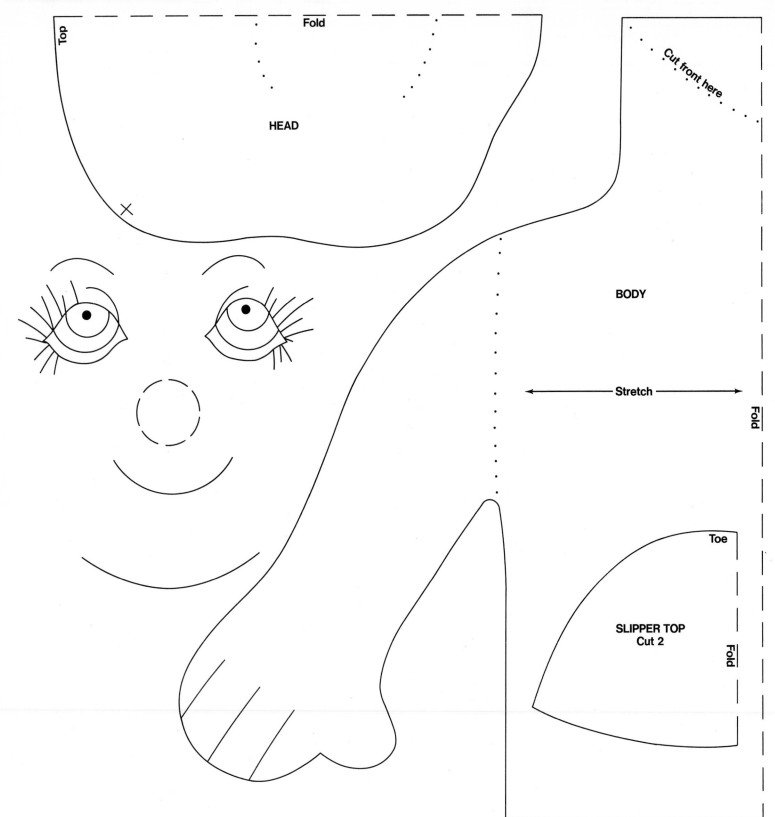

Top

Fold

Cut front here

HEAD

BODY

Stretch

Fold

Toe

SLIPPER TOP
Cut 2

Fold

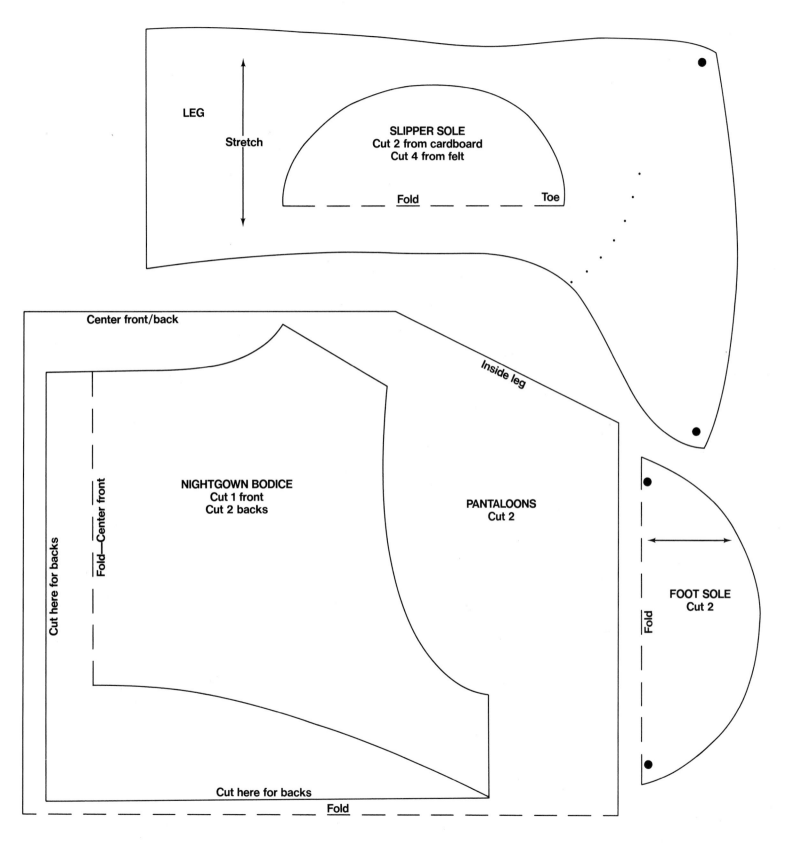

LEG

Stretch

SLIPPER SOLE
Cut 2 from cardboard
Cut 4 from felt

Fold

Toe

Center front/back

Inside leg

Cut here for backs

Fold—Center front

NIGHTGOWN BODICE
Cut 1 front
Cut 2 backs

PANTALOONS
Cut 2

Fold

FOOT SOLE
Cut 2

Cut here for backs

Fold

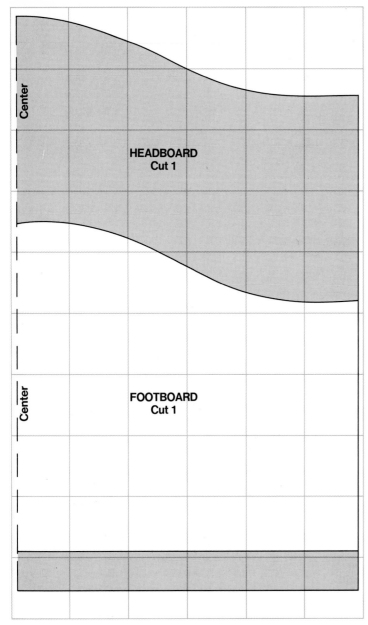

Center

HEADBOARD
Cut 1

Center

FOOTBOARD
Cut 1

1 Square = 1 Inch

Headboard

¼"×½" Groove

Closet pole

⁹⁄₁₆" Fir filler strip

60°

Mattress frame

Finishing nail

1¼" No. 6
Wood screw

❖

DOLL BED

Shown on page 156.
Finished size is 11⅞x21⅜ inches.

MATERIALS
Two 8¾-inch and two 13-inch
 closet poles (bedposts)
Four 2-inch-diameter finials
 (bedpost tops)
¼-inch hardboard in the
 following dimensions: One
 12×20-inch rectangle
 (mattress rest); one
 9⅜×11⅝-inch rectangle
 (headboard); one
 5¼×11⅝-inch rectangle
 (footboard)
Two 10½-inch and two 20-
 inch lengths of 1x2-inch
 pine (mattress frame)
Two ⁹⁄₁₆x1½x11⅛-inch fir
 fillers (frame)
Four ¼x⅝-inch fir fillers in
 lengths to fit (posts)
Table saw; low-angle block
 plane; finishing nails
No. 6 wood screws
Brads; wood glue
Wood putty
Red high-gloss enamel

INSTRUCTIONS
Cut the ¼ × ½-inch groove
in the closet pole before cutting
pole into required lengths. Enlarge and transfer the patterns
for the footboard and headboard, *left*, onto ¼-inch hardboard; cut out.

Glue pieces into the grooves,
3 inches from the ends. Allow
to dry while assembling the
mattress frame with finishing
nails and glue.

Attach the hardboard mat-
tress rest to the frame with
brads and glue. Shape the
frame filler pieces from a 2-foot
piece of 1×2 by planing it
down to ⁹⁄₁₆ inch thick. Cut the
pieces to finished length with a
60-degree miter at each end.
Center and attach these to the
foot and headboard parts of the
mattress frame.

Align the bottom of the mattress frame with the bottom of
the headboard; attach frame to
headboard with three 1¼-inch,
No. 6 wood screws and glue.
Screw through the inside of the
mattress frame. Attach the footboard the same as the headboard. Cut filler pieces for the

exposed grooves in closet pole; glue in place. Fill cracks around filler pieces with wood putty.

Set nails, fill holes, and then sand all surfaces smooth. Attach finials to pole tops with glue, and paint the bed with high-gloss enamel.

---❖---

EMBROIDERED PILLOW

Shown on page 157.
Finished size, excluding border and ruffle, is 15¾x20 inches.

MATERIALS
¾ yard of white fabric (front, backing); embroidery floss in red, green, and yellow
¼ yard of green fabric
⅞ yard of red pindot (ruffle)
2½ yards of yellow piping
Embroidery hoop and needle
Dressmaker's carbon paper
Tissue paper
Polyester fiberfill

INSTRUCTIONS
Enlarge pattern, page 164, onto tissue paper. Transfer pattern, centered, onto a 22x26-inch piece of white fabric.

EMBROIDERY: Using three strands of floss, refer to photograph and work outline stitches. Using red and green floss, work running stitches, cross-stitches, straight stitches, and French knots as desired on coverlet. Use satin stitches on holly berries (red), stars (yellow), and flower centers (red or green).

ASSEMBLY: Trim piece to 16¾x21 inches. All measurements include ½-inch seams.

For the border strips, cut two 2½x22-inch and two 2½x26-inch strips from green fabric.

Sew strips to pillow, mitering corners; trim and press. Sew yellow piping in place.

Cut rectangle from the white fabric for the backing to match the pillow top.

For the ruffle, cut four 7x40-inch strips from red pindot fabric; sew short ends together to form a tube. Fold tube in half, wrong sides facing and matching raw edges; baste the edges together. Gather ruffle to fit pillow; sew in place.

Sew pillow front to pillow back, leaving an opening for turning. Trim seams, clip, and turn. Stuff with fiberfill and sew opening closed.

---❖---

TEDDY BEARS

Shown on pages 156–157.
Large bear is 21 inches tall; small bear is 9 inches tall.

MATERIALS
For the large star-face bear
¾ yard of baby-wale brown corduroy
1 square of pink felt (inner ears, cheeks, hand and foot pads)
Felt scraps in tan (outer eye, nose) and brown (inner eye)
Embroidery floss in tan and white; polyester fiberfill
Beanbag pellets
Tissue paper; dental floss
1½ yards of 1-inch-wide ribbon
For the small bear
¼ yard of baby-wale brown corduroy
Scrap of pink fabric (inner ears)
Black felt scrap (nose)
Black beads (eyes)
Black embroidery floss
Polyester fiberfill
Beanbag pellets

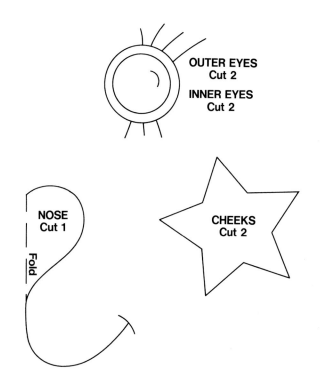

INSTRUCTIONS
Patterns for the bears are on pages 174 and 175. For the small bear, trace the patterns; for the large bear, enlarge the patterns onto tissue paper.

Cut patterns from fabrics as indicated in materials list.

All of the patterns include ¼-inch seam allowance unless otherwise noted. Sew all seams twice, using small stitches and with right sides facing. Use dental floss to sew openings closed and to sew head and limbs to body.

BODY: Sew center fronts together, then center backs; clip curves. Sew front to back at sides.

Sew base to body, matching sides and center; clip and turn. Set aside. For small bear, stuff body.

ARMS: *For large bear,* topstitch hand pads to arms, reversing placement. Sew arms together in pairs, leaving tops open; clip and turn. Stuff, leaving tops of arms unstuffed. Sew the arms to neck sides, matching the raw edges. Stuff the body with pellets, leaving an empty space at body top.

For small bear, sew arms as for large bear except do not add the hand pads. Attach to body neck as directed for large bear.

HEAD: Sew center backs together. Sew front darts; trim. Sew forehead to each head side from A to B. Then sew center fronts together from B to C. Sew front to back; clip, turn, and stuff. Use floss to hand-sew across base of head, holding stuffing in place.

LEGS: *For large bear,* topstitch edge of pads to leg backs, reversing placement.

For both bears, sew darts; clip instep dart and trim remaining darts. Layer legs together in pairs, with leg front on top. Sew from A to B. Break stitching, fold darts toward leg top; sew from C to D. Break stitching
continued

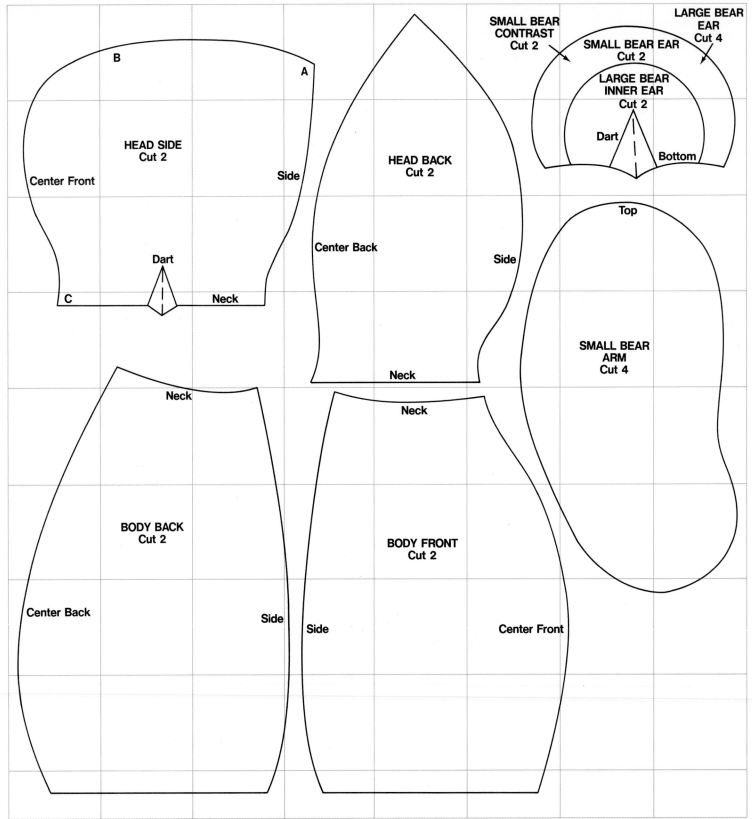

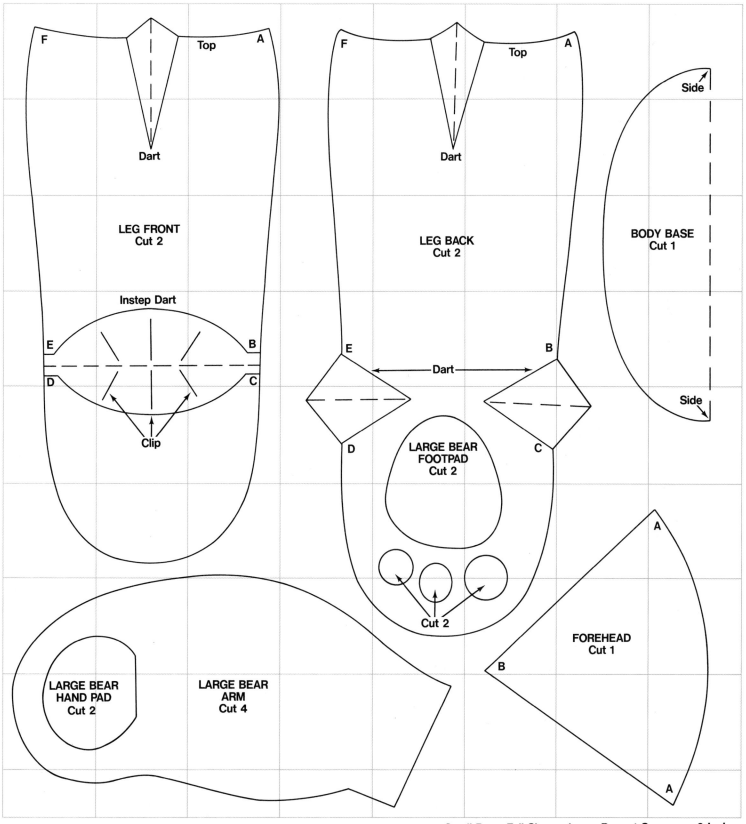

LEG FRONT
Cut 2

F Top A

Dart

Instep Dart

E B

D C

Clip

LEG BACK
Cut 2

F Top A

Dart

E B

Dart

D C

LARGE BEAR
FOOTPAD
Cut 2

Cut 2

BODY BASE
Cut 1

Side

Side

FOREHEAD
Cut 1

A

B

A

LARGE BEAR
HAND PAD
Cut 2

LARGE BEAR
ARM
Cut 4

Small Bear: Full Size   Large Bear: 1 Square = 2 Inches

175

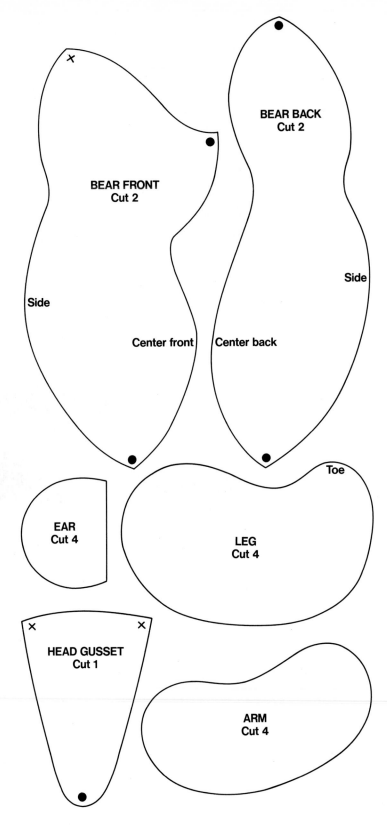

again; fold darts toward toe. Sew from E to F.

Clip, turn, and stuff feet firmly with fiberfill; use pellets for leg tops, allowing an empty space at the tops. Turn raw edges in and whipstitch closed. Sew legs to front of body base.

EARS: *For large bear,* topstitch edge of inner ears to ears.

For small bear, cut two ears from pink fabric (inner ear), and assemble same as outer ear: Sew darts; trim. Sew together in pairs, leaving bottoms open; clip, turn, and stuff lightly. Turn raw edges in and whipstitch closed; sew to head.

FACE: *For large bear,* handsew eyes, nose, and cheeks to face. Use three strands of floss to chain-stitch smile, straightstitch eyelashes, and outlinestitch eyebrows.

For small bear, sew bead eyes and oval felt nose in place. Embroider the smile using black straight stitches. Tie ribbon into bow around neck.

MINIATURE TEDDY BEARS

Shown on pages 158–159. Finished bear is 3½ inches tall.

MATERIALS
Scraps of red and brown
   calico fabrics
Polyester fiberfill
Black beads (for eyes)
Black **DMC** embroidery floss

INSTRUCTIONS
Trace full-size pattern, *left,* onto tissue paper. (*Note:* Pattern includes ¼-inch seam allowances.)

With right sides facing, pin body fronts together and sew center front seam between dots; repeat for body back. With right sides facing, sew head gusset to head from top of head (at X) to nose (at dot). Repeat on opposite side of head. Sew body side seams, leaving opening on one side for stuffing. Clip curves, turn, and stuff. Stitch opening closed.

Sew legs together in pairs, right sides facing, leaving opening for turning. Clip curves, turn, and stuff. Stitch opening closed. Sew to body. Follow same procedure for the arms.

With right sides facing, and leaving bottoms open, sew ears together; turn. Turn under raw edges and slip-stitch closed. Attach ears to head.

Sew on bead eyes. Use two strands of embroidery floss to satin-stitch the nose and work straight stitches for mouth.

WOODEN ADVENT CALENDAR

Shown on pages 158–159. Calendar measures 1³⁄₁₆x1⅞x42 inches.

MATERIALS
One 13-foot lattice strip,
   1³16x ¼ inches
24 brass upholstery nails
2 picture hangers
2 squares of white felt; scraps
   of green felt
Red adhesive-back numbers
   (½ inch tall) and letters (1
   inch tall); red acrylic paint
Spackling compound

INSTRUCTIONS

Cut three strips of lattice, *each* 42 inches long. From remaining lattice, cut 24 divider strips, *each* 1⅛ inches long.

Using wood glue, affix two of the 42-inch strips (top and bottom) to the outside edge of the third strip (back) and a divider strip to each end to create a long horizontal box. Allow to set and dry. Fill in corners with spackling compound and allow to dry. Sand smoothly; paint box using red acrylic.

Fill in the front edge of each divider strip with spackling compound; allow to dry; sand. Paint each divider red.

Divide and mark off 1¾-inch intervals along top edge of box. Using wood glue, affix the 22 divider strips to inside of box at these intervals.

Paint entire box with glossy polyurethane; allow to dry.

Hammer 24 brass nails to top of box, centering a nail over each section, ⅜ inch from front edge. (*Note:* If the nails are too long, set the nail first, then remove it; clip off end to make nail shorter, then hammer nail into initial starting hole.)

Attach the picture hangers to back of box approximately 3 inches in from each edge.

Trace pattern, *right;* cut out 24 white felt flaps; transfer designs to flaps. With green thread, add a decorative machine-stitch around the outside edge of each flap. Press straight edge up ½ inch and cut a small slit in top of flap as indicated on the pattern.

Apply the adhesive numbers to each flap, ¾ inch from folded edge.

Apply adhesive letters to the underside of each flap to spell

MERRY CHRISTMAS TO YOU, skipping flaps 1, 7, 17, 20, and 24. Cut holly from green felt; using white glue, apply to these flaps. Add berries cut from adhesive scraps.

Apply white glue to flaps along top ½ inch; affix to bottom edge of box. Fill each of the 24 sections with miniatures or small candy. Cover each section by slipping slit of flap over the brass nail.

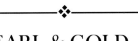

PEARL & GOLD BEAD BALLS

Shown on page 160.
Finished ornaments are 4¾ inches in diameter.

MATERIALS

2- or 3-inch-diameter plastic foam balls; white glue for plastic foam; hangers
5-mm metallic gold or white pearl prestrung beads (two 60-inch strings of beads cover one ball)

INSTRUCTIONS

Spread white glue over half of one ball. Pull the slack from the prestrung beads; apply the beads to the glued area in a spiral fashion. Pin the beads in place.

Prop the ornament up on a small jar until it is dry. Invert ornament and apply glue to the remaining half. Repeat beading process.

Trim the ends of the bead string; tuck the end in and glue in place. Insert an ornament hanger.

BEADED SNOWFLAKE ORNAMENTS

Shown on page 161.
Finished ornament is 4½ inches in diameter.

MATERIALS

8x8-inch squares of 14-count Aida cloth in assorted colors (1 for *each* ornament)
White glass beads
Beading needle
Embroidery floss in colors to match fabric
Embroidery hoop
Masking tape
White backing fabric
15 inches of white piping (trim)
Polyester fiberfill
⅛-inch-wide white satin ribbon
Graph paper
Dressmaker's carbon paper
Tissue paper

INSTRUCTIONS

Chart pattern, *below*, onto graph paper. Chart shows one fourth of the design. Flop the design three times to complete the mirror image in the remaining three quadrants.

Tape the raw edges of the fabric with masking tape to prevent raveling. Locate the center of the pattern and the center of the Aida cloth.

From the center point, begin working half cross-stitches using a beading needle and a single strand of floss (floss color should match fabric). Pull the thread up through the fabric, insert bead on needle, then reinsert needle into the fabric to complete half cross-stitch.

After stitching, use a compass to draw a circle with a radius of 2¼ inches onto tissue paper. Center tissue atop wrong side of stitchery; transfer the circle using dressmaker's carbon. Add ½-inch seams.

Cut out the stitchery and a matching back from white fabric. Sew piping to stitchery. Sew front to back, right sides facing; leave an opening for turning. Trim and clip the seam allowance every ⅛ inch; turn. Press, stuff lightly, then slip-stitch the opening. Attach a ribbon loop for a hanger.

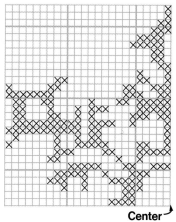

Center
1 Square = 1 Stitch

CROSS-STITCH ORNAMENTS

Shown on page 162.
Finished ornaments are 3¼ inches in diameter, excluding edging.

MATERIALS

White hardanger
DMC embroidery floss as follows: dark green, No. 937; medium green, No. 470; light green, No. 472; red, No. 606; dark blue-violet, No. 792; medium blue-violet, No. 793; light blue-violet, No. 794; light yellow, No. 744; dark yellow, No. 742; navy, No. 939; cream, No. 712; ecru, No. 543; beige, No. 950; and white
Embroidery hoop and needle
11 inches *each* of narrow cording (piping) and ½-inch-wide lace for each ornament
Red fabric (backing and piping)
Polyester fiberfill
Tissue paper; compass; graph paper
Felt-tip markers; dressmaker's carbon

INSTRUCTIONS

Transfer the chart, *right,* onto graph paper using felt-tip markers, if desired.

Use one strand of floss to work cross-stitches over one thread of hardanger.

Using a compass, draw a circle with a radius of 1⅝ inches onto tissue paper. Center pattern atop wrong side of stitchery; transfer pattern to stitchery using dressmaker's carbon paper. Add ½-inch seams. Cut out the embroidery and a

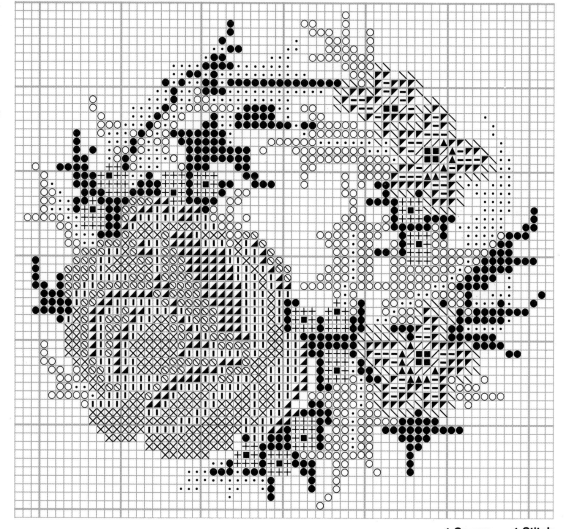

1 Square = 1 Stitch

COLOR KEY

◉	Dark Green	⊘	Light Yellow
⊡	Medium Green	▲	Dark Yellow
◎	Light Green	▣	Navy
⊞	Red	◪	Cream
⊟	Dark Blue-Violet	①	Ecru
◩	Medium Blue-Violet	⊠	Beige
◫	Light Blue-Violet	⊗	White

a matching back (red fabric). Cover piping with red fabric.

Sew piping and lace to stitchery. Sew front to back, right sides together; leave opening. Trim and clip seam; turn. Press; stuff. Sew opening closed. Attach monofilament loop.

❖

FOIL ROSE ORNAMENTS

Shown on page 162.

MATERIALS
For one rose
One 4x8-inch sheet *each* of gold and silver Cindus foil, one 8x9-inch sheet *each* of gold and silver Sophisticrepe, and 1 yard of ½-inch-wide silver Sophisticrepe (available from Cindus Corp., 515 Station Ave., Cincinnati, OH 45215)

22 inches of 20-gauge stem wire; fine wire

Spray adhesive; tacky glue

INSTRUCTIONS
Trace the patterns for the leaf and petal, *below*.

Spray the *wrong* side of silver and gold Sophisticrepe with adhesive; fuse together.

FOR THE ROSE: With the grain running from point to base, cut out nine petals. To shape each petal, stretch the center to form a "cup"; curl each side of tip outward. (*Note:* When assembling the rose, make four inner petals with silver facing inward; reverse for the five outer petals.)

Cut a 6-inch piece of stem wire; roll the base of one petal around one end; bind tightly with fine wire. Wrap the second petal around the first.

For each of the remaining petals, make a tiny pleat at the bottom to prevent the foil from tearing. Bind the petals evenly around the base, securing each petal with fine wire. Set the petals aside.

FOR THE LEAVES: Cut three leaf bottoms from silver foil paper and three leaf tops from gold. Cut an 8-inch piece of stem wire.

Make the first leaf by spraying the wrong sides of the gold top and the silver bottom with adhesive. Lay one end of stem wire down the entire center on the wrong side of the silver leaf. Affix to the gold top.

Cut two 4-inch pieces of stem wire. Attach a leaf to each as before; set aside.

TO FINISH: Glue one end of the ½-inch-wide strip of silver Sophisticrepe to the base of the rose. Wrap the stem; cut off any excess. Glue the end and set rose aside.

On the long leaf stem, glue one end of the silver Sophisticrepe strip near the base of the leaf; wrap the stem 1 inch, then lay the stems of the remaining leaves alongside the main stem. Continue wrapping the stems for 2 inches.

Place the leaf stem alongside the rose stem; continue wrapping to the end. Cut off the excess and secure end with glue. Shape stem as desired. Use to decorate gifts or place in tree.

VICTORIAN HEARTS

Shown on page 163.
Hearts are approximately
3 inches across.

MATERIALS
Velveteen fabric scraps in a variety of deep colors
Assorted silk flowers and leaves
1 yard of ⅛-inch-wide gold metallic ribbon
Polyester fiberfill
Thread
Fabric glue
Heavy paper

INSTRUCTIONS
Draw a heart pattern about 3 inches wide, adding ¼ inch for seam allowances.

Cut the heart front and back from a velvet scrap. Stitch the front and back together with right sides facing, leaving an opening for turning. Clip seam; turn. Stuff with fiberfill. Blindstitch the opening closed.

Glue a ribbon around the heart edge; using 10 inches of ribbon, make a large loop at the top of the heart for a hanger; secure in place. Then add four smaller loops using 2 inches of ribbon for each loop; secure in place. Curl the long free ends of the remaining ribbon over a scissor blade.

To finish, glue assorted flowers and leaves onto the heart as desired.

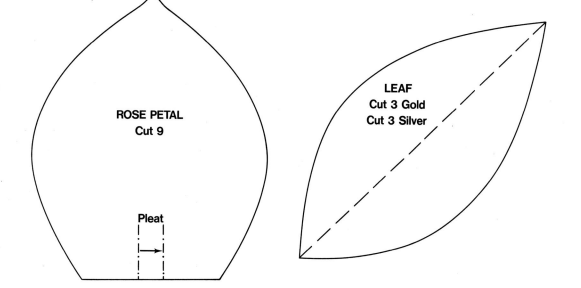

ROSE PETAL
Cut 9

Pleat

LEAF
Cut 3 Gold
Cut 3 Silver

PACKAGING

Making bazaar offerings attractive and appealing with a few added touches can effectively boost your sales.

Once bazaar merchandise is ready to sell, you will want to display it so that shoppers take notice. This is especially important at large fund raisers, where there is a lot of competition for sales and patrons' attention is easily diverted. By making your products look special—perhaps just by adding a trim or two—they become more enticing to passersby.

Labeling products

Each item for sale should be individually priced and identified. This prevents confusion at point of sale and provides identification in case items stray from one booth to another.

One way to label merchandise is to use purchased tags. Available in many sizes at office supply outlets, tags come with string attached, ready to be marked and tied to an item. They are sold in bundles and are relatively inexpensive.

You easily can incorporate bookkeeping functions into tagging items. For example, if more than one craftsperson is contributing to sales of an individual booth, tags can include coded information so that profits are divided fairly. Simply add the initials of the craftsperson to the tags.

Or you might add small adhesive-backed dots (with each party assigned a particular color) or adhesive-backed stars to a corner or the reverse side of

the tags. At the time of sale, refer to the code when the transaction is recorded.

Tags may also be handcrafted. Using heavy paper and scissors or a paper cutter, cut out

rectangles. Then, with a paper punch, make a hole in the end or in a corner and thread a length of string, yarn, or ribbon through the hole. Tie the tag onto the merchandise.

For a more interesting or personalized tag, have sheets of paper quick-printed so that the tags can be produced in quantities, cut out, and attached to merchandise using string or yarn. Include your name and an address or telephone number where you can be reached if the customer has an inquiry about your merchandise.

You might want to print a variety of prices to align with the merchandise you have, or leave a percentage of them plain so that prices can be written in. If space permits, add a small drawing or illustration.

Another way to produce eye-catching tags is to use white or colored card stock (such as plain index cards) cut to a variety of sizes. Decorate tags with rubber-stamp illustrations (use purchased stamps or design your own), small drawings, or stickers. (Educators' supply outlets sell many styles of stickers in bulk quantities.)

Wrapping gifts economically

Many bazaar offerings are such natural gift items that providing wrapping makes your merchandise more attractive and salable. If this option is suitable to your merchandise, appoint one or more wrappers to work inside your booth or at another location at the bazaar. Or, join forces with other booth operators and set up a central wrapping area for customers.

Purchase patterned wrapping paper in bulk from paper wholesalers, or use bulk rolls of plain white or colored paper.

You can dress up a plain wrapped package with a variety of trims. Consider adding a plaid ribbon bow or colored cord trim to a brown paper package. Or, affix a small lace doily to a pastel package and trim it with a bow tied from a ribbon scrap.

Look to wholesalers in your area for inexpensive products to use for imaginative trims. Investigate materials that paper suppliers, party goods merchants, and floral supply wholesalers have to offer. Many of these businesses have crea-

tive consultants who might be able to help with packaging ideas and tips.

Providing bags and boxes

Delicate or easily soiled items are best displayed and sold in plastic wraps. For small items such as Christmas ornaments or hand-decorated stationery, use see-through bags; secure packages with adhesive labels indicating the price.

Large-size transparent bags work best with soft, flat items such as apparel or stuffed toys. Seal large bags with tape, or gather the top edge and tie with a ribbon bow.

For bulkier items, paper bags work best. These are available in bulk quantities from wholesalers. Check the Yellow Pages for a supplier near you. Because suppliers may limit orders to large quantities, consider joining forces with other booth operators to get a reasonable number of bags for your use, in sizes suitable for your merchandise.

Boxes intended for smaller gifts are available from stationers or wholesalers. Cartons for large projects can be gathered from grocery stores and stored out of the way until needed. Moving companies also sell heavy-duty cartons for transporting your merchandise to and from the bazaar.

Keep a stack of newspapers handy to cushion merchandise in bags and boxes.

The expense of wrappings and other packaging efforts is part of your overhead. Incorporate these packaging expenses into the purchase price for each item or add an extra charge for a gift-wrapped box.

Organizing your space

How packaged materials are displayed depends in large part on the type of merchandise you have.

If you have many similar items, such as dozens of crocheted snowflakes or simple wooden toys, keep the bulk of the merchandise out of sight or away from the hands of shoppers. Display this extra merchandise at the back of the booth (either hanging or on shelves) or store it beneath tables or counters to keep it fresh and clean for those who ultimately purchase it.

If you have many kinds of items for sale, but only one or two of each, you'll want at least one of the items on display at all times. When planning booth space, allow for display of these types of items. For example, a stack of sturdy cartons, each painted and with one end left open, makes for good display, and the cartons are useful for transporting goods and equipment as well.

Any bazaar merchandise available only by special order, such as a quilt or beautifully dressed doll, should be prominently displayed along with fabrics or styling options for customers to see.

Building a booth

Some of the simplest bazaar booths are nothing more than tables set up in rows. Churches and schools often have a supply of folding tables. Additional tables are available from local rental agencies.

Or, you can make inexpensive portable table space from everyday materials. Begin with bases for tabletops; use sawhorses, wooden crates, or

inverted garbage cans. Bases made from containers such as garbage cans or boxes can also double as containers for merchandise and supplies. Top the bases with planks placed side by side, pieces of plywood, or hollow-core doors.

Make display space attractive (and provide concealed storage) by draping tables with fabric. Felt is a good choice for draping and backgrounds because it requires no sewing to finish edges, and it is inexpensive, comes in many colors, and is available in 72-inch widths from larger fabric stores. To prevent creasing, roll up the felt when it's not in use.

PACKAGING

Our collection of special wraps turns the simple paper bags and boxes you can find anywhere into party-style packages.

Plain brown bags can be transformed into country wraps, *above*, with the addition of paper doilies, lace, dried flowers, and ribbons. The tag on the rabbit features a simple motif that reflects the theme of a country sale. Photocopy this design (or another from pages 184 and 185) to embellish tags for your booth or handbills for your bazaar.

Glazed bags, *right*, lend themselves to sprinkles of glitter, stickers, or novelty closures such as pencils or candy sticks.

For Christmas bazaars, decorate boxes and bags with holiday greetings in metallic adhesive letters, *opposite*, glitter, and other symbols of the season.

Instructions for these projects begin on page 184.

COUNTRY GIFT BAGS

Shown on page 182.

MATERIALS
Brown lunch bags
Scraps of eyelet lace and ribbon
Paper doilies
Nylon net
Potpourri

INSTRUCTIONS

LACE TRIMS: Trim about ¾ inch from top and sides of a lunch bag; remaining long front edge is to be trimmed with lace. Cut eyelet (or other type of lace or trim) to 1 inch longer than width of bag. Pin to paper bag along front edge, turning ends under ½ inch at each side. Machine-stitch.

SACHET TRIMS: Cut a 10- to 12-inch-diameter circle of nylon net. (Use a dinner plate for a pattern.) Pour about ⅓ cup of potpourri on center of net. Gather net and secure potpourri in center with a ribbon; tie into bow. Fold over edges of bag and staple or pin sachet to front.

PAPER-DOILY TRIMS: Fold over paper bag to close. Fold a 5-inch-diameter paper doily over the edge so that about two-thirds of the doily falls to the front. Staple closed. Trim with a bow.

Cut off corners of square or rectangular doilies; complete as for bags with round doilies.

GIFT TAGS

Shown on page 182.

MATERIALS
Typing paper
Paper cement
Paper punch
Scraps of ribbon or cord

INSTRUCTIONS

Use illustrations, *right* and *opposite*. Make a photocopy of page to use as a master; use as good a copier as is available so that subsequent reproductions are sharp.

Reduce illustrations on a reducing photocopier to desired size for gift tags. It may be necessary to make one reduction and then reduce it again.

Position illustrations on a sheet of typing paper, leaving enough space in between for trimming designs and folding them to create small cards. Have the page printed at a local quick-print shop.

Cut out tags; punch a hole in corner and thread with cord.

KIDS' GIFT PACKAGES

Shown on pages 182–183.

MATERIALS
Glazed paper bags in assorted colors, with or without handles
Stick candy
Pencils with novelty trims
White glue; tisssue paper
Glitter in assorted colors

INSTRUCTIONS

GLITTER BAGS: Lay out bag on newspaper or in a shallow box. Drizzle glue onto bag front in an abstract design. Shake glitter onto glue until all glue is covered thoroughly. Let glue set; shake off excess glitter onto newspaper or into box. Return glitter to container.

CANDY AND PENCIL BAGS: Fold over top edge of bag to form a 2½- to 3-inch

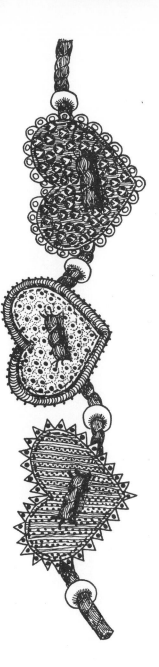

flap. With a sharp knife, make two vertical slits through both flap and bag, about 1½ inches long. Slide candy or pencils through slits to close the bag.

HOLIDAY PACKAGES

Shown on page 183.

MATERIALS
Glazed paper gift bags with or without handles
Glazed cardboard gift boxes
Scraps of ribbon
Metallic paper adhesive letters
Trims for boxes (jingle bells, stickers, candles)
Florist's wire, glue
Metallic glitter, ornament

INSTRUCTIONS

GREETING BOXES: Affix letters on box top to create greeting. Add sticker trims. Glue on ribbon bows or attach jingle bells with florist's wire.

CANDLE-TRIMMED BOXES: Wire together two pairs of hand-dipped candles at the wicks. Wire to top of box; add bow.

GLITTER STAR BAG: Drizzle glue onto front of gift bag into a star shape. Complete as for Kids' Glitter Bags, *left.*

ORNAMENT BAG: Attach ribbon to ornament; tape to inside of bag.

BELL-AND-BOW BAG: Tie a big plaid bow onto bell with clapper. Wire bow and bell to front of glazed paper bag.

SPECIAL TRIMS FOR CHRISTMAS

Simple gifts with mass appeal distinguish what sells best at Christmas bazaars and crafts sales. This chapter offers a variety of holiday gifts, ornaments, and trims that are sure to become favorite items for your group to make and sell year after year.

A booth with a prominent display of the clever sponge-painted trees, *right*, is sure to attract a lot of attention. They're simply cut from scraps of pine and painted with a base coat of acrylic paint. The textured effect is the result of lightly sponging on areas with a subtly contrasting green paint.

The charming Santa Claus figure, also painted with acrylics, is cut from a shape identical to one of the four tree patterns. Both the tree and the Santa shapes can be cut in a variety of sizes.

How-to instructions for projects in this chapter begin on page 194.

These bears are simple to make because you need to mix only a few colors of bread dough clay.

With a little practice, even a novice sculptor can style these bread dough bears with personality plus. Each of the bears is a variation of the same design, which begins with shaping the tummy and torso and adding a head, legs, and arms. Miniature props and dough "greenery" (created with a garlic press) complete the ornaments. A paper clip inserted before baking serves as a hanger.

The impact of these Christmas stitchery projects results from bright, bold, and cheerful colors and shapes.

Patchwork triangles pieced with precision make up the tree pillow, *above*, and the place mats, *opposite*, based on the Flying Geese pattern.

The crochet pattern used for the afghan, *above*, makes it predominantly white on one side and red and green on the other.

Put scraps of embroidery floss to economical use and make the counted cross-stitch ornaments, *opposite*.

With
all good
wishes
for
Christmas

May your Christmas be
one you will always prize
With every deed and thought
turned happy-wise............

Victorians take deserved credit for artfully combining elaborate detail, lush textures, and charming sentiment with a marvelous sense of style.

The focal points of this collection of ornaments are an array of antique greeting cards and Victorian-style reproductions.

Sources for the postcard-style greeting card used for the framed ornaments are antique shops specializing in Victoriana or makers of cards reproduced from these illustrations for today's buyers. Either kind may be mounted on stiff paper, and framed with braid- and lace-trimmed paper. Use foam squares to raise the design from the card, creating a shadow-box effect.

Gold metallic paper doilies form the background for the circular ornaments. Accent these with lace-edged circles covered with velvety, red adhesive-back paper. Then layer the circles and glue them together with squares of foam tucked between the elements to add thickness and dimension to the ornament. Add a glossy ribbon loop for hanging.

SPONGE-PAINTED TREES

Shown on pages 186–187.
Finished sizes are 8½, 5⅜, 11¾, and 13¾ inches tall.

MATERIALS
1x12-inch pine scraps
Acrylic paints in a variety of
  greens; brushes; sponges
Jigsaw; paper

INSTRUCTIONS
  Enlarge designs, *opposite* and
right, onto paper (use Santa tree
outline for one design). Transfer to wood and cut out with a
jigsaw. Sand, wipe clean, and
apply two coats of base color.
  Pour contrasting paint into a
bowl; using a sponge, dab paint
on trees.

PAINTED SANTA

Shown on page 187.
Finished size is 8⅝ inches tall.

MATERIALS
Scrap of 1x9-inch pine
Acrylic paints; brushes
Jigsaw; paper

INSTRUCTIONS
  Trace the design, *opposite,*
and transfer it to wood scrap;
cut out with a jigsaw. Sand all
edges smooth, wipe clean, and
paint with acrylics, referring to
photograph for colors.

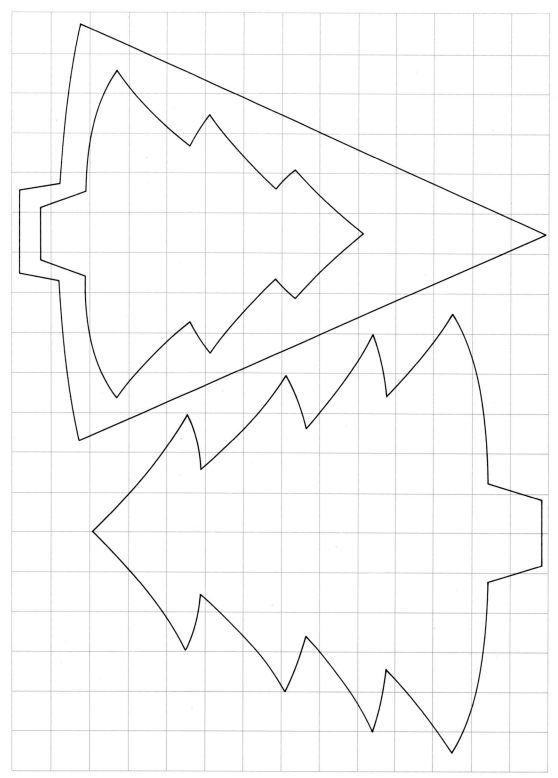

1 Square = 1 Inch

BREAD DOUGH TEDDY BEARS

Shown on pages 188–189. Finished size of bears is approximately 3½ inches tall.

MATERIALS

Paste food coloring in red, green, brown, and black
Red and white acrylic paints
Paper clips; side cutters
Black, red, and white bugle beads; miniatures
Miniature cookie cutters
Garlic press; rolling pin
Waxed paper; plastic bags
Foil; cookie sheet
Crafts knife; table knife
Fimo clay (optional; available in crafts stores)
Fine paint brush; paraffin
Coffee can; hot-glue gun

INSTRUCTIONS

Note: **This project uses hot paraffin. Do not leave melting paraffin unattended.**

TO MAKE BAKER'S CLAY: Knead 2 cups of flour, 1 cup of salt, and 1 cup of cold water until smooth; add water or flour if necessary to form a medium-stiff dough. Separate clay; knead in a small amount of paste food coloring until tint is satisfactory. Put dough in plastic bags to prevent drying.

TO BAKE AND FINISH: After shaping bears (see instructions below), bake until dry (several hours) in a 325° oven.

Following manufacturer's directions, melt wax in a coffee can set in a pan of water. Loop pipe cleaner through wire in bear; dip bear into paraffin. (Wax on bear cools quickly; rub off drips with your hand.)

TO MAKE BEARS: Refer to photograph and shape all bears atop foil same as for Bear with Gingerbread Man; add details to each bear according to specific instructions below. Slightly moisten pieces to join. (*Note:* Fimo clay or bread dough may be used to make miniatures.) For hanger, use side cutters to cut paper clip in half; insert in head. Dry and finish according to the instructions above.

For bear with gingerbread man

Roll red dough to golf ball size (tummy). Flatten one side for back. Roll coil ½ inch thick and 2½ inches long for legs; fold in half and attach under tummy. Turn up ends for feet.

For each arm, roll a coil ½ inch thick and 2 inches long; join to body. Bend up and over the tummy; leave space for gingerbread man. Press in place.

Roll a quarter-size ball for head; join to body. Roll two tiny balls for ears; press on head, indenting centers. Roll tiny brown ball (nose) and tinier black ball (snout); join to head. Add black beads for eyes.

Using miniature cookie cutter, make a medium-size gingerbread man out of light brown dough. Press to middle of the tummy, between paws. (Paint mouth on bear and details on gingerbread man after baking.) Use white beads for pajama buttons. Insert hanger.

For bear holding wreath

Use brown dough for body. Make a green coil ¼ inch thick and 4 inches long; form circle. Place on tummy. Cover with pine needles—short lengths of green dough squeezed through a garlic press.

Cut out tiny red hearts using miniature cookie cutter; place on wreath. Make red bow, cut-

ting and shaping with crafts knife. Press on top of wreath.

For bear holding garland

Make red bow and place on head. Roll a 7-inch-long (¼-inch-diameter) green coil for garland. Drape across bear's tummy with ends on sides of bear. (See photograph.)

Refer to the bear holding wreath for making pine needles; press into garland. Make tiny gingerbread men and hearts using miniature cookie cutters. Press onto garland.

For bear holding stocking

Shape a small ball of red dough into a stocking that is ¼ inch thick and 1 inch long. Insert and rotate end of ballpoint pen to open top of stocking. Insert a small ball of foil to prevent closing while baking.

Make cuff for stocking using white dough; flatten while applying. Make small gingerbread man out of light brown dough; place gently in stocking. (*Note:* After baking, add purchased miniatures of your choice, securing them with the hot-glue gun.)

For Mama bear holding tiny angel bear

Drape body with red dough thinly flattened to 3x6 inches. Gather slightly at neckline. Add collar of white dough, pressing out shape with fingers. Add white beads for buttons.

For slippers, use garlic press to make short lengths of green dough atop feet. Press ovals of green on bottom of feet.

Make angel same as large bear, referring to photograph for scale. Cut elongated ovals in half for wings; flatten and press to dress at sides. Press angel to Mama, between paws.

For sleeping bear

Make the body from green dough. Place a 1-inch square of white dough under bear's head for pillow. Roll out a 4x5-inch piece of red dough for blanket and drape across body, starting under the paw; leave some of the pajamas showing.

Add tiny bear. Place hook in pillow and also in blanket by feet so that ornament will hang horizontally.

For bear holding blanket and small bear

Make body from green clay. Attach red beads for buttons. For blanket, flatten red clay to a 3x4½-inch rectangle. Refer to photograph to join to body.

CHRISTMAS PILLOW

Shown on page 190. Finished size is 14x14 inches, excluding ruffle.

MATERIALS

⅛ yard *each* of green pindot and red cotton fabrics
½ yard of white cotton or muslin
1 yard of ¾-inch-wide white eyelet ruffle
1¾ yards of 1½-inch-wide white eyelet ruffle
Polyester fiberfill or 14-inch-square pillow form
15-inch-square piece of quilt batting; cardboard
Quilt frame; thread
Water-erasable marking pen

INSTRUCTIONS

Use ¼-inch seams throughout. Sew pieces together with right sides facing, unless otherwise indicated.

To begin, transfer the triangle pattern, *below*, onto cardboard for template. Add ¼-inch seam allowance. Cut 21 triangles from green fabric and 15 from white fabric. Following the diagram, *bottom, right,* join triangles into rows along long edges. Press the seams toward green. Sew the rows together, matching the points; press the seams toward green.

Cut two ⅝x14½-inch strips of red fabric; fold in half lengthwise; baste raw edges to long edge of patchwork triangle. Cut the narrow eyelet ruffle into two 14½-inch pieces. Baste one ruffle over red strip, bound edge flush with strip. Stitch and press. Repeat for other side.

Make a template for a triangle with a 12-inch base and 6-inch side (13⅜-inch diagonal). Add ¼-inch seam allowances and cut two from white fabric. Sew to long sides of patchwork "tree." Press seams toward tree. For border, cut red fabric strips 1½ inches wide and long enough to edge entire pillow top. Sew one side at a time; press seams toward red.

Trace pattern for star. Trace three stars on each side of tree on the large white triangles.

Cut batting and white cotton (or muslin) slightly larger than the finished pillow top. Sandwich batting between fabric lay-ers; baste. (Or clamp layers securely in a quilting frame.) Hand-quilt with quilting thread around small triangles and next to border. Quilt stars.

From white fabric, cut pillow back same as top. Baste wider eyelet ruffle to pillow top. Pin backing to pillow top; leave opening for turning. Sew, clip, and turn. Insert pillow form or stuff with fiberfill. Slip-stitch opening closed.

❖

CHRISTMAS AFGHAN

Shown on page 190.
Finished size, excluding border, is approximately 47¾x56½ inches.

MATERIALS
Coats and Clark 4-ply hand-knitting yarn (100-gram skeins): 5 skeins of No. 689 forest green (A), 7 skeins of No. 1 white (B), and 4 skeins of No. 921 vermilion (C)
Size F aluminum crochet hook

Abbreviations: See page 81.
Gauge: With larger needles over dc, 4 sts = 1 inch; 2 rows = 1 inch.

INSTRUCTIONS
Note: To change color, work last yo of last st before color change in new color. Beg with Row 2, when working dc 2 rows below, be sure to draw first lp long enough to finish st at same height as previous st.

With A, ch 193. *Row 1:* Dc in fourth ch from hook, * ch 1, sk 1 ch, dc in next 5 ch. Rep from * across to last 3 ch, ch 1, sk 1 ch, dc in each of next 2 ch, changing to B on last st; ch 3, turn.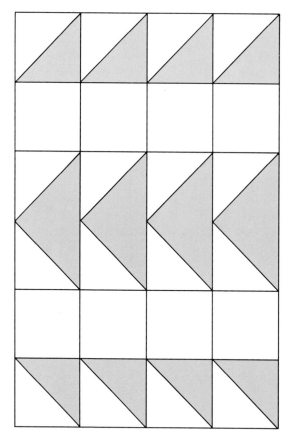

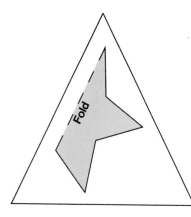

Fold

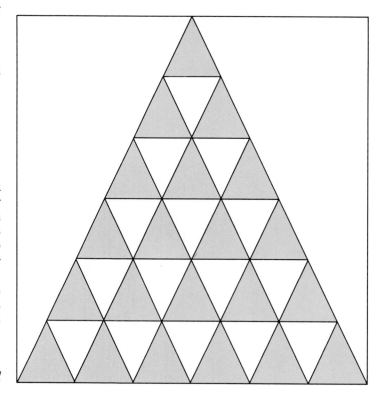

continued

Row 2: Sk first dc, dc in next dc, * working over ch-1 of previous row, dc in ch st 2 rows below (in foundation ch), dc in next 2 dc, ch 1, sk dc, dc in next 2 dc. Rep from * across to last 3 sts (turning ch counts as last st), end working over ch-1 of previous row, dc in ch 2 rows below, dc in next dc, dc in top of turning ch, changing to C in last st; ch 3, turn.

Row 3: Sk first dc, dc in next dc, * ch 1, sk dc, dc in each of next 2 dc, working over ch-1 of last row, dc in dc 2 rows below, dc in each of next 2 dc. Rep from * across to last 3 sts (turning ch counts as last st); ch 1, sk dc, dc in next dc and dc in top of turning ch, changing to B in last st; ch 3, turn.

Row 4: Sk first dc, dc in next dc, * working over ch-1 of last row, dc in dc 2 rows below, dc in each of next 2 dc, ch 1, sk next dc, dc in each of next 2 dc. Rep from * across to last 3 sts; working over ch-1 of last row, dc in dc 2 rows below, work dc in each of last 2 sts, changing to A in last st; ch 3, turn.

Rep rows 3 and 4 for pattern, alternating C and A in Row 3 until total of 113 rows are completed, ending with row worked in A. Fasten off.

BORDER: *Rnd 1:* With right side facing, join A to beg corner sp, ch 1. [Working along side edge, sc in edge of first row, * ch 1, sc in edge of next row. Rep from * along side edge to last row. Work (ch 1, sc, ch 1) in corner, sc in first st of upper edge, ch 1, sk 1 st, ** sc in next st of upper edge, ch 1, sk 1 st. Rep from ** across, ending with sc in last st, (ch 1, sc, ch 1) in corner st.] Rep bet [ ]s for last 2 sides, join with sl st in first ch of rnd. Ch 1.

Rnd 2: Work (sc, ch 1) in each ch-1 sp of previous rnd, work sc, ch 1, sc in each corner st. Join with sl st in ch at beg of rnd. Ch 1.

Rnd 3: Rep Rnd 2, do not ch at end of rnd; fasten off.

PATCHWORK PLACE MATS

Shown on page 191.
Finished size is 12¼x18¼ inches.

MATERIALS
For four place mats
1 yard *each* of white cotton and 44-inch-wide fleece
½ yard *each* of green pindot and red cotton fabrics
1⅛ yards of medium-weight white cotton; cardboard

INSTRUCTIONS
Use ¼-inch seams. Join all pieces with right sides facing, unless otherwise indicated.

For each mat, make the following cardboard templates: a 3-inch square; a triangle equal to half of a 3-inch square (cut diagonally) and a large triangle made from the two triangles *above* (with a 6-inch base and 4¼-inch sides).

For *each* mat, add ¼-inch seam allowances and cut patterns from fabrics as follows: 4 large green triangles, 8 small green triangles, 16 small white triangles, and 8 white squares.

Stitch one small green triangle to a small white triangle along longest edge. Repeat seven more times; press seams toward green side. Stitch longest side of the small white triangle to both sides of the large green triangle. Press toward the green side; repeat three times.

Following the diagram, page 197, *top, right,* sew pieces together to form rows; press. Sew rows together, joining seams carefully; press toward green.

For border, cut strips of red fabric 1 inch wide; sew to edges of mat. Press seams toward red.

Cut piece of fleece the same size as the mat top; baste to the underside of the mat. Machine-quilt layers around the outer edges and triangles. Or quilt by hand, using white quilting thread.

Cut a 12½x18½-inch piece of medium-weight white fabric for backing. Sew to mat top, right sides facing; leave opening. Turn, clip corners, and slip-stitch opening closed; press.

CROSS-STITCH ORNAMENTS

Shown on page 191.

MATERIALS
Scraps of 14- and 18-count white Aida cloth
DMC floss in the following colors and numbers: dark green, No. 699; light green, No. 702; red, No. 666; dark brown, No. 3371; and white
Assorted mini crafts frames
¼-inch-wide grosgrain ribbon

INSTRUCTIONS
Note: Half-cross stitches are shown on color key as one half the symbol for that color. Always work the half-cross stitches perpendicular to the brown backstitching.

Use 18-count Aida and two strands of floss for the tree design; use 14-count Aida and three strands for the remaining designs. Beginning at center of design, work *each* stitch over one thread of fabric. Leave approximately 3 inches of fabric unworked between designs.

For the snowman, work the tassel with red; work the fringe on his scarf with dark green backstitches. Remaining backstitches are worked with brown.

Insert finished designs into frames; trim and tape excess fabric to back.

VICTORIAN PAPER & LACE ORNAMENTS

Shown on pages 192–193.

MATERIALS
6-inch-diameter gold metallic doilies (optional)
Thin cardboard; red adhesive-backed velour paper
¾-inch-wide lace; ⅛-inch-wide satin or metallic ribbon (hangers)
½-inch-thick plastic foam
Old-fashioned Christmas cards and circular gift tags

INSTRUCTIONS
Peel protective backing from velour paper and press atop cardboard. For the round ornament, cut out a 3½-inch-diameter circle from cardboard-backed velour. Turn under ¼ inch on raw edges of short ends of lace. Glue lace to back of circle. Glue red circle to center of gold doily, if desired; attach hanging loop.

Glue a lace-trimmed Christmas card or gift tag atop foam; glue to red circle. Trim with gold braid if desired.

For the rectangle ornament, cut a rectangle from cardboard-backed velour approximately 1 inch larger than card. Glue card atop foam; glue foam to velour rectangle. Trim with braid and lace as desired.

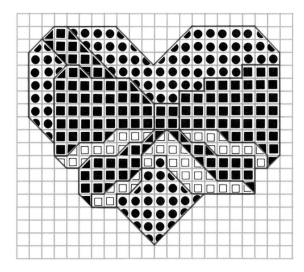

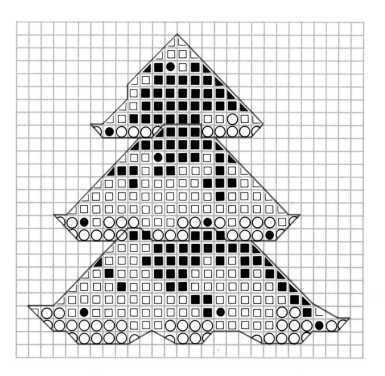

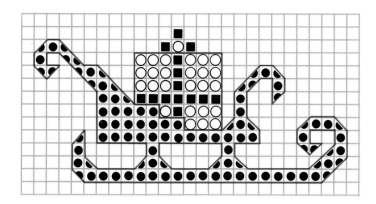

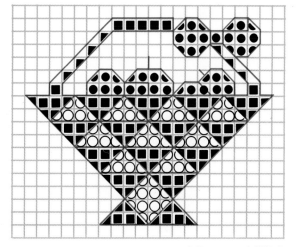

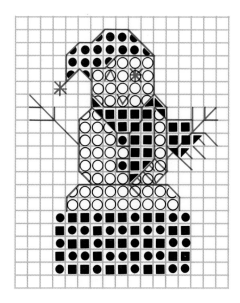

1 Square = 1 Stitch

COLOR KEY

- ■ (699) Dark Green
- ◪ (699) Dark Green Half Stitch
- ▣ (702) Light Green
- ◱ (702) Light Green Half Stitch
- ● (666) Red
- ◪ (666) Red Half Stitch
- ◎ White
- ◡ White Half Stitch

HOLIDAY PARTY DELIGHTS

Seasonal decorations sell well throughout the year, but are especially sought after at early spring and late summer bazaars. This chapter features an assortment of fanciful and festive trims and favors for St. Valentine's Day, Easter, and Halloween.

Cards and loving mementos, like the collection of greetings shown here, are the best kinds of valentines to give and receive. The cross-stitch heart is worked both on a square of even-weave fabric (made into an elegant pillow) and on scraps of perforated paper as the focal points of greeting cards. Reproductions of Victorian stationery are also used for cards, and are accented with paper doily trims. The folk art motif is used as an embroidery pattern for heart-shape sachets and a woodburned plaque.

Instructions for projects in this chapter begin on page 206.

Spring hats, egg hunts, and a parade of bunnies like these mean only one thing— Easter is on the way!

Diligent work at the *barre* has paid off for the lively ballerina bunnies, *above.* They're stitched from cotton and dressed in authentic tutus, headpieces, and toe shoes.

The quartet of bunnies, *opposite,* is designed to serve as a centerpiece for an Easter dinner table or to nestle under an egg tree.

Rely on this happy assortment of Halloween characters to ward off the night's spooks and hobgoblins.

Not at all scary, the puppet centerpiece figures, *above,* can double as party favors or prizes. The bat, cat, pumpkin, and ghost figures have simple embroidered features.

No Halloween get-together is complete without a witch. Place the witch doll, *opposite,* complete with her own pumpkin, near the door to welcome only good spirits.

SPECIAL
VALENTINES

Shown on pages 200–201.

MATERIALS
Cross-stitch valentines
Perforated paper
Even-weave fabric; backing
  fabric; lace; fiberfill (pillow)
Embroidery floss in desired
  colors; embroidery needle
Graph paper; felt-tip pens in
  colors to match floss
Embroidery hoop (optional)

Paper collage cards
Paper doilies; printed material
  such as antique calling and
  greeting cards; stickers
Charcoal paper or card stock
  in assorted colors

Folk art wooden heart
9x10-inch piece of ¾-inch
  pine; tracing paper;
  sandpaper
Woodburning tool; jigsaw

Folk art sachets
5½x6½-inch piece of white
  linen
Embroidery floss in desired
  colors; needle and hoop
Lace; water-erasable marking
  pen; tracing paper
Potpourri; fiberfill

INSTRUCTIONS
Cross-stitch valentines
 Transfer the design, *right, below,* to graph paper using felt-
tip pens (*Note:* Right side of
design is a mirror image of left
side.) Count to center of the design and the perforated paper
or fabric; begin working cross-
stitch border using two strands
of floss. (*Note:* Use backstitch on
green stitches inside border.)
continued

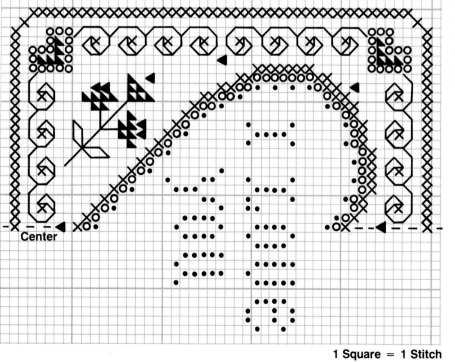

COLOR KEY
⊠ Dark Pink
◯ Light Pink
▼ Yellow
• Lavender
◢ Blue

1 Square = 1 Stitch

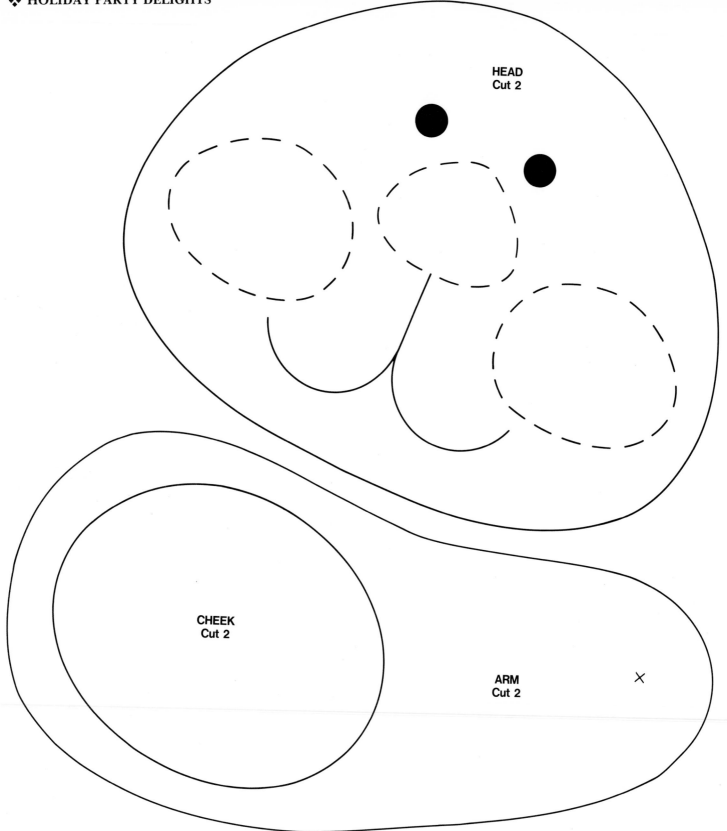

HEAD
Cut 2

CHEEK
Cut 2

ARM
Cut 2

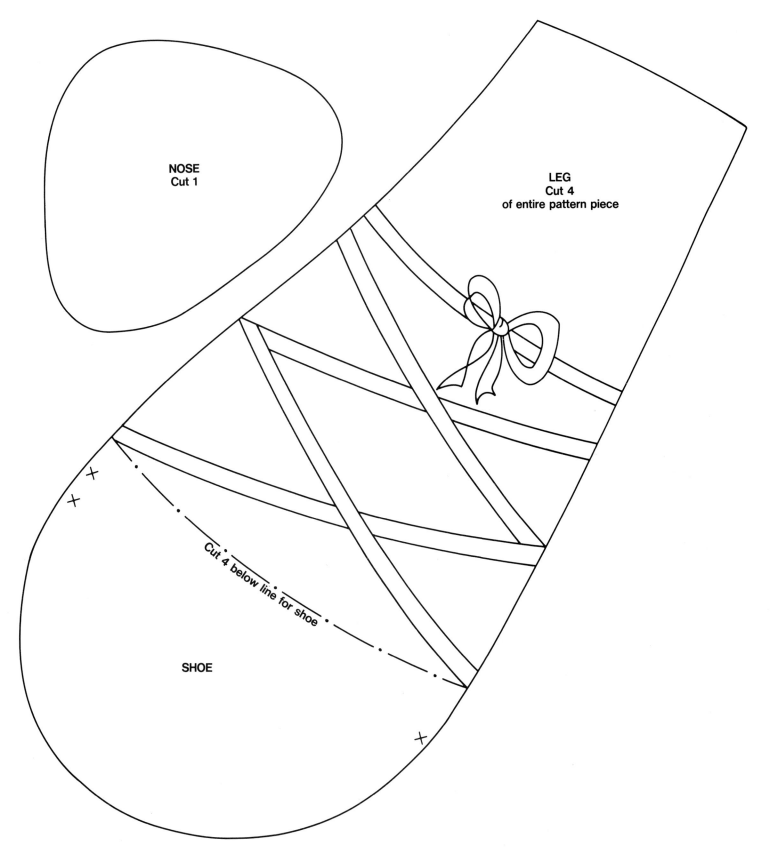

NOSE
Cut 1

LEG
Cut 4
of entire pattern piece

Cut 4 below line for shoe

SHOE

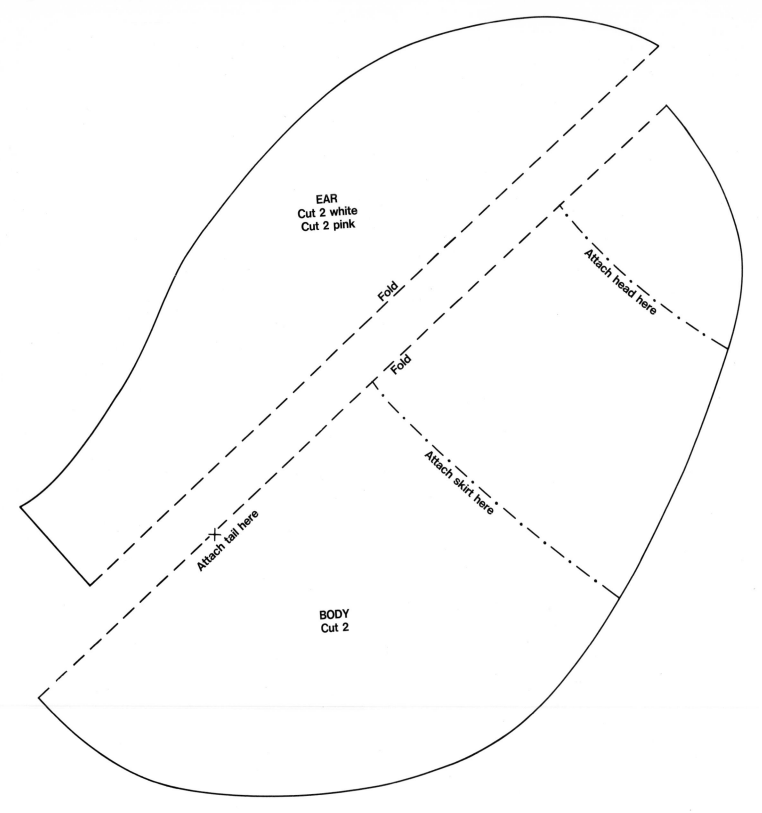

EAR
Cut 2 white
Cut 2 pink

Fold

Fold

Attach head here

Attach skirt here

Attach tail here

BODY
Cut 2

If making pillow, cut backing fabric to match front. Sew together with right sides facing; leave opening. Stuff; close opening. Edge with lace.

Paper collage cards

Cut cards from charcoal paper or card stock; fold in half. Arrange collage elements as desired. Spray back of pieces with adhesive; set in place. Add bows, if desired.

Wooden heart

Trace heart, page 206; cut from pine using jigsaw. Woodburn lines.

Sachets

Trace the design, page 207; transfer to linen, using water-erasable marking pen. Place the linen in hoop and embroider, using two strands of floss.

Cut out heart ½ inch from outline; cut backing to size. Stitch front to back, right sides facing; leave an opening. Turn and stuff lightly with fiberfill and potpourri. Sew opening. Trim with lace.

❖

BALLERINA BUNNY

Shown on page 202.
Finished size is 25 inches tall.

MATERIALS

⅓ yard *each* of white polished cotton and satin in desired color
4 yards of ⅛- or ¼-inch-wide satin ribbon (shoelaces); 1 yard of 1- or 1½-inch-wide satin ribbon (bow for head)
10x14-inch piece of pink cotton or satin and stiff interfacing
1 yard of netting (tutu)

Pink embroidery floss (mouth)
Two ⅜-inch black shank buttons (eyes); fiberfill; thread; tracing paper
White 4-ply yarn; 5-inch square of cardboard (tail)

INSTRUCTIONS

Trace the patterns on pages 208–210. Add ½-inch seam allowance to all pieces and cut from fabrics.

To sew arms, place pairs together with right sides facing. Stitch, leaving tops open. Clip seams; turn, press, and stuff. Sew opening closed; set aside.

Turn under top raw edge of satin shoe fronts and backs. Sew the shoes atop leg pieces where indicated. Next, place pairs of legs together, right sides facing; stitch, leaving tops open. Clip seams, turn, and stuff. Baste opening closed.

Sew legs to body front at markings (raw edges even).

With legs downward and leg area open, stitch body back to front with right sides together. Clip seams, turn, and stuff. Blindstitch the bottom closed, turning in raw edge of back over tops of legs.

Place pairs of ears together, right sides facing, atop interfacing. Stitch, leaving open at bottoms; turn and stuff. Baste the opening closed. Set ears aside.

For head, outline-stitch the mouth using two strands of pink floss. With ears facing downward (pink toward face) and raw edges even, stitch ears to head front. Turn ears up.

Place head back atop front, right sides facing; stitch head, from outside of one ear around to other ear. Clip seam, turn, and stuff. Turn under raw edge of head. Blindstitch opening.

Gather edges of nose and cheek pieces; stuff, and pull threads closed. Pin nose and cheeks to face; hand-stitch in place. Sew eyes to face. Using thread doubled twice, sew head to body front atop dashed lines as shown on pattern.

To finish, cut narrow ribbon in half. Fold one length in half in a V shape; slip under the middle of center back of shoe; stitch securely. Wind ribbon around each leg; tie bow in front. Hand-stitch arms securely to body.

To make the tutu, fold net in half lengthwise. Fold again and press crease along one length (top of tutu); gather edge to fit waist. Pin in place, with opening at back. Tack to body. Cut bottom edge to open; pull the layers apart for fullness.

Make pom-pom tail by wrapping yarn around cardboard; slip off, tie at center, and cut loops. Trim; tack to back at X.

Tie bow and tack to head.

❖

BUNNY CENTERPIECE

Shown on page 203.
Finished size is 9 inches tall and 10 inches in diameter.

MATERIALS

⅓ yard *each* of four pastel fabrics; scraps of contrasting fabric (inner ears) and brown felt (noses)
Thin pipe cleaners; 4 small baskets; white glue
Acrylic paint (eyes); paintbrush
Easter grass and silk flowers
2½ yards of ribbon; fiberfill
White buttonhole twist

INSTRUCTIONS

Trace patterns, page 213, and add ¼-inch seam allowances. On the body, trace the pattern to match the A-B markings on the head to make one pattern piece. Cut two bodies from *each* of the pastel fabrics. Sew first color to second color at center seam. Trim seam; press open. Repeat for matching set. With right sides facing, sew around bodies, leaving the bottoms open between dots. Clip curves and clip top of center seam; turn. Repeat for third and fourth colors.

Place first pair of bunnies atop second pair; sew over the center seam line to connect them. Stuff each bunny firmly; hand-sew opening closed.

Cut four paws from *each* of the four fabrics. Sew pairs together, leaving open at underarm. Stuff; hand-sew the opening closed. Backstitch fingers from paw edge to dots. Blindstitch paws to bodies.

Cut two outer ears from *each* of the pastels and two inner ears *each* from contrasting fabrics. Sew together with right sides facing; leave open at the bottom. Trim, clip, and turn. Blindstitch openings, leaving a small opening at one side for pipe cleaner. Topstitch.

Cut pipe cleaners into 3½-inch pieces; insert into spaces between topstitching and outside seams. Make small pleat in bottom; blindstitch ear to head. Bend ear into desired shape.

To finish, cut felt noses; glue in place. Run three strands of buttonhole twist through the cheeks for whiskers.

Refer to the photograph and paint eyes using artist's brush and acrylic paints.

Place Easter grass and flowers in baskets. Tie bow around each bunny's neck.

HALLOWEEN PUPPETS

Shown on page 204.
Finished sizes are from 5¼ to 9 inches tall.

MATERIALS

¾ yard of white fabric (linings, ghost); ¼ yard *each* of yellow (cat) and dark gray (bat) fabrics; ⅓ yard of orange fabric (pumpkin)
Scraps of green (pumpkin stem/leaf) and black (pumpkin face) fabrics
18x45-inch piece of firm, bonded sheet batting
Three ½-inch black buttons (ghost's eyes and mouth)
Two ½-inch triangular black buttons (cat's eyes)
Two 5-mm white beads (bat's eyes); embroidery floss in black and white
Fiberfill; fusible webbing

INSTRUCTIONS

Trace designs, pages 214–217. Add ¼-inch seam allowances; cut from fabrics. Sew pieces together with right sides facing, unless directions state otherwise.

GHOST: Baste body pieces to batting. Sew button eyes and mouth on front. Sew lining to *each* body piece across lower edge only; open flat. Sew body front to back through all layers, leaving an opening between dots. Turn; sew opening.

CAT: Make same as ghost, adding button eyes and embroidering face and paw lines before sewing front to back.

PUMPKIN: Cut pumpkin pieces as indicated on pattern (see cutting diagram on page 216). One set of pieces (fabric, lining, and batting) is the face. Cut left arm from second set and right arm from third set.

Cut the face appliqués from black fabric and fusible webbing; fuse to front. Satin-stitch around edges.

Baste each body piece (front and sides) to batting. Sew darts.

Sew batting to one stem and leaf piece. Join stem and leaf pieces, leaving open between dots. Turn; topstitch on dotted lines. Pin stem and leaf to top of front, raw edges even. Pin remaining side pieces to front; sew through all layers between Xs. Join center back seam.

Sew darts on lining pieces; join as for body, leaving open between dots along one edge. Pin lining to pumpkin, right sides facing; sew bottom edge. Turn through opening; stitch opening. Tack lining top to inside of pumpkin behind stem.

BAT: *Note:* Flaps are openings for insertion of fingers for puppet movement. Fold one *flap* piece, wrong sides together, along fold line; baste raw edges. Baste batting to wrong side of one *wing* piece. Position flap atop right side of wing; baste together. Repeat for second wing.

With flap side of one wing piece and right side of one of the remaining wing pieces facing, sew together, leaving open between the dots. Turn. Repeat for second wing. Baste wings together, flap sides facing, along straight edge.

Sew bat front center seam. Add bead eyes. Using three strands of white floss, straight-stitch mouth and fangs. Sew backs together, leaving open between Xs. Sew front to back; turn and stuff firmly. Insert wings in back opening, and sew opening closed.

WELCOME WITCH

Shown on page 205.
Witch is 31 inches tall.

MATERIALS

Variegated gray novelty yarn (hair)
6x16-inch piece of cardboard
Polyester fiberfill
3 squares of peach felt (face, hands, and nose); 2 squares of orange and 1 square of gold felt (pumpkin); scrap of green felt (pumpkin)
4⅝x16-inch piece of black and orange fabric (apron); 3x12-inch piece of striped fabric (stockings)
1 yard of 1-inch-wide ruffled eyelet (apron, legs); ½ yard of black felt (body, hat, boots)
1 yard of 1-inch-wide orange ribbon (shoes, hat)
Two ⅜-inch black buttons with shank (eyes)
Red embroidery floss (mouth)
Nylon thread

INSTRUCTIONS

Enlarge patterns for hat and body, and trace remaining full-size patterns, pages 218 and 219; cut from fabrics. When stitching, sew all pieces with wrong sides facing, unless otherwise indicated.

For legs and shoes, stitch the stockings together at the sides, right sides facing; turn, press, and stuff lightly. Stitch shoe fronts to backs, leaving tops open; stuff lightly. Insert bottom of stockings into top of shoes; stitch to close. Baste lace around tops of stockings.

Sew body front to back, leaving bottom open; stuff lightly. Pin top of stockings between body pieces at dots; sew.

For apron, turn under hem on one long edge; attach eyelet. Hem short sides. Gather top to 7 inches. Cut a 2x20-inch strip for waistband and fold in half lengthwise, right sides facing. Sew a ⅛-inch seam, leaving ends open; turn. Turn raw ends to inside; stitch ends. Center the right side of apron top on length of waistband; stitch.

For arms and hands, overlap arm pieces on hands ⅛ inch; stitch across. Sew arm fronts and backs together, leaving an opening at top. Stuff hands lightly and stitch fingers. Stuff arm; stitch closed. Tack arms to sides of body at dots.

Embroider mouth. Crease the center of the nose, then pin and stitch nose to face. (*Note:* Leave bottom open.) Sew head front to back, leaving open at top. Stuff lightly and stitch closed. Sew on eyes. Tack head to body front along dashed lines on pattern.

For hair, wind yarn into a thick bundle around cardboard; slip off carefully and tie in middle with a piece of yarn. Sew yarn to head.

Fold hat in half lengthwise and sew edges; turn. Place seam to back and tack on head. (*Note:* Pull felt brim wider at edges. Crumple hat in several places and turn up front brim to uncover face.)

Cut out pumpkin eyes, nose, and mouth. Insert the piece of gold felt between front and back of pumpkin; sew around edge, leaving open at top. Stuff lightly.

Cut vine along cutting lines. Bunch big end of vine and leaf together and insert in opening; sew pumpkin closed. Tack pumpkin to hands.

Cut orange ribbon in thirds. Tie bows; tack to hat and shoes.

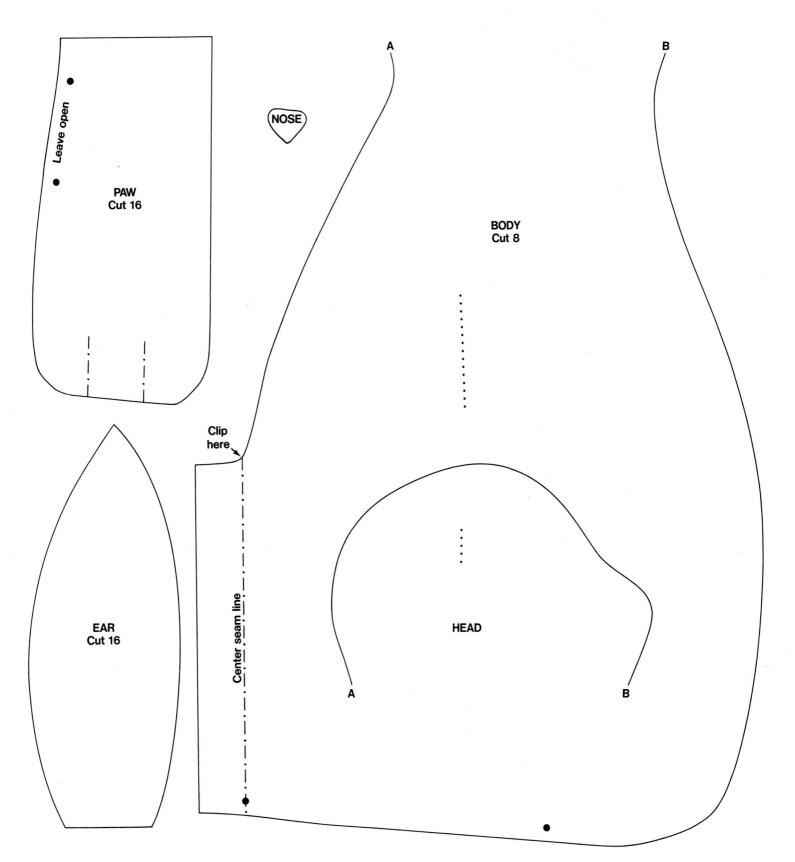

Leave open

PAW
Cut 16

NOSE

A

B

BODY
Cut 8

Clip
here

EAR
Cut 16

Center seam line

HEAD

A

B

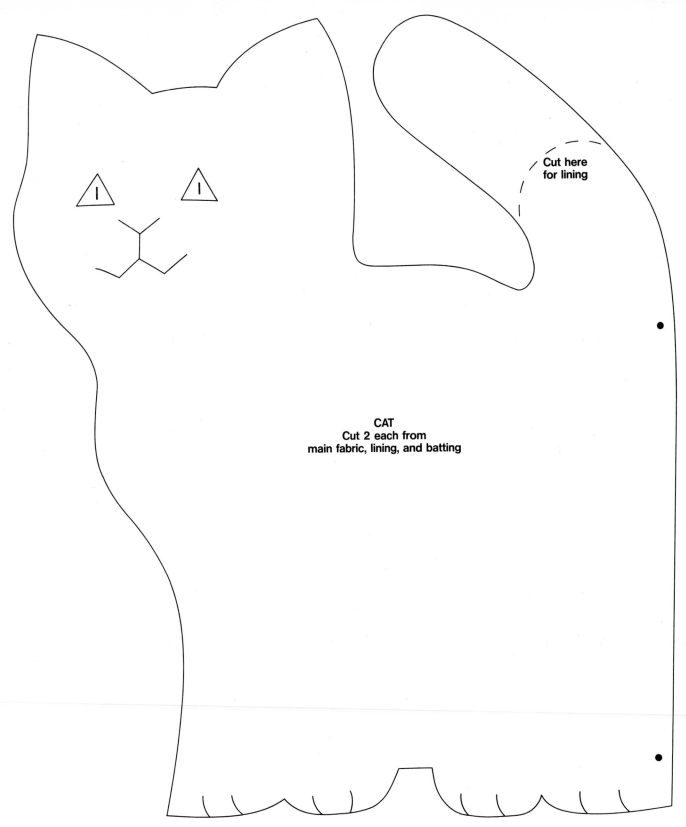

Cut here
for lining

CAT
Cut 2 each from
main fabric, lining, and batting

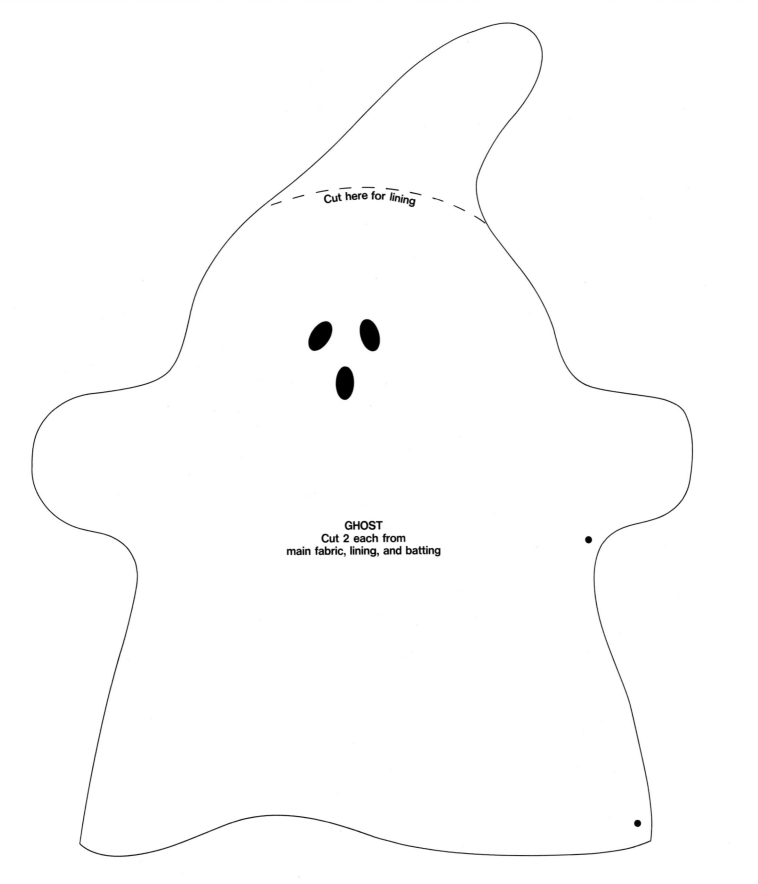

GHOST
Cut 2 each from
main fabric, lining, and batting

Cut here for lining

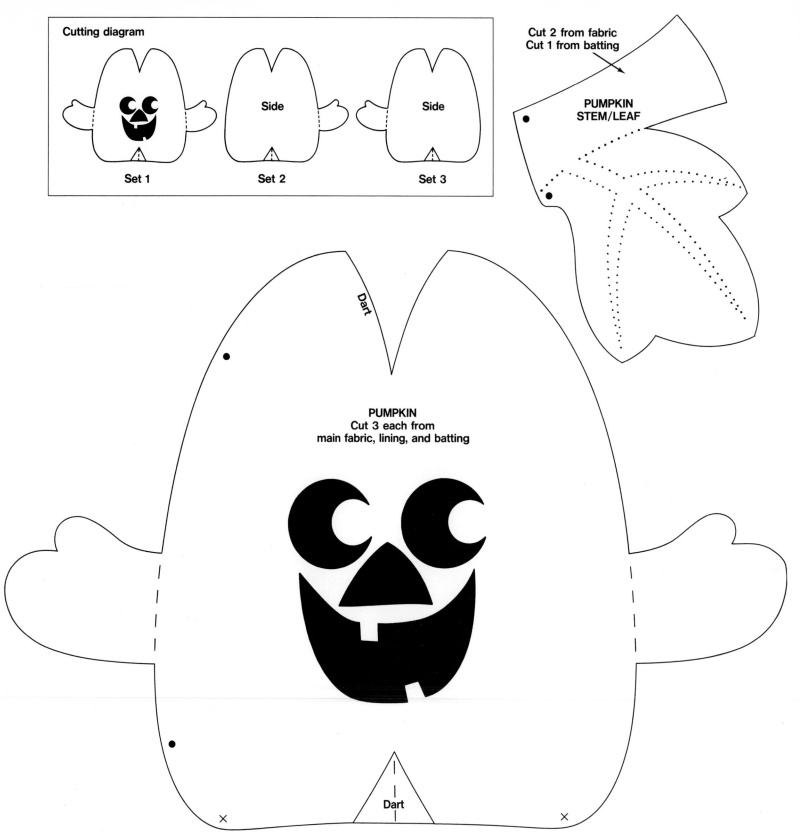

Cutting diagram

Side

Side

Set 1

Set 2

Set 3

Cut 2 from fabric
Cut 1 from batting

**PUMPKIN
STEM/LEAF**

Dart

PUMPKIN
Cut 3 each from
main fabric, lining, and batting

Dart

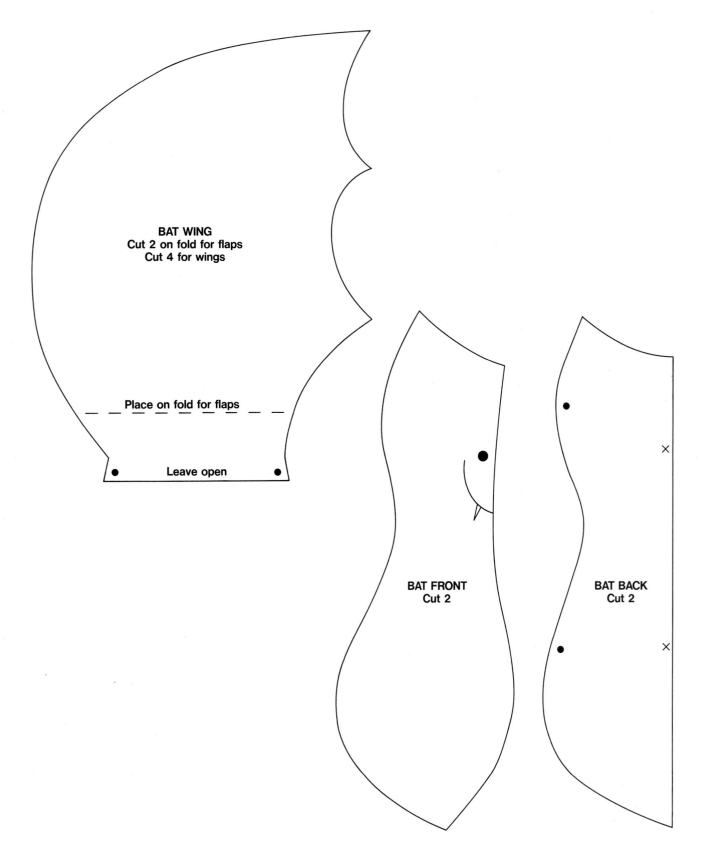

BAT WING
Cut 2 on fold for flaps
Cut 4 for wings

Place on fold for flaps

Leave open

BAT FRONT
Cut 2

BAT BACK
Cut 2

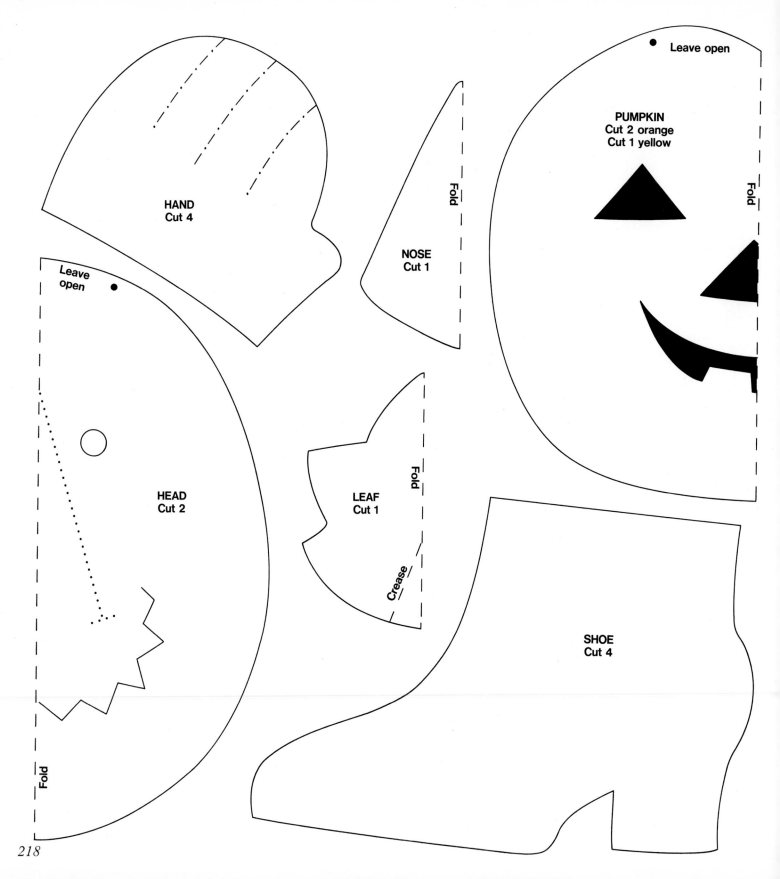

HAND
Cut 4

NOSE
Cut 1

Fold

Leave open

PUMPKIN
Cut 2 orange
Cut 1 yellow

Fold

Leave
open

HEAD
Cut 2

LEAF
Cut 1

Fold

Crease

SHOE
Cut 4

Fold

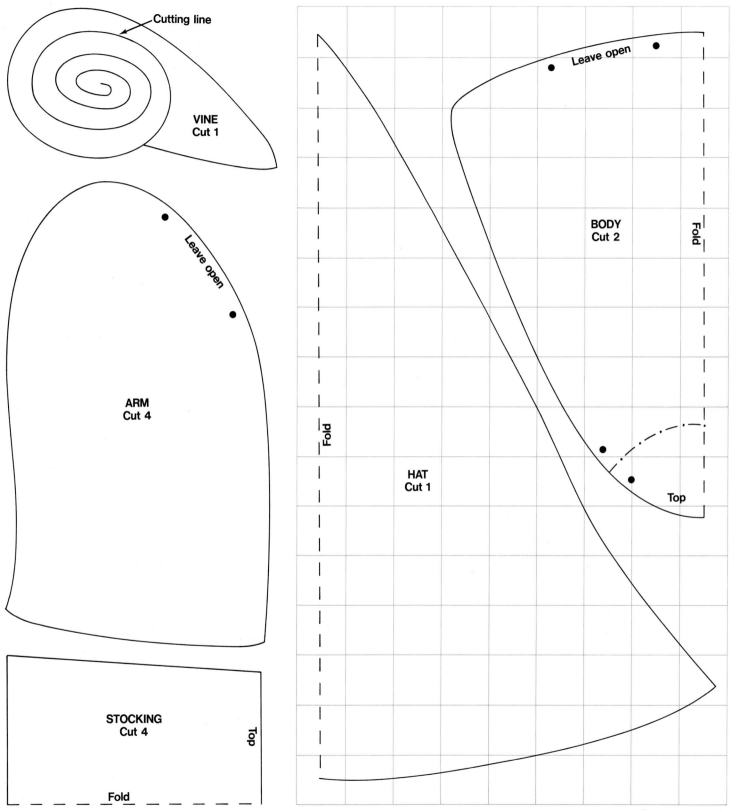

Cutting line

VINE
Cut 1

ARM
Cut 4

Leave open

STOCKING
Cut 4

Top

Fold

Fold

HAT
Cut 1

BODY
Cut 2

Fold

Leave open

Top

1 Square = 1 Inch

CREDITS

We would like to express our appreciation and gratitude to the many people who helped us with this book. Our heartfelt thanks go to each of the artists and artisans, who enthusiastically contributed designs, ideas, and projects.

Thanks, also, to the photographers, whose creative talents and technical skills added much to the book. In addition, we are happy to acknowledge our debt to the companies, institutions, and individuals who provided materials for projects, locations for photography, or in some other way contributed to the book.

❖

DESIGNERS

Donna Barnett-Albert—48–49, patchwork projects

Barbara Bergman—156, bedding

Sandi Blake—115, dogs

Taresia Boernke—114, bear; 156–157, bears

Gary Boling—32–33, publicity projects; 180–181, packaging ideas

Jerry Brown—160, bead balls

Nancy Buckley—191, cross-stitch tree trims

Linda Joy Center—12, vest

Chris Chennault—32, banner; 204, puppets

Kerri Christensen—83, apple backpack

Pat Cody—82, school sacks

Christopher Cravens—186–187, wooden trees and Santa

Joan Cravens and Sally Mavor—138–139, frames

Jane DiTeresa—15, rabbit toys

Hugie Dufresne—67, crocheted edging

Phyllis Dunstan—14, kittens; 76–77, message board; 78–79, pencil box, nap mat, overnight bag, slippers; 112–113, mouse family; 116, doll; 156, doll; 158–159, advent calendar

Martha Ehrlich—106, kids' group projects

Pam Elfritz—38–39, ink-on-paper designs

Linda Emmerson—36–37, boxes and cards; 107, beanbag toss game

Mary Engelbreit—152–153, embroidered picture; 154, stockings; 155, ornaments; 157, pillow

Dorothy Everds—80–81, pajama bag dogs

Dixie Falls—12, child's sweater; 52, handkerchief case and sachets; 53, hardanger box

Pat Gardner—51, pillows

Phyllis Giberson—40, roosters

Nina Gordon—188–189, ornaments

Meryl Griffiths—36–37, fraktur picture

Diane Hayes—200–201, cross-stitch design

Rebecca Jerdee—6–7, wooden house blessing; 8–9, painted finishes on bowls, trivets, frames; 11, checkerboard; 13, heart hanger; 14–15, furniture

Robyn Knibbe—85, animal sweatshirts

Nellie Kwas—67, note cards

Judy LaSalle—117, dolls; 202, ballerina bunnies; 205, witch

Dorothy Main—68–69, gift and note cards

Sally Mavor—136–137, alphabet quilt; 140, bibs

Sally Mavor and Joan Cravens—138–139, frames

Sally Mavor and Judith Veeder—136–137, tote bag; 140, pincushion; 141, rabbit pillow toys

Lina Morielli—190, afghan

Beverly Rivers—41, dolls

Sarah Robinson—10–11, paper cutouts

Diane Schultz—52–53, pillow dolls

Mimi Shimmin—84, sweatshirt; 200–201, sachet and plaque

Margaret Sindelar—62–63, caddies and plastic envelopes

Rhoda Sneller—86–87, computer patchwork projects; 190–191, pillow and place mats

Sara Jane Treinen—138, ice-cream cone hang-ups

Ciba Vaughan—50, picture; 200–201, cards;

Judith Veeder—13, tote bag; lap robe; 158–159, bears

Judith Veeder and Sally Mavor—136–137, tote bag; 140, pincushion; 141, rabbit pillow toys

Sue Veigulis—13, patchwork skirt

Bonnie Wedge—203, centerpiece

Nancy Wilhelmson—192–193, Victorian ornaments and picture

Jim Williams—161, ornaments; 162, cross-stitch ornaments

Don Wipperman—156, doll bed

Pamela Woods—162, foil roses; 163, hearts

Mary Zdrodowski—66, mirror and jar lid

PHOTOGRAPHERS

Hopkins Associates—Cover; 36–39; 48–49; 64; 66–67; 114; 117; 152–159; 163; 203

Mike Jensen—76–89

Scott Little—115; 200–202; 204

Perry Struse—6–15; 40–41; 50–53; 62–63; 65; 68–69; 77; 112–113; 116; 136–141; 160–162; 186–193; 205

ACKNOWLEDGMENTS

Ames Public Schools
Northwood Elementary School
Ames, IA 50010

Jerry Brown

C.M. Offray and Son, Inc.
261 Madison Avenue
New York, NY 10016

Dan River Fabrics
111 West 40th Street
New York, NY 10018

Living History Farms
Des Moines, IA 50322

The Octagon Center for the Arts
Ames, IA 50010

INDEX

For photographs, see pages noted in **bold** type; remaining page numbers refer to how-to instructions and patterns.

Have BETTER HOMES AND GARDENS®
magazine delivered to your door.
For information, write to:
MR. ROBERT AUSTIN
P.O. BOX 4536
DES MOINES, IA 50336